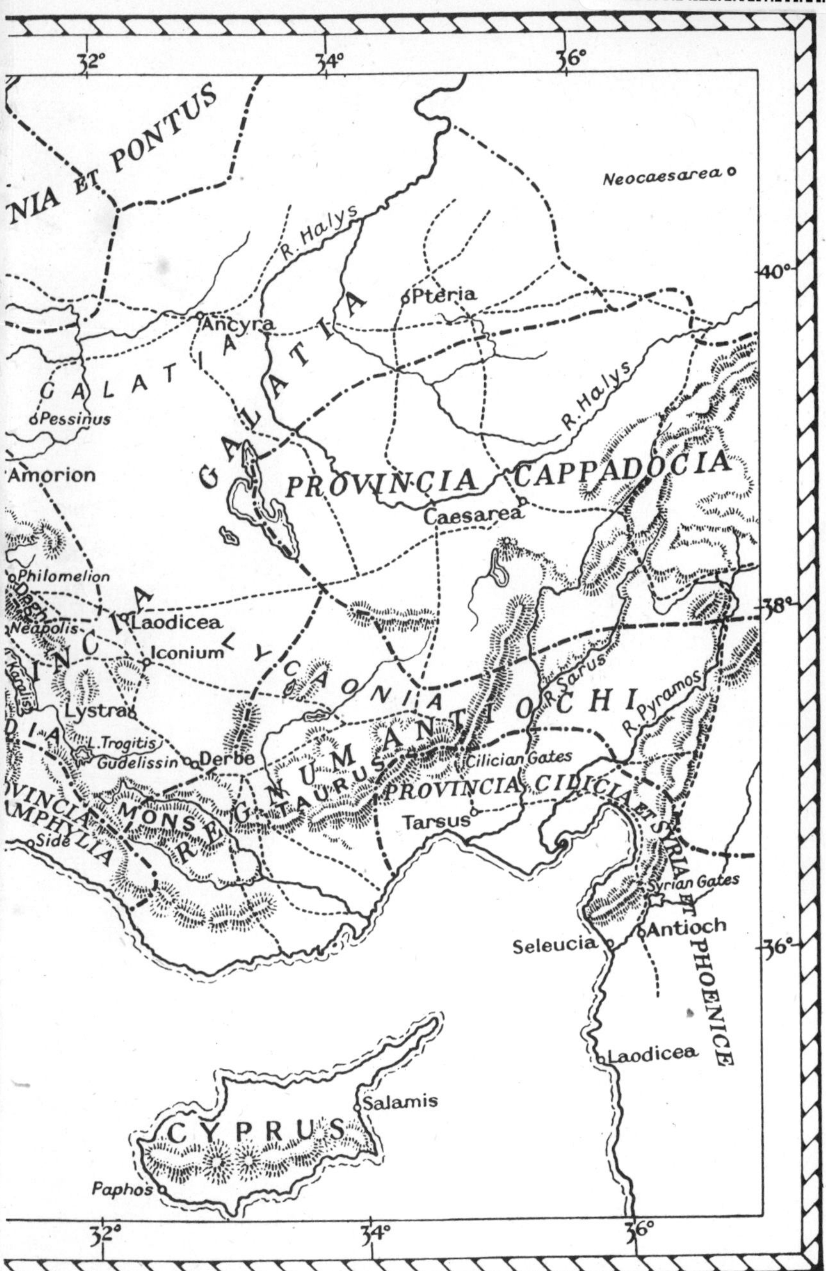
32°
34°
36°
40°
38°
36°
NIA ET PONTUS
Neocaesarea
R. Halys
Pteria
Ancyra
GALATIA
G A L A T I A
Pessinus
R. Halys
Amorion
PROVINCIA
CAPPADOCIA
Caesarea
Philomelion
Neapolis
Laodicea
Iconium
LYCAONIA
R. Sarus
REGNUM ANTIOCHI
R. Pyramos
Lystra
L. Trogitis
Gudelissin
Derbe
Cilician Gates
TAURUS
MONS
PROVINCIA CILICIA ET SYRIA ET PHOENICE
Tarsus
Side
AMPHYLIA
Syrian Gates
Antioch
Seleucia
Laodicea
Salamis
CYPRUS
Paphos

GLADSTONE'S
LIBRARY

FIDE ET VIRTUTE
W. E. Gladstone
St. Deiniol's Library
Hawarden, Clwyd
Founded by
The Rt. Hon. W. E. Gladstone

GLADSTONE'S
LIBRARY

AN INTRODUCTION TO THE NEW TESTAMENT

AN INTRODUCTION TO THE NEW TESTAMENT

BY

KIRSOPP LAKE

D.LITT., PH.D.
Corresponding Member of the Berlin Academy

AND

SILVA LAKE

PH.D.

LONDON

CHRISTOPHERS

22 BERNERS STREET, W.1

MELBOURNE : SYDNEY : WELLINGTON : CAPE TOWN : TORONTO

First Published in Great Britain, February, 1938.
Reprinted (revised) November, 1938.

Printed in Great Britain

HOWARD LEHMAN GOODHART

Philoniani fortasse sanguinis
spiritus certissime heredi
grato animo
D D D
auctores

CONTENTS

MAPS

PREFACE

IN this book we have sought to give the generally accepted results of modern study of the New Testament, but no attempt has been made to build on that basis, to deal with the theological, philosophical or ecclesiastical problems which are inevitably related to it, or to do more than briefly indicate the problems which remain.

The construction of the book calls for little explanation. The first part discusses the literary facts and critical problems concerned with the various books of the New Testament—Gospels, Acts, Epistles and Revelation. The second part deals with the background, Jewish and Gentile, against which the New Testament must be set. Finally, there are appendices on Chronology, Topography, Literary Evidence and Bibliography.

It is our hope that this *Introduction* may be of use to three classes of readers: first, to those who approach it as relatively elementary students; secondly, to teachers who desire a foundation on which to build for themselves. It is for these latter that references have been freely made to more detailed books, especially in German, which are essential to them, though not likely to be of great service to their pupils.

The third class is somewhat different. Most of our colleagues would agree, we think, as they approach the close of their active professional careers, in recognising that few of their students remember distinctly, if at all, the facts which they have heard in the lecture room. Five years after they have taken their degrees, they have lost all active knowledge of them. But they have a dim recollection that they once heard something; some of them think occasionally of the subsequent discussions, and some have perhaps not wholly forgotten the lecturer. Moreover, there are times when they wish to recall the facts more clearly. There are a few in whom the teacher has a deeper, though not always articulate, interest, and we hope that some of them may find a use for this book.

There are some topics, treated briefly in this book, which we should like to have elaborated but for considerations of space. Needless to say, we could have discussed at much greater length such questions as *Formgeschichte* criticism or the dates of the Gospels; we hope, however, that in cases like these we have given sufficient indication where the subjects may be further pursued. On a somewhat different footing is the suggestion which has been made to us by friends who have read these pages that the scale of the treatment of the Gospel of John is, compared with that of the Synoptic Gospels, the Acts and the Pauline Epistles, something less than adequate. To that our reply is that while there have been from time to time attempts to analyse this Gospel and to make it reveal the secret of its composition, most of those attempts have soon been recognised as failures, and none of them have reached the state of relative certainty which is found in considering the problems of the Synoptic Gospels.

This is, at any rate partly, explicable by the difference between the Gospel of John and the Synoptics. The Synoptic Gospels are a group; their relationship is obvious even when their details are doubtful; while the Gospel of John is a unit in which no such aid to its analysis is furnished. We would point out that the great Old Testament scholars of the past had precisely this difficulty to overcome, and overcame it. We would suggest that there is no direction in which the attention and activity of the younger generation of scholars could be more fruitfully turned than that of the elucidation of the problems in the Gospel of John. The field is white unto harvest.

K.L.

S.L.

ABBREVIATIONS

S.A.B. (or S.B.A.) ... *Sitzungsberichte der Akademie zu Berlin*
Beginnings .... *The Beginnings of Christianity,* Foakes-Jackson and Lake
C.I.G. .... *Corpus Inscriptionum Graecarum*
C.I.L. .... *Corpus Inscriptionum Latinarum*
Earlier Epistles ..... *The Earlier Epistles of St. Paul,* K. Lake
G.G.A. .... *Göttingische gelehrte Anzeigen*
Hastings .... *Dictionary of the Bible*
Hauck-Herzog ..... *Real-encyclopädie für protestantische Theologie und Kirche*
I.C.C. .... *International Critical Commentary*
I.G. .... *Inscriptiones Graecae*
J.B.L. .... *Journal of Biblical Literature*
J.T.S. .... *Journal of Theological Studies*
Juster .... *Les Juifs dans L'Empire Romain*
L.H.B. .... Lietzmann's *Handbuch*
Meyer .... *Kritisch-exegetischer Kommentar über das Neue Testament*
P.G. .... Migne, *Patrologia Graeca*
P.L. .... Migne, *Patrologia Latina*
Pauly-Wissowa ..... *Real-encyclopädie der classischen Altertumswissenschaft:* neue Bearbeitung
Schürer (or G.J.V.) .. *Geschichte des jüdischen Volkes im Zeitalter Jesu Christi,* E. Schürer
Strack-Billerbeck ... *Kommentar zum Neuen Testament aus Talmud und Midrasch*
Streeter .... *The Four Gospels,* B. H. Streeter
T.U. .... *Texte und Untersuchungen zur Geschichte der altchristlichen Literatur*

PART ONE

THE BOOKS OF THE NEW TESTAMENT

CHAPTER I

The Synoptic Gospels: The Literary Facts

THE gospels of Matthew, Mark and Luke are commonly called "synoptic,"—a phrase perhaps more often used than understood. It is derived from attempts to arrange the text of the gospels as a synopsis,[1] which, by the use of three or four parallel columns, would enable any student to see at a glance the different form given by each Evangelist to any episode of the gospel story. It soon became clear that Matthew, Mark and Luke lend themselves to this form of treatment, but John does not. Therefore Matthew, Mark and Luke are called "the synoptic gospels" in distinction from John, the fourth gospel.

The questions to be considered in connection with the synoptic gospels are: Who wrote these books and what material did the authors use? What was the special purpose of each?

The evidence on these questions is of two kinds. First, internal evidence found in the book itself; secondly, external evidence found in other writers. Internal evidence is, of course, the older, being that of the gospels themselves; external evidence may be extremely valuable, but it is often hard to distinguish between external evidence derived ultimately from

[1] The use of the word seems to be due to J. J. Griesbach (1774) who published a "synopsis" of the Gospels of Matthew, Mark and Luke, so that they could be "seen together." Hence arose the custom of calling them the Synoptic Gospels, though Griesbach does not actually use the phrase, nor does it appear to be known who did so first. For the general study of the Synoptic Gospels, H. Lietzmann's *Handbuch* and the last editions of Meyer's *Kommentar* are excellent and probably better than anything in any other language. In English C. G. Montefiore's *The Synoptic Gospels* is the best. It can be supplemented by W. C. Allen's and A. H. McNeile's commentaries on Matthew, H. B. Swete's commentary on Mark, B. S. Easton's *The Gospel according to St. Luke.* Advanced students can profitably consult J. Wellhausen's commentaries, and A. Loisy's *Les Évangiles Synoptiques.*

persons who knew the facts about the gospels at first hand, and that which is an intelligent formulation of internal evidence, to which it really adds nothing, however early it may be.[2]

INTERNAL EVIDENCE

The most important internal evidence is given in the titles of the gospels. Each is described as "the Gospel according to——." "Gospel" means "good news" [3]; in the Epistles it clearly means "the good news about Jesus" and should be so interpreted in Mark i.1, "the beginning of the Good News about Jesus." Thus we have documents described as the good news about Jesus according to Matthew, Mark or Luke, i.e. in the form given to it by these three persons. If these titles be part of the documents, this is the oldest evidence for their authorship. It does not, of course, identify the authors,—for the names are all common enough (Luke perhaps the least so), but it names them. Why should this testimony not be accepted? No reason has ever been shown, for the view that antiquity tended to anonymous books is contrary to evidence, and it is most unlikely that the second Gospel, for instance, ever circulated without the name of Mark attached to it.

What conclusions about the authors might reasonably be drawn from the gospels, as they stand, by anyone who knew them and the other books of the New Testament but nothing else? Such a reader would find a Matthew, who was at first a publican (or custom-house officer) in Galilee, but became an Apostle. That would identify the author of the Gospel according to Matthew. In Acts xii.12 ff. he would find Peter in the house of John Mark's mother, and in I Peter v.13 a Mark connected with Peter in Babylon, which would be taken

[2] See Cadbury in *Beginnings*, Vol. II, p. 250.

[3] This use appears to be almost, though not quite, specifically Christian. The word is found in earlier Greek as "the reward for good news," but it is used as "good news" just often enough to make it probable that it was obtaining this sense in popular circles about the end of the first century B.C. In the Christian era it was so firmly attached to "the Gospels" that it became obsolete otherwise.

(probably correctly) to mean Rome. It would be possible to deduce that the Gospel according to Mark was Petrine and Roman. But Mark's connection with Peter is less obvious than with Paul, whom he actually accompanied on the first missionary journey, especially if I Peter be not accepted as genuine.[4] Similarly in Colossians iv.14 he would find a Luke who was a physician and a companion of Paul, whom he would take as the author of the third gospel.

Roughly speaking, this is also what "tradition" (i.e. external evidence) states. It is all in the New Testament. That is not a reason for rejecting it; on the contrary, it is an admirable reason for accepting it, but it means that the identifications may have no more authority than they would if we made them ourselves.

But internal evidence can go further, if the synoptic gospels be compared with each other. That comparison was not made, or was made only for other purposes, until the end of the eighteenth century; but since then profitable work has been done on the subject, the results of which can be counted as part of the internal evidence, for they are not the inventions of critics but are implicit in the gospels themselves.

The situation inherited from antiquity was this. The close relationship of the synoptic gospels was recognised, but it was held that, since they were all infallibly inspired and accurate, they could not contradict or correct each other. Matthew was the oldest, Mark was next and Luke was the latest of the three. Some even thought that Mark was an abbreviated though correct edition of Matthew. In the nineteenth century, however, this opinion was seen to be wrong and it became clear that Mark was used both by Matthew and Luke.[5]

[4] See pp. 165 ff.

[5] The first step was taken in a very famous article by Karl Lachmann in *Studien und Kritiken* for 1835, pp. 570-90. This article really established the priority of Mark, but the point was driven home in a long discussion summarised by H. J. Holtzmann in *Die Marcus-controversie* in the *Archiv für Religionswissenschaft,* X, and in his *Einleitung.* The best German summing up of the whole question is probably Wernle's *Die synoptische Frage.* It was not given much consideration in England until an epoch-making article by F. H. Woods in *Studia Biblica,* II, pp. 59 ff. in

The method of proving this is complicated in detail but simple in principle. The material common to Matthew, Mark and Luke is arranged in three parallel columns in such a way that when the same story comes in all three gospels the three forms of it are placed side by side. Attention is first paid only to the order in which the paragraphs are arranged and not to their wording. It is then clear that the order of passages found in all three gospels is sometimes Matthew and Mark against Luke and sometimes Luke and Mark against Matthew, but never Matthew and Luke against Mark. This is *prima facie* evidence that both Matthew and Luke copied Mark.

There is, however, a subordinate problem. If the wording of the paragraphs is studied, rather than the order, the same phenomenon often emerges, namely that Mark is in the majority. The combination Matthew-Luke is less usual than the combinations Mark-Matthew and Mark-Luke, but it is no longer true that it is never found. When the divergent form is found in Mark, such passages are known as "secondary features of Mark."[6] If the absence of such phenomena proves the originality of Mark in the one case, their presence might be supposed to prove the opposite in the other, and the two arguments might be considered as contradictory. This, however, is scarcely sure. The facts are more in favour of Mark than statistics would show, because Mark is written in rather rough, bad Greek which almost any two editors would be likely to correct in the same way. Thus many of the agreements between Matthew and Luke can be regarded as a nat-

---

1890, but after this Sanday in Oxford and Swete and Armitage Robinson in Cambridge popularised the theory. It was admirably set out in F. C. Burkitt's *The Gospel History and Its Transmission* and in his *The Earliest Sources for the Life of Jesus*. There is a very important discussion in W. C. Allen's commentary on Matthew, but the best modern treatment in any language is B. H. Streeter's *The Four Gospels*, pp. 150-331. For the proper study of the question a "synopsis" of the Gospels is quite indispensable (see Bibliography, App. E) Huck-Lietzmann's is probably the best, and there are also excellent ones by Burton-Goodspeed and by J. M. Thompson.

[6] See Allen's commentary on Matthew in the *International Critical Commentary*, F. Nicolardot's *Les procédés de redaction dans les trois premiers évangelistes*, Streeter's *Four Gospels*, pp. 295 ff. and Sir John Hawkin's *Horae Synopticae*, 2nd ed. pp. 114 ff.

ural coincidence in literary correction. There remain, however, a few passages which cannot be so explained. Some of them (though it is not yet clear which they are) may be regarded as pointing to corruption in the text of Mark, and the question passes from the realm of the synoptic problem to that of textual criticism. In our opinion, there are not a few places in which the text of Mark as we have it today is probably corrupt and in these cases the agreement of Matthew and Luke may give the original text of Mark. But the problem of the harmonisation of the text is very difficult.

It is possible that this is the solution of the whole question, but there are those who doubt it. They may be divided into three groups: *a.* those who think that our Mark is a second edition of the original Mark used by both Matthew and Luke; *b.* those who think that Luke was acquainted with Matthew as well as with Mark; *c.* those who think that Mark was translated from an Aramaic source and was known in both forms to the editors of Matthew and Luke, who corrected the Greek by the Aramaic. We believe that there is more evidence against than in favour of any one of these three theories, but each has behind it the authority of competent scholars.[7] In any case, the general priority of Mark is a firmly established result.

Thus, so far as the narrative common to all three gospels is concerned, we have the first edition in the Gospel of Mark, so that in these paragraphs Matthew and Luke are valuable not as additional, and independent, accounts of the same event, but as early Christian editions of the original story. Their importance lies in their changes, for by studying them we can see the reaction of the early Christian mind to the earliest Christian tradition,—or, more accurately, to the facts of history.

One illustrative example may be taken from the very beginning of the gospel story. According to Mark, John the Baptist came baptising with a "baptism of repentance for the re-

[7] For *a.* most of the older books give a summary, but the theory has now very few supporters; for *b.* E. Simon's *Hat der dritte Evangelist den kanonischen Matthäus benutzt?* This view was held but, we believe, never published, by Professor J. H. Ropes; for *c.* see especially C. C. Torrey's *Our Translated Gospels.*

mission of sins," and men of all districts came out to be baptised by him, confessing their sins. Whatever may be the real meaning of the passage, and whatever may have been the real intention of John's baptism, it is obvious that this passage would imply at first sight that all who were baptised recognised their sinful nature. When, therefore, the story says that Jesus came to be baptised by John, the inference is obvious that he also recognised himself as a sinner. Few conclusions would be more shocking to the early Christian mind; moreover, the suggestion that John the Baptist ever communicated anything to Jesus, most of all that he gave him forgiveness of sin, would have been repugnant to early Christians.[8] The Gospel according to Matthew, in editing Mark, endeavours to eliminate this suggestion from the narrative. It makes Jesus come to John and John to say to him, "I have need to be baptised of thee, and comest thou to me?" Jesus replies, "Suffer it for the moment, for thus it becomes us to fulfill all righteousness," implying that in his case baptism was not a remission of sins but was undergone as a part of the complete fulfillment of righteousness, and that he was not a sinner but a perfectly righteous man. It is obvious that we have here a second edition of the original narrative, which tried to reconcile the story with Christian ideas about the nature of Jesus.

The question whether Mark used written sources has again been revivified in the last few years.[9] This problem was more or less forgotten when it was generally agreed that Matthew and Luke used a Mark substantially identical with the canonical gospel. Certainly they did, but the canonical Mark may be a translation from Aramaic or it may be a composition made up of previously existing Greek sources.

[8] A definite evolution can be traced in the accounts of John's relation to Jesus. In Mark he baptised Jesus, apparently without knowing him, and this is probably true also of Q (Cf. Matt. xi.2-6 = Luke vii.18-23). In Matthew the text of Mark is emended so that John recognises Jesus as his superior. In Luke John is the cousin of Jesus, but otherwise the Marcan account is not emended, though it is expanded. In John no baptism of Jesus is recorded, and John is merely a witness of the descent of the Spirit into Jesus.

[9] This question is also dealt with by the exponents of *Formgeschichte*, see pp. 18 ff.

Prof. Torrey and the late Prof. Burney are the leading exponents of the former view. The evidence for it is of two kinds. First, there is the assumption that the Apostles preached first to Jews in Palestine, and therefore talked and wrote Aramaic. This assumption can easily be pressed too far. Except in exclusively Jewish circles, Greek was probably the chief language of Palestine and all the evidence goes to show that the Apostolic preaching succeeded in Greek circles, not in Aramaic ones. Secondly, it is widely held that the text of the gospels contains Semitic idioms and phrases which show that it is a translation. This also is a dangerous argument. The writers of the gospels were probably Jewish by descent, and their Greek was doubtless Jewish-Greek. But the fact that their Greek was bad does not prove that it was a translation. Nevertheless, though the case for Aramaic originals may have been exaggerated, it should not be neglected. Unfortunately, a superficial study of the subject is worthless and few know enough Aramaic or even Greek to pursue it independently.

The case for the belief that earlier Greek or Aramaic sources lie behind Mark will always depend on the answer given to two questions, often put but not yet finally answered:

i. Does Mark vi.31-vii.37 represent a written tradition of the same events as are described in Mark viii.1-ix.1? Starting from the obvious similarity of the accounts of the feeding of the five thousand and the four thousand, some such analysis as the following has been suggested, on the basis of the theory that Source A and Source B can be distinguished. It will be seen that the similarity is sufficient to suggest two sources, but not to prove them. In any case, the question remains whether the doublets were written or oral.

Source A	Source B
The gathering of a crowd	
Mk. vi.31 ff. = [Mt. xiv.13 Lk. ix.10-11]	Mk. viii.1 = [Mt. xv.32] *not in Luke*
The feeding of the crowd	
Mk. vi.34 ff. = Mt. xiv.15 ff. Lk. ix.12 ff.	Mk. viii.2 ff. = Mt. xv.32 ff. *not in Luke*

The passage to Bethsaida (?) in Peraea	
Mk. vi.45 ff. = Mt. xiv.22 ff. *not in Luke*	Mk. viii.10 = Mt. xv.39 *not in Luke*

Encounter with the Pharisees	
Mk. vii.1 ff. = Mt. xv.1 ff. *not in Luke*	Mk. viii.11 ff. = Mt. xvi.1 ff. *not in Luke*

Journey to North	
Mk. vii.24 ff. = Mt. xv.21 ff. *not in Luke*	[Mk. viii.22 ff. *not in Mt. nor Luke*] Mk. viii.27 = Mt. xvi.13 ff. Lk. ix.18 ff.

ii. Are the prophecies of the Passion in Mark viii.31, ix.31 and x.33 three versions of one original saying? It might seem so, but it should be remembered in any case that Jesus' prophecy of his rejection in Jerusalem is not likely to have been made on only one occasion. Writers, inflamed by the fact that *littera scripta manet* are inclined to make a statement once; teachers, if they wish to be remembered, repeat the same thing over and over again. Moreover, a Christian missionary would be more interested in what Jesus did or said, especially if it bore on the message about Jesus, than in the circumstances under which he did or said it.

The further study of the synoptic problem soon shows that there is much material common to Matthew and Luke, but not found in Mark, which is almost verbally identical in the two gospels. How can it be accounted for? There are only three possibilities: i. Luke knew Matthew; ii. Matthew knew Luke; iii. both had a common source other than Mark.

i. It has been suggested that Luke used and compressed Matthew, adding at intervals such extra material as he had found. The main objection to this is that it assumes that the Gospel of Matthew as a whole (allowing somewhat for textual evolution) lay before Luke, who selected and rejected a little here and a little there. But Luke's selections and his rejections are not easily intelligible on this hypothesis, which implies that he treated Matthew in a very different way from Mark.[10]

It is, of course, possible to make this theory more tenable by suggesting that the "Matthew" used by Luke was not our Matthew, but an earlier form which did not contain the Nativity chapters, or that the original Luke had no Nativity story. The difficulty, however, remains, that it implies that Luke knew and rejected the Sermon on the Mount and the magnificent parables peculiar to Matthew. Again, it is possible to say that the "original" Matthew did not contain these parables. But if Matthew is trimmed down to this extent it loses so much that the "original" Matthew becomes Mark *plus* the parts which are also in Luke. This would mean merely that Luke knew a combination of Mark and something else, and it is then difficult to see why Luke should be supposed to have looked up the Marcan parallels in Mark, and so rarely have followed Matthew in these sections.

ii. Matthew used Luke. The objections to i. apply even more strongly here and this theory has rarely, if ever, been suggested.

iii. Therefore, since both these possibilities are untenable, only the third alternative remains,—that both writers used a document, which must have been in Greek,[11] containing *some or all* of the material found in both. This is the simplest theory, but the difficulty is in the words italicised,—*some or all*. The document suggested is usually called Q (the initial of the German *Quelle*, 'source'); it might equally well be several documents or one. The main objection to the theory of Q is that we know how Luke and Matthew treated Mark. Both

[10] See note 6 on p. 6.

[11] The close verbal agreement of the Gospels is impossible if they are *independent* translations of Aramaic. That does not exclude the possibility that the Greek Mark or the Greek Q, used by Matthew and Luke, were translations from Aramaic. See C. C. Torrey's *Our Translated Gospels*. The strongest evidence that Matthew and Luke used a Q which was a translation from Aramaic seems to us to be the use of διχοτομῆσαι in Matt. xxiv.51 and in Luke xii.46. This verb can mean nothing except "cut in pieces," and makes no sense in the context. It must be a misunderstanding. It is certainly easier to postulate a mistranslation from Aramaic in the original Greek Q, than a corruption in Greek. See Torrey, pp. 155 and 157.

took relatively long sections and copied them with only small changes. But, in the case of Q, Matthew took a series of short passages and put them together, or, alternatively, Luke split up the continuous text of Q and distributed it among various contexts. Why did they (or at least one of them) treat Q so differently from Mark? We know of no satisfactory answer. From time to time, there is a revival of the old theory (suggested by Eichhorn and popularised by Schleiermacher) of a number of little documents combined in one way by Matthew and in another by Luke. This partly answers the conditions of the problem but does not explain the recurring agreements in sequence which exist in the non-Marcan as well as in the Marcan sections:

e.g. Luke	vi.20-23	=	Matt.	v.2-12
"	—.27-36	=	"	—.44-48
"	—.41-42	=	"	vii.3
"	—.43-44	=	"	—.16-17
"	—.46-49	=	"	—.21
"	vii.1-10	=	"	viii.5 ff.

These sequences are the kernel of the problem and the last word has not yet been said.

Assuming, then, as a working hypothesis,[12] that Matthew and Luke made use of a common source (or complex of sources) to be called Q, what were its contents, how did Matthew and Luke use it, and was it known to Mark?

i. What were the contents of Q? There is no way of answering this question with any approach to accuracy. The best proof of this is to consider what a miserable failure would result from any attempt to reconstruct Mark from Matthew

[12] There is no such agreement as to Q as there is as to Mark. Out of a mass of literature the following especially demand attention: A. von Harnack, *Beiträge,* II, *Sprüche und Reden Jesu* (translated as 'the Sayings of Jesus'); J. Wellhausen, *Einleitung,* pp. 65-89; W. C. Allen, *Commentary on Matthew;* Sir J. Hawkins, *Horae Synopticae,* especially pp. 107 ff.; *Oxford Studies in the Synoptic Gospels,* especially pp. 141-208 (but pp. 165-184 have been superseded by Streeter's *Four Gospels,* in which he explains that he has changed his opinion). Streeter's *Four Gospels* is much the most lucid and comprehensive treatment in English.

and Luke, if Mark were not extant, and we tried to reconstruct the obvious common sources of Matthew and Luke.[18] We should reach a document omitting nearly 25% of Mark, but including all which we now think may have come from Q. Therefore, the temptation must be resisted of following any mechanical system such as accepting only passages found in both Matthew and Luke.

That Q cannot be certainly reconstructed is as clear as that it once existed. It should be noted, however, that two sections in Matthew, the Sermon on the Mount (Matt. v.1-vii.29) and the Instructions to the Twelve (Matt. x.5-xi.1) lead up to narratives which are also found in Luke but not in Mark, so that Q can hardly have been merely a collection of sayings. On the other hand, neither in Matthew nor in Luke is there any hint that Q ever contained an account of events in Jerusalem. It would therefore seem probable that it was a collection (collections?) of stories illustrating the teaching which Jesus had given to the multitude in Galilee.

ii. The method of its use in Matthew and Luke is equally obscure. Two extreme positions are possible. Either Matthew preserved Q as faithfully as he did Mark, while Luke cut it up into shorter pieces and connected each piece with a narrative-setting which he either invented or found elsewhere; or Luke preserved Q as faithfully as he did Mark, giving the narrative-setting as he found it, and Matthew usually left out the narrative-setting and collected the sayings so that they formed long discourses. As between these two positions, the second is perhaps the more probable, though there is no real evidence and there can be no final conclusion.

iii. That Mark and Q probably overlapped, in the sense that they both told some of the same stories, is possible. For instance the stories of the Baptism and Temptation in Matthew and Luke seem to have come from a common Greek source, which was not Mark. Whether this was, for instance, the same document as that which provided the Sermon on the Mount is quite another question. For this reason, it is desirable to em-

18 See Burkitt in *Beginnings*, Vol. II, pp. 106 ff.

phasize that if we use Q to designate the non-Marcan material common to Matthew and Luke, it must be taken to mean the *source or sources* used by the Evangelists, without prejudging which of the two (source or sources) is preferable.[14]

In addition to Mark and Q, Matthew and Luke each have much material not found elsewhere.[15] This certainly did not come from Mark, and at least some of it would, with varying degrees of probability, be excluded from any reconstruction of Q. The most important parts of this material are as follows:

i. Both Matthew and Luke give an account of the birth and ancestry of Jesus. These accounts obviously come from different sources, for they agree only in three points. First, they regard the conception of Jesus by the Virgin Mary as the miraculous act of God, not of man—so that Joseph in both stories is only the husband of Mary, not the father of Jesus; secondly, they place the birth of Jesus in Bethlehem; thirdly, they trace the ancestry of Jesus (though in different ways) to David.

Matthew tells the story of the Birth in the Manger, the Magi, the Massacre of the Innocents and the Flight into Egypt. Luke tells of the Annunciation (for which Joseph's dream seems to be a surrogate in Matthew), the Shepherds, the Angelic Chorus and Jesus' childhood. He also tells the story of the birth of John the Baptist.

It has often been argued that there is a glaring contradiction between the genealogies, which have the descent of Jesus through Joseph, and the rest of the narrative which seems to be written to prove that Joseph was not the father of Jesus. But this criticism is to be treated with reserve. To the Jewish mind, a man's children were those born of his wife, not those physically generated by him. It was quite possible to regard Jesus as the son of Joseph, given to him miraculously by the spirit of God through his wife. Parallels can be found in

[14] See also p. 11.

[15] Once more, the best discussion of the subject is in Streeter's *Four Gospels*, pp. 242 ff., even if his "four document" theory be emended by writing "source" for "document."

Philo in the stories of the birth of Isaac, of Samson and of Samuel, in all of which the Biblical narrative is interpreted as meaning that the child was conceived through the supernatural act of God. For this reason, it is not necessary to postulate separate sources for the genealogies and for the rest of the nativity stories either in Matthew or in Luke.

The difference between the two narratives did not much trouble ancient interpreters, who intertwined them into a continuous story, but the difference between the genealogies was a real difficulty to them. This, however, was generally explained by assuming that Luke gives the legal descent of Joseph, the putative father of Jesus, through Eli from Nathan, the son of David, and that Matthew gives his physical descent through Jacob from Solomon.[16]

There is a noticeable difference in style as well as in content between the Matthean and the Lucan narratives. The Lucan account is full of Old Testament thoughts, and it is natural that many scholars have thought that it is a translation from Aramaic or Hebrew. Against this, however, is the insuperable objection that all the Semitisms in it and the phrases borrowed from the Old Testament, especially in the poems, are found in the Septuagint.[17] It is, therefore, more probable that it is 'translation' Greek, not translated Hebrew, deliberately

16 The explanation can be traced back to Julius Africanus quoted by Eusebius, *Eccl. hist.* I, vii.5. The argument is clearer in paraphrase than in translation. The point is that among the Jews if a man died childless his brother was charged with the duty of begetting children by the widow, who was still reckoned as the wife of the deceased. Such children were legally regarded as the sons of the dead brother, though known to be actually the children of the living one. This happened in the case of Joseph. He was legally the son of Eli, physically of Jacob. A further complication was that Eli and Jacob were only half brothers. They were the sons of the same mother, Estha, but Eli was the son of her second husband Melchi, descended from Nathan the son of David, and Jacob was the son of her first husband Matthan, descended from Solomon, the son of David. Thus Matthew, giving the physical descent of Jesus, traces it through Jacob to Solomon, but Luke (who avoids the word "begat"), giving the legal descent, traces it through Eli to Nathan.

17 See Sir John Hawkins, *Horae Synopticae*, pp. 154 ff. and, for a convenient collection and discussion of all quotations from the Old Testament by the writers of the New, Turpie, *The Old Testament in the New*, London, 1868, still very valuable as a book of reference.

adopted by the author in imitation of similar stories (e.g. that of Hannah, the mother of Samuel) in the Old Testament. Whether it was composed by Luke or someone else is likely to be always an open question. Harnack argued in his *Lucas der Arzt* that the vocabulary is specifically Lucan; he scarcely proved his point, but established a good case.

The Matthean narrative is a more doubtful question. The story as a whole is told in simple Greek with nothing to prove that it is a translation, but also nothing to prove that it is not. The question really turns on the quotations from the Old Testament, which are adduced to prove the fulfillment of prophecy.[18] Unlike the much more numerous citations and allusions in Luke, these are not all or even mostly from the Septuagint, but seem usually to be independent renderings, sometimes perhaps of a text varying from the Masoretic. If they are an integral part of the narrative they do not prove that the whole was translated from Hebrew or Aramaic, but they make this view not improbable. If they are merely insertions, this argument falls to the ground, and that they are insertions is suggested by the fact that similar quotations from the Hebrew Old Testament are found throughout Matthew, in places where the ground-text, taken either from Mark or Q was certainly used by Matthew in Greek, even if the possibility be conceded that these documents are translations.

The theory has often been suggested[19] that these Matthean quotations from the Old Testament, proving the fulfillment of prophecy, were taken from an early collection of *Testimonia,* or proof-texts from the Old Testament. There is much to favour this view, which we accept as almost certain, but there is no decisive proof of it.

ii. The material combined with Mark and Q in Matthew or Luke, but not in both, may be divided into two categories. There are in each gospel a number of parables and a smaller number of episodes which are not recorded elsewhere. It is

[18] They are usually introduced by the phrase "That it might be fulfilled."

[19] Especially by J. Rendel Harris. Cf. his *Testimonia.*

conceivable that some, or even all, of this material really belonged to Q or even to Mark. The suggestion that any of it comes from Mark is, however, very improbable, for there is no valid reason for thinking that there ever was an earlier form of Mark (the Ur-Marcus theory) of which the present text is an abbreviation. All the evidence, such as it is, points the other way. Nor is the suggestion that any of it comes from Q very convincing, though the case is different. Judging from the way in which Matthew and Luke used Mark, there is great probability that each left out different parts. Therefore, it is antecedently probable that some sections originally belonging to Q are now extant only in Matthew and others only in Luke. The difficulty is that we cannot identify these sections. Is it likely that any one who found in his source the parable of the Prodigal Son deliberately omitted it? Or that he left out the parable of the Wise and Foolish Virgins? Surely not. But if not, it would seem either that Matthew and Luke used, in addition to Mark and Q, special sources which contained a collection of parables, or, perhaps less probably, that each collected them for himself.[20]

A more difficult question is raised by two sections in Matthew:

In v.17-44 there is an extended discussion of the Law and its meaning, introduced by the assertion that Jesus was not come to destroy the Law, but to "fill" it.[21] Naturally there has always been much dispute whether this passage is taken from Q or belongs to the peculiarly Matthean material, and whether it represents the authentic teaching of Jesus or is that of a Jewish Christian.

20 See also pp. 41 and 45.

21 The Greek might mean to "keep" or to "supplement." Probably the latter, for the teaching of Jesus in the context shows that he was consciously giving an interpretation of the Law which made it harder. Most people manage to avoid murder; few succeed in abstaining from anger. It should be noted that the usual rendering "fulfil," inevitably implies 'I am not come to destroy the Law, but to fulfil the Prophets.' This is doubly wrong. There is nothing in the context about fulfilling prophecy, and the phrase "Law or the Prophets" in Matt. v.17 merely means "Scripture" generally.

In x.5-16 are the instructions to the Twelve not to go to the Samaritans or Gentiles.[22]

Both these passages are found only in Matthew. In any case, they throw light on Matthew's point of view; if they were originally in Q and omitted by Luke, they would also illuminate Luke's point of view. Unfortunately, this is just the question which cannot be answered. Luke may have "omitted" them, because he did not know them. In favour of the view that the substance of these passages is authentic, though the Matthean form may be secondary, is the fact that Luke seems to have been acquainted with part of their contents (e.g. cf. Luke xvi.17; Matt. v.18.

A somewhat different approach to the gospels was made in America by a group of scholars headed by Prof. B. W. Bacon and in France by A. Loisy. To us it seems that they were apt to minimise the importance of the facts on which Holtzmann and his followers had built, and to emphasise Pauline influence even in the Gospel of Mark, where to us it seems noticeably lacking. But they made a permanent contribution by urging that the influence of the community should be noted in the gospel story, as, for instance, in the Quartodeciman controversy in relation to the variation in the gospels in the story of the Passion.[23]

The point to be remembered is that the gospels were not written as "pure history" but as missionary propaganda, and reflect the problems, conditions and controversies of the early communities. The weak spot in the *Quellenkritik* of the end of the nineteenth century was that it studied the gospels as a literary problem rather than as a reflexion of early Christian life. It is extremely valuable to use the gospels and Acts as representing the questions raised in the Apostolic age and the

[22] See *Beginnings,* Vol. I, pp. 314-318, and Burkitt's criticism in his *Christian Beginnings,* p. 135. We now agree with Burkitt.

[23] Bacon's book, *The Beginnings of the Gospel Story,* should be studied, together with Loisy's *Les Évangiles Synoptiques* as the best examples of a penetrating criticism different from the dominant school. It has been in the main ignored, except in America, but advanced students will find it suggestive.

answers given to them. For instance, it is clear that the listeners to the Apostles asked such questions: How do you know that Jesus was the Messiah? Why did he not announce it to the people in Galilee? What did he say about this and about that? Obviously to reconstruct the answers to these questions is more important than the definition of Q.

A notable step forward in approaching the gospels in this way was made by a group of scholars in Germany, including Dibelius, Bultmann and K. L. Schmidt, who have adopted for their method the name *Formgeschichte* (form criticism).[24] The method has been used also, with differences, by Lightfoot, Vincent Taylor and Dodd in England and by Easton and Riddle in America. The name was borrowed from specialists in mediæval German literature who classified and dated popular stories according to their form—the way in which a story is introduced, or ended, and so forth.

The method and results of this study were first applied (by Gunkel) to the Old Testament, and afterwards to the New. It tries to go behind the gospels and, by considering the way in which stories were told, enable us to see each story of what Jesus did or said as a unit by itself,—rather than part of an organic whole. It is argued that the stories in Mark, for example, may have been in circulation, in a written form, before Mark used them. It is possible; but there seems to us to be no evidence of it, and the general unity of Marcan style is against the view. Ultimately the whole question resolves itself into a comparison between the stories and their contexts.[25] Theories that there were written collections of parables etc. are purely hypothetical. As hypotheses they deserve discussion, but, as Burkitt was fond of saying, "it is possible to draw too many conclusions from the fact that if you are going to tell that sort of story, that is the sort of way in which you would tell it."

In the hands of its more successful exponents, such as Dibelius, *Formgeschichte* does not reject the results of the

[24]See *Bibliography* for some of the main books. The best introduction to the subject in English seems to us to be B. S. Easton's *The Gospel before the Gospels.*

[25]The best general criticism of the whole method is in Burkitt's *Jesus Christ*, 1932, especially p. 70. The importance of the Epilogue in this book is far greater than its size would suggest.

previous criticism, but tries to go beyond it, especially in the case of Mark, to discover earlier written sources of the gospels and to discount the accuracy of the canonical narratives. So far as Matthew and Luke are concerned, this is partly a new attack on the problem of Q etc. from a different angle. So far as Mark is concerned, it is partly the revivification of *Ur-Marcus*. Its most solid and undoubtedly permanent achievement is that it has brought more imagination into the question and reminded us of the actual conditions of the period between the Passion and the writing of the gospels.

How did Christianity spread? By controversy and teaching. The Apostles said, "Jesus is the Messiah and he will be the Judge at the End of the World. His story proves the truth of the statement." Acts, in the speeches of Peter and Paul, gives in epitome examples of the Apostolic preaching, but there must have been many stories used by the missionaries to drive home their message. Mark undoubtedly contains a collection of these stories. They can be classified by various names,[26] but the fact that a terminology originally used for classifying the tales of folk-lore can also be used for stories in Mark does not prove anything except that it can be used.

Some critics of this school apparently think that Mark shows few signs of chronological arrangement. To us it seems that, on the contrary, Mark's plan is broadly but clearly chronological. The suggestion is also made that the teaching of Jesus was circulated with varying contexts of narrative; this is very probable and admittedly there are places where there is inconsistency in the story as we have it. Most of these inconsistencies were pointed out in the generations between Baur and Wrede. In some respects, the constructive studies of the synoptic gospels, from Holtzmann to Streeter, are an interim, —to our mind a very successful one,—and the *Formgeschichtliche* school is taking up again the work of more detailed study, and quite correctly reminds us that the gospels represent missionary and controversial activity. Papias knew this,

[26] Such as "paradigms" and "apothegms" and "paraenese." There is an excellent criticism of the use made of these terms in E. Fascher *Die formgeschichtliche Methode*.

but some scholars had forgotten it. It also points out that the connection between any given story and its context is likely to be weak, for preachers, like raconteurs, sometimes make up a context to fit a story on the one hand and their audience on the other.

But there seems to us a tendency to exaggerate this last point, especially when it is tacitly implied that it was the ethical teaching of Jesus which was the main element in Apostolic teaching. On the contrary, unless we are prepared to abandon all the evidence of Acts and of Paul, it was the teaching about Jesus,—that he was the divine Saviour and Judge,—which conquered the world.

There is perhaps also a tendency to read too much of modern conditions into the reconstruction of early Christianity. *Formgeschichte* speaks of "the community" and of "preaching." This inevitably suggests a congregation which cherished established opinions and preachers who voiced them. But the Apostles were creating opinions by authoritative pronouncement; it was not preaching in the ordinary sense; moreover, there was not "a community", but a group of communities.

The truth is that the whole *Formgeschichte* movement points to a deep difference of opinion, rather than to purely literary questions. The final result of criticism before 1914 was to paint a picture of Jesus as the herald of the End, believed by his followers to have thought that he was the eschatological Son of Man who would preside at the Judgement, though he had concealed the fact from the populace by speaking in parables. As Schweitzer pointed out, this is a Jesus who belongs to the first century and cannot live in the twentieth.[27]

Schweitzer was not really the first to see this. The fact is often overlooked that the difficulty was clearly perceived by the radical school in Holland and Germany,[28] who insisted not merely that the Jesus of the synoptic gospels was unimportant for religion, but that he was a literary fiction and

27 In his *Quest of the Historic Jesus.*

28 Such writers as Drews, van Manen, Oort, Bolland and G. van der Bergh van Eisinga in Europe and W. B. Smith in America, who all felt that they were assisting the Christian religion by destroying a myth on which it had once been nourished, but was now being poisoned.

could be shown never to have existed, because he did not explain the Christianity of the second century. The answer to this school was that the synoptic gospels, if they were fiction, were inexplicable as Christian documents and absurd as Jewish or heathen ones. Rapidity of evolution explains the difference between the gospels and the second century.

The answer was adequate and the radical school is, therefore, if not dead, at least suffering from low vitality. But the problem remained. The picture of early Christianity which was attractive to Lutherans of the Schleiermacher-Ritzchlian school in Germany, was of missionaries who converted the heathen by proclaiming the ethical teaching of Jesus. The difficulty in maintaining this position is that early Christian literature, especially Acts, paints an entirely different picture. It shows missionaries preaching a supernatural Lord who is the Saviour and will be the Judge. Is it possible to prove that there was a period before the writing of the gospels when a different message was preached? If so, how did the "paradigms" and "apothegms" make the transition to Mark, with its perfectly clear, even if unpalatable story, so consistent with the picture in Acts?

On the other hand, this criticism should not be pressed too far. There is a danger that the adherents and opponents of *Formgeschichte* may misinterpret each other. If we understand Dibelius correctly, he would say that the Apostles converted the world by eschatological teaching; the result was Christian communities and in those Christian communities the non-eschatological discourses were the chief subject of preaching. The gospels, generally, represent the second stage. We would, on the other hand, think that Mark, in the main, represents the first stage,—teaching for conversion,—and that there is much of this stage even in Matthew. But doubtless Matthew and Luke also contain much of the second stage and possibly more than we have realized. How much more? Where is John to be placed? These are the fascinating problems which the future will discuss.

EXTERNAL EVIDENCE

It is now desirable to take up the tradition of the Church and see how far and how credibly it amplifies the information given by the gospels themselves.

Few students realise that for the period between the crucifixion of Christ and the Edict of Milan we have only two books written as ecclesiastical history,—all the rest are either didactic or polemical. These two books are the Acts of the Apostles and the Church History of Eusebius. Fortunately, Eusebius was a very careful collector of evidence, who quotes verbatim and had the best possible means of finding what evidence existed. A few details, but very few, can be added from other writers.

Let us extract from this very scanty material[29] the facts which it states about each evangelist and compare it with the internal evidence discussed above.

According to Papias, Mark wrote down the teaching of Peter about Jesus. He did not write it according to *taxis* (order), and he did not compile the *logia* (oracles) of the Lord, but he made no mistakes. This evidence would be clearer if we knew the meaning of the essential phrases *taxis* and *logia*. *Taxis* means orderly arrangement, but it may refer either to chronological order or to correct composition. The latter view is not impossible, for the word was a technical term for proper literary arrangement.[30] If so, Papias' statement is confirmed by the internal evidence. The Gospel of Mark is the least literary of the three, and would have pained the feelings of any educated Greek. Nevertheless, this ingenious explanation does not quite satisfy. Anyone reading the Greek of Eusebius with no knowledge of the problem would almost certainly say that the meaning of Papias is that Mark wrote down scattered episodes with no effort at order, and that Mark is in this respect a contrast to someone else who *did* write in order.

The criticism implied by Papias was that Mark was uncorroborated by some other document which he knew, and he ex-

29 See Appendix C.

30 See F. H. Colson, *Journal of Theological Studies*, XIV, pp. 62 ff.

plained this as due to lack of *taxis* in Mark, the importance of which he admitted. He says that Mark is, nevertheless, valuable, because he made no mistakes; the Gospel is all true, though not written in proper *taxis*. Unfortunately, the effect of Papias' statement has been to establish the view that Mark is a disjointed collection of episodes. This is not confirmed by the facts. Mark seems to have a clear idea that Jesus was journeying through the country. He does not give notes of time, but many consecutive notes of places.

The full force of the problem is seen if it be remembered that the internal evidence of Mark does not confirm the view that it was written with no regard to chronological order. This view, therefore, cannot be mere deduction, but must repeat a very early criticism of this form of the Gospel on the basis of comparison with some other which was alleged to be superior to it in this respect. But which gospel was it which supplied the standard? So far, no convincing answer has been given.

The other point is at least a little clearer. Papias contrasts Mark, who did not make a collection of the Lord's *logia,* with Matthew, who did. But does that mean our Gospel of Matthew? If so, the previous problem would be in some ways easier, but, as will be seen,[31] it is quite improbable that Papias (not Eusebius) can have meant this. Moreover, the exact meaning of *logia* is difficult; all that is known is that Mark did not have a collection of them and Matthew did, but the further discussion of this point belongs rather to the treatment of Matthew.

Clement and Irenaeus add to the evidence of Papias that Mark wrote in Rome, but Clement thinks that Peter was still there when the Gospel was written, and Irenaeus that he and Paul were both dead.

There is a remarkable unanimity about this tradition and though the statement that Mark's gospel represents the teaching of Peter might have been deduction from I Peter v.13, this view is not very satisfactory. Anyone who had only the New Testament would be more likely to guess Paul as Mark's source of information. But no one ever did. Therefore, there is a presumption that on this point we have a remnant of real

[31] See pp. 25 f.

tradition, not of deduction, and neither the internal evidence nor the statements about Mark in other books, looked at in order to test the Petrine theory, gives any reason for doubt.

According to Acts, Mark was a young man living in Jerusalem. He was a cousin or nephew of Barnabas and therefore possibly a Cypriote and probably a Greek-speaking Jew. He accompanied Barnabas and Paul on their first journey, but quarreled with Paul and afterwards went off with Barnabas. If the Pastoral Epistles can be trusted, Paul and he were later reconciled, and I Peter refers to him as Peter's "son." Such are the facts about Mark; the question is how they compare with the evidence of the Gospel itself.

Mark i-xi cannot be the personal observations of Mark, but there is nothing in these chapters which might not have been derived from Peter. Peter is a prominent figure in the Gospel from beginning to end, and may well have told Mark everything contained in it. The Baptism and Temptation must go back to Jesus himself, but why not through Peter? Thus, the first part of the book may really be, as Loisy called it, the Faith of St. Peter, as related by Peter to Mark or to congregations of which Mark was a member. There seems, however, to be a distinct difference in character after chapter xi and it is possible that from here to the end of the book the basis of the narrative is the actual observation of Mark. It has been suggested that Mark was the young man at Gethsemane, who witnessed the scene in the Garden. Scarcely anyone else would think it worthwhile to interrupt the story of the Passion by explaining that he escaped arrest by leaving his clothes behind.

According to Papias, Matthew wrote the *logia* [32] in the Hebrew tongue and each translated it as best he could.

The meaning of the word *logia* is often discussed, largely because imperfect attention to the Greek evidence led some of the earlier critics to take it as 'sayings', with an implied antithesis to 'actions.' But the early Christian use is to give the word its ordinary force in classical Greek,—'oracles.' It is used in this sense of the Old Testament in I Clement. There is,

[32] See above, pp. 23 f.

therefore, considerable force in the theory held by Rendel Harris and, at least at one time, by F. C. Burkitt, that Papias used it to describe a collection of 'oracles' or 'proof-texts' from the Old Testament. This might be the source of the 'proof-texts' so often found in Matthew, which differ from most other quotations in the New Testament by being taken from the Hebrew text, not the Septuagint.

The chief objection to this theory is that there are not enough of these proof-texts, even in Matthew, to make up a book, and it is decidedly weakened if we have to supplement it by saying that the editor of the first gospel only took over part of the collection, though he borrowed the name of its maker as the title of his edition.

An alternative view is that one of the other documents incorporated in our Matthew was the *logia* collected by the original Matthew. If so, Q would seem to be the most probable. Of course it was used in Greek both by Luke and our Matthew, but it may have been originally Aramaic. Possibly, but hardly probably, there is a trace of some tradition to this effect in the note found in many Greek manuscripts, that the gospel was written by Matthew in Hebrew and translated by "John,"—whoever he may have been.

Papias says nothing about Luke's gospel, and the general tradition that Luke was a companion of Paul and a physician is obviously derived from Colossians. It was also often stated that Luke came from Antioch. This is probably based on the Western text of Acts xi.27 f. There has been much controversy as to whether Luke-Acts show that Luke was a companion of Paul and a physician.[33] The latter point has been settled negatively by H. J. Cadbury, who destroyed all the arguments of Harnack in *Lucas der Arzt,* but the former is open to much discussion.

The comparison of Acts with the Epistles seems unfavourable, though scarcely fatal to the theory that the writer of Acts

[33] The case for the belief that the editor of Luke-Acts was a companion of Paul is based on the We-clauses in Acts, and has been argued with the most enthusiasm by Sir William Ramsay in his *St. Paul, the Traveler and Roman Citizen,* and other books. The opposite case is to be found in the *Beginnings of Christianity,* Vol. II (pp. 298 ff.) and Vol. V, (pp. 194 f.).

was a companion of Paul. It is also doubtful whether the emphasis in Luke xxiv.39 on the fact that the risen Jesus had a body of flesh is compatible with knowledge of the Paul who wrote in I Cor. xv that flesh and blood cannot inherit the Kingdom of God.

Thus, the results of an inquiry into the first question formulated on p. 3, "Who wrote these books?" can be tentatively answered as follows: Mark was probably written by a man of that name and the internal evidence corroborates the tradition that he represented the teaching of St. Peter. The authorship of Matthew is less certain, as the earliest tradition mentioning his name does not seem to deal with the gospel as we have it now, but more probably with one of its sources. Finally, Luke may well have been written by a man of that name, but the internal evidence renders it doubtful whether he was a companion of Paul, or merely used the diary of someone who was.

The second question, "What material did the authors use?" can similarly be answered as follows. Both Matthew and Luke used Mark, in approximately the same form as we have it now, and another document (or documents) usually called Q. Although it cannot be accurately defined its contents were discourses rather than narratives. Both gospels probably also used special sources of their own, but the extent of these sources, and whether they were documents or merely traditions is a very doubtful point.

A theory similar to that of the Ur Marcus (see p. 20) has been suggested, notably by Streeter, to the effect that between the sources of Luke and the present form of the Gospel there should be postulated an intermediate form to which the name is given of Proto-Luke, and a similar postulation of a Proto-Matthew has also been suggested. This is an interesting suggestion, but it has not met with very wide support, and it seems to us that the facts on which it is based are sufficiently explained by the recognition that Matthew and Luke each used a source peculiar to himself (see page 14 ff.).

CHAPTER II

The Plan and Purpose of the Synoptic Gospels

THE purpose of this chapter is to describe the general plan which seems to have been followed by each of the three authors of the synoptic gospels, in order, so far as possible, to discover their main purpose in writing.[1]

It is, of course, clear that they purposed to give an account of the life of Jesus, but this account was necessarily intended to justify Christian opinion of the time, as well as to satisfy Christian curiosity. What this opinion and curiosity were can be seen best from the selection of incidents and the general arrangement of each gospel.

THE PLAN AND PURPOSE OF MARK

Mark gives a connected narrative of the general course of the life of Jesus, arranged as follows:

i. Mark i.1-13: A short description of John the Baptist, leading up to the Baptism of Jesus and his temptation in the wilderness. The main point of this section is that at his Baptism, Jesus heard a "voice from heaven," the customary Rabbinic phrase to describe a divine revelation, announcing that he was appointed "Son of God." "Son of God" is a curiously ambiguous phrase. In the Old Testament it often means an angel (cf. Gen. vi.4, Job i.6) but in the Wisdom of Solomon it often means a 'good man,' and in Ps. ii.7 it apparently means an 'anointed' Davidic king.[2]

[1] It is absurd to suppose that everything which was known was related in the Gospels. It is this which gives strength to the argument that episodes such as the *Pericope de adultera* or the *Man working on the Sabbath* may be perfectly true, though not part of the original text of our Gospels.

[2] See pp. 204 f.

ii. Mark i.14-iii.6: Jesus' ministry of healing and preaching in the synagogues of Galilee, of which, however, only Capernaum is mentioned by name. To this period belongs the call of Andrew, Peter, James and John. The main features are the demons' immediate recognition of Jesus as the "Holy One of God," the healing of disease and a quarrel with the Rabbis, who were angry because Jesus did not observe the law of the Sabbath and blasphemed by claiming to forgive sins. This quarrel drove Jesus out of the synagogue and forced him to adopt a different kind of ministry.

iii. Mark iii.7-vii.23: The ministry of Jesus by the shore of the sea of Galilee and on the hills. It includes the appointment of the Twelve Apostles, a refutation of the charge made by Scribes from Jerusalem that Jesus was a demoniac himself, a short collection of parables and an explanation of them, a miraculous calming of the sea, some more miracles of healing, instructions to the Twelve, the story of Herod and John the Baptist, the feeding of the five thousand and more controversy with Scribes.

iv. Mark vii.24-ix.29: The sequence of events in this section is somewhat confused. As it stands, it describes:

a. The withdrawal of Jesus to Phoenicia and the healing of a Syrian woman's demoniac child.

b. How Jesus "went out from the districts of Tyre through Sidon to the sea of Galilee, through the midst of the districts of Decapolis." This is very difficult, but not geographically impossible.[3]

c. The feeding of the four thousand, after which Jesus went by boat to an unknown place, Dalmanutha, obviously somewhere on the shore of the Lake. It has often been suggested that this is a doublet of the feeding of the five thousand.

d. Jesus then went again to the north to Caesarea Philippi, where Peter acknowledged him as the Messiah, but apparently regarded the term as having a content other than Jesus accepted.

[3] See p. 271.

e. The Transfiguration on the mountain, when the mission of Jesus was again revealed by a "voice from heaven" as at the Baptism, but this time not to Jesus only but to Peter, James and John.

f. The healing of the demoniac child whom the disciples had been unable to cure.

v. Mark ix.30-xi.15: The journey of Jesus from the north through Galilee along the Jordan Valley to Jericho and so to Jerusalem. This is a straightforward account of a journey from one point to another. It was (cf. ix.30-50) not a missionary journey as long as Jesus was in Galilee, but nevertheless a growing crowd followed him, and though he is not said to have given any definite teaching, answers are recorded to questions on marriage, the requirements for entry into Life Eternal (especially in relation to wealth) and on precedence in the Kingdom. Thus Jericho was reached and Jesus healed a blind beggar, Bartimaeus.

From Jericho they went on the road to Jerusalem. This is a climb of almost 4,000 feet in a distance of less than twenty miles. The steepest part is probably the last, especially if, as seems to have been the case, the road went over the side of the Mount of Olives, and Jesus felt too tired to go on. A donkey was therefore fetched from a village in the neighborhood, and he rode up on it. It is doubtful whether Mark means that he rode into Jerusalem,[4] for though John and possibly Matthew and Luke thought of this as a triumphal entry into Jerusalem, probability would suggest the opposite. Anyone standing at the bottom of the eastern side of the Mount of Olives might well feel incapable of going any farther, but to go down from the hill-top into Jerusalem would not require any help. In fact, it is more tiring to ride an ass *down-hill* than it is to walk.

vi. Mark xi.15-xii.44: A series of discussions and episodes in Jerusalem. Of these the most important is the first, which describes the "cleansing of the Temple," when Jesus endeavoured to turn out the people who were selling animals for sacrifice or changing money. The reason for these vendors

[4] See p. 257.

in the Temple was that it was illegal to offer any beast for sacrifice which was imperfect, and to make certain that the beasts were perfect, it was generally advisable to purchase an animal from the Priests who examined and guaranteed it. This was undoubtedly a source of great income to the Priests. In the same way, it was illegal to offer any money to the Temple except the sacred Jewish coinage, and for that reason the ordinary money in secular use was changed by the representatives of the Priests at the door, doubtless for a suitable commission. The possibilities of profit in these two forms of commerce are obviously large and were the foundation of the fortunes of the great High-priestly families.[5] It will therefore be seen at once how dangerous a step Jesus took in protesting against such traffic, and it is not difficult to conclude that it was this rather than his quarrels with the Scribes which led to his death.

It should especially be noted that the previous narrative is not explicit as to the number of those who came up with Jesus from Galilee, though the implication seems to be that there were many more than the Twelve. But the story of the cleansing of the Temple and the hesitation of the Priests to arrest Jesus are unintelligible unless we recognise that he was at the head of a large and determined crowd.[6] No one man, or even thirteen, could have turned out the merchants and bankers and prevented free passage through the Temple, and if they had tried their arrest would have followed immediately.

vii. Mark xiii.1-37: The Apocalyptic address to the disciples. It has often been disputed whether this is an integral part of the Gospel of Mark or not. Many have thought that it was taken bodily from some other source, others that it can be

[5] The chief ones were the Boethusians, the family of Annas, the family of Kantheras and the family of Phabi, see *Beginnings,* Vol. I, p. 33.

[6] The conduct of the festival of Nebi Musa in modern Jerusalem is very illuminating to those who see it. The inhabitants of all the towns march into Jerusalem, shouting "So and so is a good man" or something similar. Everyone is excited and the police have a delicate task to observe order without inciting to riot. To arrest a leader during the day would be very inadvisable; but it is possible, if necessary, in the night. Probably the police of Jerusalem looked on "the Galileans" much as the police of today regard the deputations from Nablus or Hebron.

divided into sections which have been pieced together by some editor. Neither view is now as popular as it was once, and to us it seems difficult to see any real reason either for cutting the chapter out or for dissecting it into sources. Apart from many exegetical difficulties, two points are especially to be noted.

First, Jesus is certain that the End is close at hand, but is not willing to claim knowledge of the exact date; it will be during that generation, but the day and the hour are uncertain. He describes signs which will precede the End, but the phraseology is sufficiently important to be noted, especially since its implication is strangely overlooked in many commentaries.

Secondly, if we follow the Authorized Version, he says that these signs are the beginning of "sorrows," but the word translated 'sorrows' really means 'birth-pains,' and an extremely important point is that Jesus was not thinking of these events as the End of the Old Age nearly so much as the Beginning of the New. His warning to the Disciples is to prepare for the New, rather than to be concerned with the Old. Commentaries should be consulted to see what arguments there are for thinking that this chapter is necessarily before or after the Fall of Jerusalem. To our mind, it seems much more probable that it is earlier than the siege of the city, and we believe that it is probably a fair representation of what Jesus said.

viii. Mark xiv.1-52: The events of the last days before Jesus' arrest. This may be divided into three parts:

a. Jesus in Bethany (Mark xiv.1-9). The main importance of this is that it indicates an anticipation of death in the mind of Jesus, without the expressed expectation of resurrection. The same point can be noted in the parable of the vineyard in xii.1-9, in contrast to viii.31, ix.31 and x.33 f. Possibly this fact grows in importance if it be held, as we are inclined to do, that Mark xi-end is the personal reminiscence of Mark, while the early chapters are his memory of what Peter told him.

b. The story of the treachery of Judas. The question has often been raised as to what it was that Judas betrayed. Two views have been popular. The first is that Judas betrayed the fact that Jesus would admit that he was the Messiah if he were directly asked. This was rendered well-known, if not originated, by Schweitzer and Burkitt. The alternative is that Judas told the Priests how they could find Jesus in a place where his arrest could be effected quietly. This is the ordinary view, and implies that the Priests were afraid to arrest Jesus during the day. Like the story of the cleansing of the Temple, it indicates the presence of a large crowd of Galileans supporting Jesus, which was dissipated by his arrest, once it was made, for the Jerusalem populace was hostile. This seems to us the most probable view.

c. The Last Supper (Mark xiv.12-25). This is connected in tradition with the institution of the Eucharist. This tradition is as old as Saint Paul. It is not explicitly stated in Mark or Matthew, though scarcely contradicted by them. The alternative, rendered popular by Schweitzer,[7] is that Jesus' words mean "the Kingdom is so near that before we meet together again it will be here: I will not drink of the fruit of the vine until I drink it in the Kingdom."

A less important point is whether the story implies that Jesus knew that Judas was the traitor; the later gospel tradition took this view, but Mark can equally well mean that Jesus felt that the traitor was "one of the twelve," who were actually eating with him, but did not know which it was.

d. Gethsemane and the Arrest (Mark xiv.26-52). Traditionally Gethsemane is just across the brook Kidron. The story has sometimes been impugned on the ground that there were no witnesses of the Agony. This seems to us slightly absurd. Doubtless there was no stenographer, but the disciples may well have known in general what was happening, and "written up" the details. The story as a whole seems extraordinarily unlike fiction.

ix. Mark xiv.53-xv.41: The trial and crucifixion of Jesus. Jesus obviously was condemned by Pilate, as at least a potential rebel, but there has been much controversy as to whether the appearance of Jesus before the High Priests was a formal trial

[7] A. Schweitzer, *Das Abendmahl.*

or a preliminary investigation with the purpose of collecting evidence before the trial in Pilate's court.[8] It may be questioned whether there is quite as much difference between the two possibilities as is sometimes suggested. In any case, the trial before Caiaphas did, in point of fact, serve the purpose of an examination which was intended to justify the handing over of Jesus to the Romans. It is also not clear in what sense Jesus was supposed to have committed blasphemy. If the Talmud be followed, blasphemy could not be committed except by the use of the name of God, which does not seem to have been uttered in the narrative as given in the Gospels.

Pilate appears to have realised that Jesus was the victim of spite, rather than a dangerous rebel. He offered to release Jesus, but the Jews asked for Barabbas, "a prisoner with the rioters who had committed murder in the riot." What riot was this? The English version renders it by "insurrection" which is too strong, but riots, which is all that the Greek means, were and are endemic in Palestine. It is at least a probable guess that the "cleansing of the Temple" was represented to Pilate as part of a riot.

Jesus was crucified, and Simon of Cyrene was impressed into service to carry the cross. Simon is described as the father of Alexander and Rufus. It is usually held that their names are recorded because they were afterwards Christians. Rufus is identified with the man of that name mentioned in Romans xvi.13, but this tradition is neither old nor important, for it is an obvious guess.

Crucifixion was a peculiarly horrible method of execution, because it was usually so lingering a form of death, sometimes prolonged for several days. But Jesus died very quickly, and the centurion appears to have thought that this was a sign of God's favour. The last words which Jesus uttered according to Mark were "My God, My God, why hast thou deserted me." No Christian could have made this up without foundation. Like the Marcan story of the Baptism it cannot be fiction for it is contrary to all Christian thought. This appears to have

[8] See R. W. Husband, *The Prosecution of Jesus,* and Lietzmann, *Der Process Jesu, S.A.B.* 1931.

been felt by Luke who substitutes, "Father, into thy hands I commend my spirit," and by John who substitutes "It is finished," though it might equally well have been said that it was only beginning. Both these later Gospels are magnificent literature, but Mark seems to have a heart-rending poignancy which stamps it as history.

x. Mark xv.42-47: The burial of Jesus. This is attributed to Joseph of Arimathea, a member of the Sanhedrin, who was "expecting the Kingdom of God." This is interpreted by Matthew, and possibly, but not explicitly, by Luke, as meaning that he was secretly a disciple of Jesus. Obviously, this may be the meaning; but it may also mean merely that he was a pious Jew, who wished to fulfill the law of Deuteronomy xxi.23, which called for the immediate burial of executed criminals.[9]

xi. Mark xvi.1-8: The Resurrection. The end of the Gospel of Mark is unfortunately missing. Exactly what happened to it is still more or less of a mystery, though the facts are plain.

In the oldest texts,–in Greek, Latin, Syriac, Armenian and Georgian,–the gospel ends at xvi.8. Not only does it end, but it appears to end in the middle of a sentence, though on that point there has been some controversy. The last two words in Greek are ἐφοβοῦντο γάρ, and it is argued, to our mind with great force, that no book ever ended with γάρ. A sentence or paragraph, or even a volume may have ended with γάρ, though this must have been rare, but not the whole composition. Moreover, it is at least a question whether ἐφοβοῦντο does not require, or at least expect, an object, so that if translated according to the best probability, it should not be rendered "For they were afraid," but "For they were afraid of–" and we should print γὰρ not γάρ.

Thus, either through accident or design, the gospel as we have it now, is probably incomplete. In favour of the view that it was accident is the fact that any one who mutilated the gospel on purpose would scarcely have left an unfinished half sentence, so that there is perhaps more to be said for the view

[9] See K. Lake, *The Resurrection of Jesus Christ,* p. 130 and pp. 173 ff.

that in some way the gospel suffered a loss of a page at a very early stage of its existence.

To fill up the obvious lacuna at the end and to conclude the narrative verses xvi.9-20 were put in at an early time. This is generally called the "longer conclusion." It is found in many early, but not the earliest, manuscripts, and appears to be a compilation based on the other gospels, especially that of Luke. One manuscript (W) expands the longer conclusion a little farther and this expansion was known to Jerome.

There was also a much shorter conclusion, which appears to have been current in the Roman province of Africa, and was known in some Egyptian localities, possibly Alexandria. This runs as follows: "But they reported immediately (*or* concisely) to the circle of Peter all that had been enjoined on them. But after this Jesus himself appeared to them, and through them sent the sacred and uncorrupted message of eternal salvation from the east to the west." There are several variants in the text of this passage but none of great importance. It is found in k, the best representative of the African Old Latin, in the Alexandrian manuscripts L Ψ, in a few other later Greek manuscripts, in the margin of the Harclean Syriac, and in some Sahidic and Bohairic manuscripts.

Neither the longer nor the shorter conclusion have any claim to be treated as genuine[10]; they are merely early attempts to fill up the lacuna.

Fortunately, it is not quite impossible to reconstruct from the rest of the Gospel what the content of the original conclusion must have been. Mark xiv.28 and the words of the young man at the tomb (xvi.6 ff.) are clearly leading up to an appearance of the risen Jesus in Galilee. From the emphasis put on Peter in the last passage, it is also probable that he played a considerable part in the events which were to come. It is generally conceded that the Gospel according to Matthew provides no trace of the genuine ending of Mark. Matt. xxviii.16-20 seem to be an editorial addition and it is generally held

[10] The discussion in Westcott and Hort's *notes* in their Greek Testament, Vol. II, is decisive, but those who enjoy controversy should read Burgon's *The Last Twelve Verses of St. Mark.*

that Matthew, like ourselves, knew Mark only in mutilated form. Similarly Luke, who does not describe any appearance in Galilee, seems quite independent of Mark. It has, however, been argued with some force that John xxi may be based on the lost conclusion and that the Apocryphal Gospel of Peter shows some traces of a knowledge of it.[11]

Thus the main result of an investigation of the end of Mark is that the gospel originally contained the story of how the disciples went to Galilee and there saw the risen Jesus. There is, unfortunately, nothing to show whether it followed the Pauline view that the risen Jesus was a spirit, or, more accurately, had a body of spirit; or whether, like Luke and John, it represented him as appearing with a body of actual flesh.

What was the purpose of this gospel? It is an account of the work of Jesus culminating in the Resurrection. It clearly intends its readers to recognise that Jesus was the "Son of God," the "Messiah" or the "Son of Man" who is to come on the clouds of heaven at the End.[12] This claim is supported by the "voice from heaven" at the Baptism (Mark i.11), by the power shown over disease and demoniacs, by the recognition of the demons (Mark i.24, iii.11, v.7), by the recognition of St. Peter (Mark viii.29), by the voice from heaven at the Transfiguration (Mark ix.7), by Jesus' own confession before the High Priest (Mark xiv.61 f.), and finally by the Resurrection.

It is, however, very noticeable that according to Mark, Jesus never made this claim in his public teaching.[13] God himself nominates Jesus and recognises him,—as do his foes, the demons. But, so far as men go, until he reaches Jerusalem, he is not recognised by any except his disciples. He tells his disciples to be silent until after his Resurrection and teaches in parables in order to conceal his Messiahship. Finally, Mark emphasises the opposition of the Scribes and Pharisees to Jesus, especially in the matter of the Sabbath.

[11] See Lake, *The Resurrection of Jesus Christ*, pp. 137 ff.; P. Rohrbach, *Der Schluss des Marcusevangeliums*, and Harnack, *Chronologie*, I, p. 696.

[12] See pp. 204 ff.

[13] Cf. Mark, iv.11 ff. and ix.9.

It would therefore seem that Mark's purpose was *a.* to show that Jesus was the Messiah, in the sense that he was the "Son of Man" who would come on the clouds of heaven at the End; *b.* to explain why this had not been known to the general public during the life of Jesus,—because he had not told them; *c.* to indicate why the Scribes had opposed him,—because he interpreted the Law differently.

It is significant that this description of the purpose implied by Mark would also serve very well to define the purpose implied by the speeches in Acts, except for three differences:— Acts has less about demons, has more quotations from the Old Testament, and does not use "Son of Man" to describe the function of Jesus the Anointed. Apart from these relatively small points, the Gospel of Mark would seem to give just such a presentation of Jesus as do the speeches in Acts attributed to Peter and Paul. Acts represents the Apostles as preaching the supernaturally endowed and divinely appointed Messiah, who would return in Judgement, and announcing his Resurrection and future coming in Judgement, not as promulgating his general teaching as to conduct. Mark gives an account of Jesus admirably fitted to confirm this apostolic message and to satisfy the desire of the earliest communities for more knowledge.[14]

THE PLAN AND PURPOSE OF MATTHEW

The basis of the Gospel of Matthew is Mark, to which the editor adds material from other sources. It is essentially a second edition of Mark, with some of the difficulties smoothed out, and with much added material put in at intervals. Almost the whole of Mark is included in Matthew, and the Marcan order is not seriously changed except in the earlier sections, where it seems to have suffered, chiefly owing to the need of fitting in non-Marcan material. In this respect Matthew differs from Luke, which is a new book written with the help of

[14] Cf. p. 95.

Mark as a source. The main additions to Mark in Matthew are:

i. Matt. i.1-ii.23: The Infancy narratives. These stories (the Miraculous Conception revealed to Joseph, the Magi, the Massacre of the children, the Flight into Egypt, and the return to Nazareth) are peculiar to Matthew, and the genealogy is different from that of Luke.[15]

ii. Matt. iii.1-iv.11: John the Baptist. Matthew has considerably added to Mark's narrative by expanding the account of John the Baptist's preaching and the account of the Baptism and Temptation. The first may be genuine tradition as to John the Baptist, the second must be either autobiographical details learned from Jesus, or very early fiction. Moreover, some of these expansions are also found, with only unessential changes, in Luke. In any case, it is derived from a source known to both Matthew and Luke, unless one of them used the other.[16]

iii. Matt. v.1-viii.13: The Sermon on the Mount and the centurion's servant. A discourse on the Law and ethics. The treatment of the Law is peculiar to Matthew but much of the ethical part is found also in Luke. The same order is generally followed by Matthew and Luke,[17] but the degree of similarity between the two gospels varies greatly in different paragraphs. Sometimes it is so verbally exact as to imply a common Greek source. Sometimes the same idea is explained in quite different words.

A noticeable feature in its arrangement is that it leads up to the narrative of the centurion of Capernaum, which is also found in Luke in the same relative position. This story is told somewhat differently in the two Gospels, but there are so many marked agreements that a common Greek source seems indicated, though opinion is always likely to differ as to whether Matthew or Luke has preserved the original form of that source.

[15] See pp. 14 f.
[16] See pp. 10 ff.
[17] See p. 12.

The importance of this is that both Matthew and Luke have this narrative, which is not Marcan, bound up with the preceding paragraphs which are most certainly derived from Q.[18] Does not this show that Q gave the "narrative-setting" for at least some of the discourses which it preserved? Most investigators think that this must be so. But this indication of a narrative-setting is as a rule characteristic of Luke, not of Matthew, and suggests that Matthew left out narrative-setting and combined cognate sayings, rather than that Luke invented narrative-settings, and distributed cognate sayings among them.

iv. Matt. x.5-42: The Instructions to the Twelve. A considerable part of this section is found in Luke x, in connection with the sending of the Seventy, and in some scattered parallels elsewhere. The commands not to go to the Gentiles or to the Samaritans are peculiar to Matthew,[19] but just as in the Sermon on the Mount Matthew ends with a narrative section found also in Luke, so, after the instructions to the Twelve, Matthew adds as a continuous narrative

xi.2 ff. The question of John the Baptist, Luke vii.18 ff.
xi.7 ff. Jesus' statement as to John, Luke vii.24 ff.
xi.20 ff. Invective against Galilean cities, Luke x.13 ff.
xi.25 ff. The "I thank thee, Father," Luke x.21 ff.

which, as the references show, is found in Luke in the same general order, and with very close resemblance to Matthew in language, though divided by other material. Clearly, these sections were in a Greek source or sources known both to Matthew and to Luke. Moreover, Luke inserts before the mission of the Seventy a short section (Luke ix.57-62) which Matthew puts at the end of the "Sermon on the Mount complex" (Matthew viii.19-22). The case for the use of a common source is convincing, but very little help is given for reconstructing the original arrangement of the paragraphs derived from it.

[18] See p. 11.
[19] See pp. 17 f.

v. After the Marcan section on precedence in the Kingdom (Mark ix.33 ff.) Matthew inserts a selection of sayings dealing in the main with forgiveness, some of which are found also in Luke. But the greater part (xviii.21 ff.) seems to be an amplification or even a correction of the simple statement in Luke xvii.4 that forgiveness should extend to seven times.

vi. Matt. xx.1-16. The parable of the Workers in the Vineyard is added to Peter's question about the rewards of the Apostles (Mark x.28 ff.). There is no parallel in Luke.

vii. Matt. xxii.1-14. The parable of the Wedding-feast is added to the parable of the Vineyard (Mark xii.1 ff = Matthew xxi.33).

viii. Matt. xxiii.1-39. To the end of the passage corresponding to Mark xii.34-40, Matthew adds a long section reviling the Scribes and Pharisees. Much of this is scattered about in Luke xi, and the case is strong for a common tradition.

ix. Matt. xxv.1-46. To the end of the section, corresponding to Mark xiii, Matthew adds three long parables, illustrating the teaching just given. These are not found in Luke, though the parable of the Talents (Matt. xxv.14 ff.) has a close resemblance to the parable of the Pounds (Luke xix.11 ff).

From vii, viii and ix it would appear that Matthew was acquainted with parables (already collected?) which were unknown to Luke, just as Luke, or his collection, was unknown to Matthew. Obviously, this is a strong argument against the suggestion that Luke had read Matthew; he was interested in parables and if he knew Matthew, why did he not borrow his best ones?

It should be noted that in this section Matthew follows Mark with considerable verbal fidelity, but adds some short episodes which inspire less confidence than the body of the narrative,—such as the guard at the tomb, the descent of the angel who spoke to the women, the earthquake and the resurrection of the saints. Moreover, Matthew shows no sign of having had a complete Mark. It would seem that his copy, like ours, stopped at xvi.8, and he supplemented it with a short account of the appearances of the risen Lord in Galilee, which seems to be deduction from Mark xiv.28 rather than independent tradition.

Clearly, the editor of Matthew was greatly interested in the teaching of Jesus, and desired to add some account of it to Mark. The historical situation implied is obvious enough. The Apostles and the group associated with them were preaching about Jesus, just as Acts relates, saying that he was the Messiah; but there must have been many in Galilee, Peraea and Syria on whom Jesus' own teaching had had a great permanent effect. Some of these may have rejected the Apostolic message, without forgetting Jesus' teaching, and may have been the forerunners of those unorthodox Jews against whom the synagogue legislated in the second century. Others, again, though converted by the Apostolic message, desired also to perpetuate Jesus' teaching, which they had heard and loved.[20] Thus the contact between the Apostolic missionaries and these Galilean hearers would have been one cause for the combination of Mark with Q and other sources.

But there was another cause of first-rate importance. The Gentile Christians, or converted Hellenistic Jews, needed a code of Law, for they had been brought up in a world which had always had one. Just as the Jews supplemented the Law by the Mishnah, so the Christians, represented by Matthew, supplemented it by the teaching attributed to Jesus. In this respect, the Gospel of Matthew is the first in a long line of Christian writings leading through the Didactic books, the Didascalia and the Apostolic Constitution to the tremendous edifice of Canon Law,–the Christian Talmud.[21]

THE PLAN AND PURPOSE OF LUKE

Matthew wrote a second edition of Mark, but Luke wrote a new book, using Mark for material but not necessarily as a guide. He obviously wished to correct Mark, especially in the second half of the Gospel. Probably Mark was one of the "at-

[20] See K. Lake, *Paul, His Heritage and Legacy*, p. 54.

[21] See further on pp. 199 ff.

tempts" to which he alludes, perhaps a little slightingly, in his preface. He believed that he knew better than Mark, apparently from inquiry into local oral tradition (Luke i.1-4). Modern critics incline to prefer Mark.

i. Luke i.5-ii.52. Luke begins his Gospel, as does Matthew, by describing the family, birth and childhood of Jesus, but gives a different account from that in Matthew, agreeing only as to the place in which Jesus was born, the supernatural nature of his birth, and his Davidic ancestry.[22] This section is obviously neither from Mark nor from any source known to Matthew. Marcion appears to have read a Gospel of Luke which had no Infancy narratives, and this may be the original form, but most scholars reject this theory.

ii. Luke iii.2-iv.13. Then, like Matthew, he takes up the Marcan story, but adds considerably to it in his description of John the Baptist and the Temptation of Jesus. Moreover, he here uses the same tradition as Matthew,[23] so that either Matthew had access to the same source as Luke or one of them used the other. The *prima facie* reason against the second view is that neither knew the other's Infancy narratives, which precede these paragraphs. It is possible that one or the other was originally written without these Infancy narratives, but there is little evidence to support this hypothesis.[24]

iii. With chapter iv.31, Luke begins to follow Mark closely and Luke iv.31-vi.12 = Mark i.16-iii.6, with no change of order except that Peter's call[25] (Mark i.16-20) is placed after the healing of his wife's mother and is told in combination with "the miraculous draught of fishes," and that the whole section is introduced by an account of Jesus in Nazareth (iv.16-30).

iv. The last section brings us to the end of the first section of Mark, where Jesus gives up the ministry in the synagogue as his habitual practice and preaches in the country and by the shore. Luke apparently recognised that there was a break

[22] See note 16, p. 15.
[23] See pp. 13 f.
[24] See also p. 14 f.
[25] See Lake's *Resurrection*, pp. 140 f.

in the story at this point, and inserts a long section, presumably from Q since it is found also in Matthew (Luke vi.20-viii.1. This is often called the *Sermon on the Plain,* to distinguish it from the much longer parallel in Matthew v.2-vii.29 called the *Sermon on the Mount.* This section presents the whole problem of Q. Not only the contents, but the ordering of the subject matter and often the phraseology render it clear that Matthew and Luke have a common tradition, but quite differently arranged.[26]

v. Luke viii.4-ix.50. At this point, Luke turns back to Mark and reproduces Mark iv.1-ix.42, except that he omits the whole section (Mark vi.45-viii.26) which, roughly speaking, is the 'northern ministry of Jesus.'

This omission of the South-Syrian or Phoenician tradition is a very striking feature of Luke's treatment of Mark. He leaves out all the northern ministry of Jesus and changes the locality of the Confession of Peter by omitting all reference to Caesarea Philippi,—so that the Transfiguration and the episodes connected with it seem to be placed in the neighbourhood of Bethsaida. It is also noteworthy in this connection that he omits all reference to the appearance of the risen Lord in Galilee, and that in Acts he tells how the Gospel spread from Jerusalem to Samaria and says that it reached Antioch, but says nothing about the long stretch between Caesarea and Antioch. Did Luke have a different and earlier form of Mark from that used by Matthew? Had his copy of Mark been mutilated in the middle as well as at the end?

vi. Luke ix.51-xviii.14. At this point, Luke leaves Mark for a long time and inserts a section of which the composition and origin are a hard problem. It begins with an episode in Samaria, and has no further geographical data (except the vague allusion in xvii.11) until Luke comes back to the Marcan tradition and in xviii.35 we find ourselves in Jericho. It is sometimes called the Peraean section, but only because it is supposed to be an amplification of the Marcan section (Mark x.1 ff.) which takes Jesus through Peraea to Jericho.

[26] See above p. 17.

As is the case with the "Sermon" section (Luke vi.20-vii.1), there is at times obvious community with Matthew. But there is much more that is peculiar to Luke, including some of the finest passages in the gospels, such as the parables of the Prodigal Son and the Good Samaritan. It is incredible that these wonderful parables were in Q and omitted by Matthew, just as it is incredible that the parables of the Ten Virgins or of the Sheep and the Goats were in Q and omitted by Luke. It seems to follow that, besides the common source, or sources, —Q—both Matthew and Luke had each seen or heard traditions of parables and discourses by Jesus which were unknown to the other.

It is, however, noticeable that this section contains a few passages found in Matthew's account of the Sermon on the Mount. This suggests two possibilities: either Luke put discourses of Jesus which he had found in Q into a narrative context which seemed to him suitable, or Matthew detached these discourses from their original context. There has been intermittent controversy for nearly half a century as to the relative probability of these hypotheses, on which there are many arguments but no decisive evidence.

vii. Luke xviii.15-xxiv.2. At the end of the long, 'special' section the writer returns to Mark and from here onwards the general parallelism to Mark is relatively close, though the variation in detail is considerable. Luke omits the episodes of the sons of Zebedee and their desire for precedence and of the barren fig-tree, and inserts a few details such as the very significant introduction of Herod into the trial of Jesus. Moreover, the language of Mark is noticeably revised,—so thoroughly that some have doubted whether Luke is actually using Mark, rather than the same general tradition, modified from other sources. The sequence of events, or rather that of the paragraphs describing them, is the same as in Mark, so that there must be a close relationship between them; but there is much more variation in detail than is found in the earlier chapters. It would seem that Luke believed that he was in a better position to correct Mark in the account of the events in Jerusalem than in the earlier narrative. It has been suggested that the women who came up from Galilee with Jesus were one of Luke's sources. Dr. Sanday used to single out Joanna, the wife of Chuza, and thought that Luke mentioned her to show that she was his informant.

viii. Luke xxiv.2-end. Here the Resurrection narratives are reached.[27] The story of the women at the tomb (Luke xxiv.2-10) is clearly based on the same tradition as Mark xvi.1-8, but is greatly modified. Luke's other narratives have no parallels. They place all the appearances of the Lord in the neighbourhood of Jerusalem and thus differ from Matthew and (by implication) from Mark, who say that the disciples saw the risen Jesus in Galilee.

It is very remarkable that the Lucan appearances of the risen Jesus do not correspond to the list given by Paul in I Cor. xv.5 ff. Luke also emphasises that the Lord rose with the same body as had been buried,—a body of flesh and bones, not a spirit (xxiv.39). Paul, on the other hand, says that flesh and blood cannot inherit the Kingdom of God, and argues that at the Resurrection all will be changed to spiritual bodies; since he states that Jesus was the first fruits of the Resurrection this implies that he too had a "spiritual body." Luke appears to be combating this view.

What purposes can be detected in Luke's treatment of his sources? The matter is complicated, but the following points will at least require notice in any final decision on the point [28]:

i. Luke, according to the preface, believed that he could improve on previous attempts to write an account of the Christian story. Since Mark was certainly one of these previous attempts, Luke must mean that he had corrected Mark. It then becomes interesting to note that these corrections mainly affect the later chapters. They probably imply three important modifications of opinion:

First, the Jews, rather than the Romans, were responsible

[27] See Lake, *Resurrection*, p. 91 ff.; Gardiner Smith, *The Narrative of the Resurrection;* and C. R. Bowen, *The Resurrection in the New Testament.*

[28] See also Cadbury's *The Making of Luke and Acts.*

for anti-Christian movements. This is seen in the introduction of Herod into the Passion narrative, and is very clear throughout Acts.

Secondly, Luke disbelieved the narrative of Mark, which made the risen Jesus appear in Galilee, and substituted for this a series of appearances in Jerusalem.

Finally, he believed that the risen Jesus had a body of flesh and blood.[29] This was not the belief of Paul and there is nothing to show that it was that of Matthew, or of Mark, but it was emphasised in the Gospel of John as well as in Luke, and became the dominant belief of Christians.

ii. It is possible that Luke held that poverty was a form of virtue.[30] This point has sometimes been overemphasised, but Acts would at least indicate that in Luke's opinion it was desirable for wealth to be held in common, so that there would be no poverty.

iii. It is possible that Luke regarded the teaching of Jesus, which he collected from Q and other sources, as a substitute for the Jewish Law. It is clear that Marcion interpreted the Gospel in this way, but it is, of course, by no means clear that Marcion was right, and, by accepting the Gospel of Luke as part of the fourfold Gospel, the Church rejected not only Marcionism, but Marcion's view of the Gospel of Luke. The interpretation of the difference between Matthew and Luke in their attitude to the Law seems to us to be one of the problems which would most repay renewed study.

iv. Far the most important feature of the Lucan writings is that the author continued the story of Jesus by adding another volume on the story of the Church,—the Acts. At the same time, he changed the importance of the eschatological teaching of Jesus by rendering it possible to postpone its fulfilment almost indefinitely. In fact, if the Gospel of Luke and the Acts be read continuously, as they should be, it is clear that the concept of the Church as a society inspired by the gift of the spirit sent from on high by the exalted Jesus is in process

[29] Cf. Luke xxiv.39.

[30] Cf. the parable of Dives and Lazarus, Luke xvi.19 ff.

of eclipsing the immediate expectation of the Parousia. The mere existence of Acts is a proof that Luke thought of Jesus as the founder of a society which would exist until a (possibly distant) Parousia, rather than as the herald of the immediate coming of the eschatological Kingdom of God,—though he still expected that the Lord would ultimately return as the divinely appointed Judge.[31]

In connection with this, attention should be given to a point which is certainly interesting and possibly important. Luke is the only evangelist who apparently prefers to call Jesus "the Lord," rather than by any other title.[32] So does Paul, but not John, except in the vocative, and—which is significant—in narrative after the Resurrection. The name seems to be a translation of an Aramaic title "Mar," preserved in I Cor. xvi.22. The very interesting point is that "Mar" in Aramaic is not a cult-title, but "Lord" is one in Greek.

To some extent, the Gospel of Luke belongs to the same category as Matthew, for it also is a combination of the teaching of Jesus with the teaching about Jesus. But,—though this may well be disputed,—it seems possible that whereas to Matthew the teaching of Jesus supplemented the Law, to Luke it replaced it. It was not a wholly wrong instinct which made the anti-Jewish heretic Marcion choose Luke as his special gospel. In general, too, Matthew has a much more Jewish background than Luke. The discussion of Jesus' teaching about the Law in the Sermon on the Mount, whether it came from Q or not, is "redolent of the soil"; surely it is authentic tradition about Jesus. Similarly, the command to the Apostles not to go to the Samaritans and Gentiles is so contrary to the later situation that it must be original. Its memory had been preserved, possibly among Jewish Christians who deprecated the method of Hellenists, but the intention of the author of Matthew was to maintain that during the life-time of Jesus the Apostles were sent only to Jewish communities, after the Resurrection they were instructed to convert the Gentiles (Matt. xxviii.19 f.).

[31] See also pp. 207 ff.

[32] See below pp. 237 f.

Finally, it is especially noteworthy that either Matthew or Luke (and possibly both) treats Q differently from the way in which he treats Mark. Mark is taken over almost in its entirety by both. Luke edits it and corrects more freely than does Matthew, but his source is still quite recognisable. Q, on any hypothesis, is treated much more freely either by one or both of the evangelists. Does this imply a more critical attitude towards Q than towards Mark? Or does it mean that Mark was already regarded as authoritative and not to be tampered with? If so, where? [33]

There remains the tantalising question, when were the Gospels written? The earliest definite evidence for this is the little scrap of John in the Rylands Library in Manchester. Papyrological experts think that this belongs to the early second century (c. A.D. 130). This fixes a *terminus ante quem.* The *terminus a quo* can be fixed only by internal evidence, and as to this there is no general agreement, but two points have been the focus of discussion.

i. Mark xiii is often thought to be a prophecy of the fall of Jerusalem, and to show that it was written before that event, though some have argued that exactly the opposite is true, and others think that Mark xiii is an interpolation from a different author. On the other hand it is thought that the parallel passage in Luke xxi 20 ff. is a re-writing of Mark in the light of the actual facts of the siege of Jerusalem. If this argument be accepted, Mark was written before A.D. 70, and Luke after it. No light is thrown on the date of Matthew, who at this point merely copied Mark (Matt. xxiv 15 ff.).

ii. It has been agreed by Krenkel and others that Luke used, and used incorrectly, statements in the *Antiquities* of Josephus as to Theudas and Lysanias. If so, Luke must be later than A.D. 90. There is little doubt as to the incorrectness of the statements in Luke, though there is still controversy on this point, but this does not prove that they are due to a careless reading of Josephus (see p. 244 f.).

[33] See Streeter, *The Four Gospels,* and B. W. Bacon's *Is Mark a Roman Gospel?* in *Harvard Theological Studies,* VII. Both are very interesting if not quite convincing.

CHAPTER III

The Gospel of John

THE tradition of the Church is that this gospel was written by John the son of Zebedee, who was the "beloved disciple" referred to in xxi as the author of the book. This tradition can be traced back as far as Irenaeus, who lived at the end of the second century. He was then bishop of Lyons in Gaul, where there was a Greek-speaking colony, but he had come originally from Ephesus. In his boyhood he had heard Polycarp, who was martyred in 155 (?), and Polycarp had said that he had known John the son of Zebedee in Ephesus. This story is not impossible, for Irenaeus probably died about 210 and may easily have been born in 140 and heard Polycarp when he was a boy of under fifteen. Polycarp was 90 in 155 [1] and therefore was born in 65. If John was thirty (and he may easily have been only twenty) at the crucifixion (A.D. 30), and died in Ephesus in A.D. 95, Polycarp may well have seen him in Ephesus.[2]

Not only is this not impossible, though it makes ample use of the possibilities of longevity, but the story fits together so well that it must contain some element of truth. The minimum is that there was *a* John in Ephesus during the boyhood of Polycarp, that is between 80 and 95 A.D.

The real reason for rejecting the tradition is purely subjective,—the contents of the gospel seem irreconcilable with the

[1] The date is given by Eusebius as 166–167, but Waddington showed that the governor of Asia in the time of Polycarp, Statius Quadratus, became proconsul in 153–154. The martyrdom was on a Saturday, and February 23rd 155 would thus be indicated. But both C. H. Turner and E. Schwartz have argued, though on different lines, that February 22nd 156, is the true date. See *Studia Biblica* II, pp. 105 ff. and *Gött. Abh.* VIII (1905) 6, pp. 125 ff.

[2] Polycarp gives his age by implication in *Martyr. Polycarpi* IX.

theory that it was written by a disciple who had been a companion of Jesus and an eye witness of his life. This view is based on the theory, now widely held, that the Gospel of Mark gives a true account of the ministry, and the Gospels of Matthew and Luke a true account of the teaching of Jesus. Thus, since the Johannine narrative is so different from them it must be largely, if not entirely, fictitious and written by a Hellenistic Christian in order to support the sacramental theology which finds a centre in the divine Jesus.

Thus, the real Johannine problem is the difference between Mark and John. The traditional theory is that Mark was early and correct, but partial and incomplete, and that John was more complete and accurate, though later. The modern theory seems to have the best of the argument, but there are many difficulties still unsolved.

The main differences between the two accounts are these:

i. According to Mark, Jesus did not begin his public ministry until after John the Baptist had been imprisoned. According to John, Jesus begins his ministry before that of the Baptist ends. Moreover, whereas in Mark John the Baptist baptises Jesus without knowing him, the Baptist's main function in John is to recognise and bear witness to him.

ii. According to Mark, Jesus began his ministry in Galilee and stayed there, or still farther north, until he finally went south. He was only a week in Jerusalem. But, according to John, Jesus went either two or three times back and forth between Jerusalem and Galilee.

iii. According to Mark, Jesus never asked the people to hold any especial opinion about himself. His desire was that they should repent, change their conduct, and so receive entry into the Age to Come. He expressly forbade his disciples to say that he was the Messianic Son of Man. According to John, on the other hand, Jesus freely announced that he was the Son of God, and demanded faith in himself. Those who believe in him will be given eternal life and Jesus will raise them up at the last day.

iv. According to Mark,—in the opinion of the disciples, not of the people,—Jesus is the Son of Man who will come in glory to judge the world. His verdict will depend on the record of conduct shown by men; not on their recognition of him. But according to John, Jesus is the supernatural Son of God. His relation to God, his Father, is unique; salvation depends on believing in him, eternal life is given by him and is impossible except to those who have been born again of Water and the Spirit and who eat the Flesh and drink the Blood of the Son of Man.

Thus external evidence, extremely good, is balanced by internal evidence pointing the other way and equally powerful. The English scholars of the middle of the nineteenth century, best represented by B. F. Westcott's commentary, endeavoured to reconcile the internal evidence to the external by emphasising the probability that the synoptic account is partial. They made John the basis of their reconstructions of the life of Jesus.

The more recent tendency [3] has been to accept the internal evidence and explain away the external tradition. The general lines on which this is done are as follows: On the evidence of Papias, a contemporary of Polycarp, there was at that time in Asia Minor a "John the Presbyter" who was not the son of Zebedee,—for he says that he took trouble to inquire what Peter or Andrew or John, the disciples of the Lord, *had said* and what John the Presbyter *was saying*. Now II John and III John both begin by ascribing their authorship to the "Elder" or "Presbyter," but according to tradition, and also according to the internal evidence of style, the Epistles of John were written by the same author as the Gospel. Is it not possible that this, rather than the Irenaean tradition is correct, and that Polycarp when a boy confused John the Presbyter with John the son of Zebedee? Partially corroborative evidence, but un-

[3] The most valuable books for the study of modern work on this subject are J. Drummond, *The Character and Authorship of the Fourth Gospel,* A. Loisy, *Le Quatrième Évangile,* W. Bauer's commentary on John in Lietzmann's *Handbuch,* J. Chapman's *John the Presbyter,* Streeter's *The Four Gospels,* pp. 363-481, and B. W. Bacon, *The Fourth Gospel in History and Research.*

fortunately partially discrepant, is found in Dionysius,[4] bishop of Alexandria, in the third century, and perhaps also in another passage in Papias. Dionysius says that the tombs of two Johns were to be seen in Ephesus, and Papias perhaps says that John the son of Zebedee was put to death by the Jews together with James his brother. Admittedly, however, the evidence for Papias' statement is not certain. His writings are not extant; they are known only through quotations, and this passage is found only in George Hamartolos and Philip Sidetes.[5] Eusebius does not mention it and they may have made a mistake, but it is a curious corroboration that the Syriac menology celebrates the martyrdom of the two sons of Zebedee on the same day.

In conclusion, one curious point may be noted in the history of criticism. Modern critics have doubted the correctness of the tradition that connects the fourth Gospel with John the son of Zebedee. But they have hardly ever doubted its connection with Asia Minor. The late Professor Bacon [6] indeed sometimes suggested that it was Palestinian, but few followed him. Yet the evidence for the Ephesian origin of the gospel is not strong apart from that which supports its Johannine authorship. Internal evidence would rather suggest Alexandria, for the gospel is extremely Philonic.

This point has been brought to the front by an amazing document published by Dr. Bell.[7] It is a papyrus of the first half of the second century: a combination of Johannine, synoptic and unknown material. The fourth Gospel therefore was read and used as a source in Egypt before A.D. 150. Exactly what the effect of this fact will be when it is fully appreciated, we cannot say, but it will certainly raise many questions.

It will already be clear that the fourth Gospel presents an

[4] See App. C.

[5] See App. C. for the evidence of George Hamartolos and Philip Sidetes. The first to call attention to Philip Sidetes was De Boor (*T.U.* V.2, pp. 167 ff.). A full summary of the facts is given in *Beginnings,* Vol. IV, p. 133. See also J. H. Bernard, *Studia Sacra,* pp. 260 ff.

[6] See his *The Fourth Gospel in History and Research,* and his *Is Mark a Roman Gospel?*

[7] H. I. Bell and T. C. Skeat, *Fragments of an Unknown Gospel and Other Early Christian Papyri,* London, 1935.

entirely different set of problems from the Synoptics. There is nothing to compare with it which belongs to exactly the same type as itself. Its analysis, therefore, cannot be compared with that of the synoptic gospels, but is much more closely akin to that of Old Testament documents in the Pentateuch.

Attempts at such analysis have often been made, but the diversity of them is the proof that they have never been very successful.

John's general sequence of events is as follows:

i. The prologue (i.1-14).

ii. The witness of John at Bethany beyond the Jordan (i.15-36).

iii. The call of Andrew, Simon, Philip and Nathaniel (i.37-51).

iv. The marriage in Cana in Galilee (ii.1-11).

v. Jesus in Jerusalem and Judaea during and after the Passover, the cleansing of the Temple, Nicodemus, John the Baptist at Aenon (ii.12-iii.36).

vi. Jesus in Samaria. The woman at the well (iv.1-42).

vii. Jesus in Cana. Cure of the son of the royal (Imperial?) officer (iv.43-54).

viii. Jesus in Jerusalem during a "feast." The Pool of Bethesda (v.1-47).

ix. Jesus in trans-Jordan and Capernaum shortly before the Passover. Jesus walking on the sea, the feeding of the five thousand, discourse in the synagogue and discussions with the disciples and his brethren (vi.1-vii.9).

x. Jerusalem. Tabernacles. The blind man. The Dedication (vii.10-x.39)

xi. Trans-Jordan. Bethany. Lazarus (x.40-xi.53).

xii. The desert by "Ephraim" (xi.54-57).

xiii. Bethany, six days before the Passover (xii.1-11).

xiv. Last visit to Jerusalem. Disputes. Discourses. Passion. Resurrection (xii.12-xx.31).

xv. Galilee (xxi.1-end).

It will be seen that this means a journey of which the main stages are: Jordan Valley–Galilee–Jerusalem–Samaria–Galilee – Jerusalem – Jordan Valley – Galilee – Jerusalem – Jordan Valley–the desert–Bethany–Jerusalem.

Many suggestions have been made to show that this scheme contains passages which are not in their original place, or which, possibly, do not really belong to the Gospel at all. Two such sections are now generally rejected, one on textual, as well as internal, evidence:

i. The story of the woman taken in adultery (vii.53-viii.12) is not found in the oldest manuscripts in Greek, though it appears always to have been present in Latin. The general consensus of textual critics is that it does not belong to the earliest history of the Gospel of John. It is also an interesting fact, the real meaning of which is not quite clear, that it is found in some manuscripts at the end of John and in others in the middle of Luke.[8] The probability seems to be increasing, the more the matter is studied, that this is one of the longest of the various short stories about Jesus which were in circulation at a very early date, but which were not taken up either into the synoptic gospels or the Gospel of John. Their origin is doubtful; they may be perfectly true stories which happen to have missed reception into the Gospels, or they may be inventions of later Christians. It is hard to see how any final decision can be reached on this point; but these stories are an important link in the evidence of those who think that the gospels as we have them are merely a selection from the stories which were circulating in the first century.[9]

ii. Chapter xxi contains the story of the miraculous draught and Peter's "second call" and has every appearance of being an appendix. The gospel seems to come to a suitable conclusion with the last verse of chapter xx, and then begins again, with some contradiction and no obvious connection between xx and xxi. It is therefore generally believed that xxi is an appendix to the gospel and not an integral part of it.

It has been suggested that this appendix to John is a survival

[8] In the Ferrar group (Family 13) it comes after Luke xxi.38.
[9] See p. 11.

of the Galilean tradition implied by the Gospel of Mark, which made the first appearance of the risen Jesus to the disciples take place in Galilee.[10] There is much to be said for this theory, though it has never been proved. Certainly, the Gospel of Mark suggests that it is leading up to a story of the appearance of Jesus to his disciples in Galilee, in some form in which Peter played a prominent part, and John xxi preserves just such a story as might have been expected. Further than that it will probably never be possible to go.

Moreover, there is a good deal to be said for the suggestion, which has been made by more than one person, that just as the first call of Peter stands by itself in Mark, but in Luke is combined with a miraculous draught of fishes, so in John the "second call" of Peter, if it may so be named, is connected with a miraculous, or perhaps we should say *the* miraculous draught of fishes, told in a slightly different way from that in which it was taken up by Luke.[11]

A third point in which an analysis might suggest that the gospel is not in its original condition is the position of chapter v. It has been suggested, especially by Wellhausen,[12] that this ought to come between chapters vi and vii, eliminating an apparently quite unnecessary journey to the Jordan Valley and to Galilee before the visit of Jesus to Jerusalem, and linking the scene of Jesus in Jerusalem and the episode at the pool of Bethesda with the block that includes vii.10-x.39. Doubtless this readjustment would be an improvement in order, but whether the evidence is sufficient to support a theory which implies that all known manuscripts have suffered corruption or go back to a distorted original may well be doubted. Authors, at least, are well aware of the fact that improvements in order are often made in the second draught of a book and not in the earliest form of it.

These three sections stand out from a multitude of other suggested corruptions, most of them smaller. Wellhausen, for

[10] See p. 36.

[11] See p. 43.

[12] In a fascinating monograph entitled *Das Evangelium Johannes,* and see also P. M. Strayer, *Some Transpositions of Text in St. John's Gospel* in the *Journal of Theological Studies,* II, pp. 137 ff.

instance, has thought that chapters xiii and xiv represent a difference of theory so great that they cannot have originally belonged to the same document as xvii ff. Though no concensus of opinion has yet been reached as to whether he is right or not, the point is certainly worth considering.

The sequence of events and places, however, is a less important part of the Gospel of John than the "signs" and discourses of Jesus. "The signs" are as follows:—

The conversion of water into wine at Cana in Galilee (ii.1 ff.).

The healing of the son of the Imperial officer in Capernaum (iv.46 ff.).

The healing of the paralytic at the sheep gate at Bethzatha in Jerusalem (v.1 ff.).

The feeding of the multitude (vi.5 ff.).

The healing of the man who was born blind (ix.1 ff.).

The raising of Lazarus (xi.1 ff.).

It will be seen that these miracles include some of healing but that there is a noticeable lack of the category most frequent in the synoptic gospels, namely the exorcism of demons. In the fourth Gospel there are many allusions to the devil, but none to demons, and above all none to demons as the cause of disease. Clearly, the purpose of these "signs" is to prove the divine nature of Jesus, and their dominant feature is that they could not have been done by any ordinary man.

The discourses represent the teaching which Jesus gave, and it is the teaching that presents the greatest difficulty in an analysis of the gospel. In the Acts, and to some extent in the synoptic gospels, it is possible to state the subject of each speech, not because there is one speech to each subject, but because, as a rule, the speech does not cover more than one topic, or at least a connected series of topics; there is more than one speech to each subject, but rarely more than one subject to each speech. In the fourth gospel, however, this is not the case. The speeches largely deal with the same subject, but there is a tendency to wander over the whole field of thought,—the value of faith, the wickedness of failing to believe, the possibility of supernatural salvation and Jesus as the only method of salvation, together with his relation to the Father, recur over and over again. It is entirely arbitrary to select one subject and say that that is the main purpose of any one speech.

It is at once clear that the purpose of the narrative is to support the teaching given in the discourses, and of the discourses to explain the implications of the narrative, and that whereas the synoptic gospels represent a form of Christianity which had been greatly modified by the middle of the second century, the fourth gospel already represents the essential doctrines of Catholic Christianity. These may be summarised as:

i. The divine nature of Jesus.

ii. The necessity for and the supernatural power of Baptism and the Eucharist.

iii. The supernatural authority and privileges of the Church.

i. The divine nature of Jesus is implied throughout the Gospel, but is most clearly stated in the prologue, in which it is laid down that Jesus is the Logos, or Word of God. Perhaps the best way to approach an understanding of the prologue to the Gospel is to consider the problems which had to be faced by an early Christian writer.

He had inherited from Judaism the belief that there is only one God, and under no circumstances could that belief be abandoned. On the other hand, he had accepted from Christian teachers the belief that Jesus was divine. How could he accept that without saying that there were two gods? Some writers, such as Justin Martyr, never produced any explanation of the difficulty, but met it by alternating the contradictory views that there was one God, and nevertheless, that Christ was a second god. The Apostle Paul appears to have put the question on one side by not using the word "God" for "Christ" but only "Lord," and unfortunately we do not know exactly what he meant by this distinction.

The solution which the writer of the prologue reached is dependent partly on a second problem, which had better be stated first. Assuming that God is a being far above all human existence, what is the means of communication between God and man? Earlier writers in the Old Testament had sometimes spoken of the "Hand of God" as the means of communication, others of the "Breath" or "Spirit" of God. The writers of the Wisdom literature went further and used Wisdom as the connecting link between God and the world.[13] Wisdom became more than a quality. It was almost, if not quite, personified, especially in the Wisdom of Solomon. It belonged to God, but it could be appropriated by man. And yet, Wisdom speaks as though it were an entity distinct both from God and man. In this case, we have Wisdom as a being distinct from, and yet never separate from God.

Another way, or rather another word, for expressing the same idea seems to have been Logos, which means either 'word,' 'saying,' or 'reason.' In the latter sense, it was peculiarly popular with Stoic writers, but it was taken over by the semi-Platonic Philo and used by him as the channel of communication between God and the world. It will be seen that there is but a verbal difference between Logos in this sense and Wisdom. It is this phrase which the writer of the prologue took over and by it he explained the course of history. Thus he solves the problem of the communication between God and the world, and at the same time solves, or at least circumvents, the problem of how there could be but one God, and yet Jesus could be God.

Finally, it should be noted that this use of Logos was facilitated by the Old Testament. In it creation is accomplished by God's speech. He *said* "Let there be light" etc. To connect this fact with the Stoic use of Logos is entirely in the spirit of Philonic exegesis. The perhaps insoluble question is whether John was interpreting the Old Testament by Stoicism, or Stoicism by the Old Testament. An almost exact parallel is given by the *Hellenistic Theology* of Cornutus who explains that Hermes is the Logos.

The question remains whether the prologue as it stands is an integral part of the Gospel, or was added either by the author himself or by someone else, in order to make plainer

[13] See Prov. viii.1 ff. and cf. p. 222.

the doctrine contained in the rest of the book. What the prologue says is that the Logos was the source of creation and the principle which had always inspired Life and Light in the world. It was constantly coming into the world, and equally constantly being rejected by those who ought to have belonged to it. Finally, the Logos had become flesh, that is to say had become a human being, and the Logos also was able to give to those who accepted it the privilege of becoming by grace what they were not by nature,—"Children of God."

The Gospel then goes on to explain how John the Baptist had been a witness to the moment when the Logos became flesh. He saw the Spirit of God descend into Jesus and remain there. At first sight at least it would seem clear that this is the incarnation of the Logos, but the word "Spirit" is used instead of "Logos" and Logos is not used again in the same sense throughout the Gospel. Does that mean that the prologue comes from one source, which may be called a Logos-source, and the rest of the Gospel from another, which may be called a Spirit-source?

This question has never yet been fully solved and is the main critical problem concerning the prologue. Is it by the same author as the rest of the Gospel, and has it always been an integral part of it? These are not quite the same question, though they are closely related.

The argument for thinking that it may come from a different source from the rest of the Gospel is that it uses a different terminology. Nowhere, outside the prologue, is the word Logos,—in the technical sense,—used of Jesus. The whole Gospel, from the beginning, is a plea for the belief that Jesus is not an ordinary man, but divine, and that his coming has introduced a new element into human life. He is the Son of God, the Life, the Resurrection, the Light of the World, the Way, no man comes to the Father except through him, and he gives men his flesh to eat that they may have eternal life. Thus there is no doubt about the divine nature of Jesus in the Gospel, but 'Son of God,' not 'Logos,' is the characteristic phrase. On the other hand, in the prologue, Son of God does not occur and Logos is the dominant word.

It is therefore a plausible theory that the prologue was put in as a preface after the book was written, because the writer thought that Logos suggested the right philosophic approach to understanding the mystery of the divine nature of the Son of God, without sacrificing monotheism, and herein he was certainly right.

But did he write this preface himself, or is it an introductory quotation from some other document? The main fact in favour of the "other document" is that the reference to John the Baptist in the prologue seems to break the rhythm, and may have been inserted in order to adapt it to the Gospel. On the other hand, the phraseology of the whole passage seems similar to that of the rest of the Gospel, and, although the word Logos is not used in its technical sense outside the prologue, the concepts of Life and Light as divine qualities which confer salvation seem to run right through the book, and to have their roots in the prologue. The reiteration of these phrases and of the ideas which they represent is the strongest argument for thinking that the prologue was written by the same author as the rest of the Gospel and was always part of it; just as, on the other hand, the marked absence of the phrase Logos and of any further working-out of the idea which it covers,—that is to say the relation of the Logos to God,—is the main reason for thinking that the prologue was originally separated from the rest of the book.

ii. The background of the Gospel is sacramental. It not only relates how Jesus taught the necessity of Baptism and the Eucharist, but implies a general knowledge of the sacraments by the readers of the Gospel.

In John iii the story of Nicodemus introduces a long discourse on regeneration, and, unless the reference to water be excised, the writer must have meant that Baptism was the means of regeneration.

Similarly in John vi the story of the miraculous feeding of the multitude introduces a long discourse maintaining that it is necessary to eat the flesh and drink the blood of the Son of

Man in order to gain Life. The reference to the Eucharist is unmistakable.

In each case the doctrine is clear. Life depends on a sacramental act, not merely on conduct. John is in this point very different from the synoptic gospels, but in complete agreement with the Christianity of Justin Martyr and later Christian writers.

Critics often think that the discourses of Jesus impressing his teaching are fictions of the author, because there is no sign of anything like them in the Synoptics. They therefore conclude that sacramental Christianity is the invention of Hellenistic Christians and unknown to Jesus or his immediate disciples. With this opinion we agree, but are fully conscious of the difficulty of accounting, on this theory, for the sudden and immediate origin and growth of sacramental Christianity, to the exclusion of any other, until the development of Protestantism. In fact, the absence of sacramental doctrine in the Synoptics remains a problem for the Catholic, and the presence of it in the Church a problem for the non-Catholic.

The traditional or Catholic position argues that, for some reason, the earlier writers,—the Synoptics,—left out the sacramental teaching of Jesus and were supplemented by the later writer, John the Apostle, who remembered discourses of Jesus which had been disregarded or not understood at the time that they were spoken. There are many books expounding this theory, but the best preparation for understanding it is to read Browning's *Death in the Desert.*

iii. The existence of the Church, that is to say the Christian community, as a society which has special and supernatural privileges is found first in the later Epistles of Paul. It would be hard to say that it is really present in the earlier Epistles. In them the Church is, of course, implied, but it seems doubtful whether it has a supernatural position such as it has in the later Epistles and still more in John, where it is, as it were, the extension of the Incarnation.

There is nothing in Mark which approaches this view of the Church and in Matthew there is, with the doubtful exception of some parables, nothing which implies the supernaturally privileged position of the Christian community and the Church. One is indeed tempted to say that in Matthew the Church is that form of community which has taken over no more and no less than the privileges of the congregation of Israel, the ancient People of God [14]; it is sometimes equated with the Kingdom of God, but further it is impossible to go. Luke marks an advance, for it certainly implies the permanent existence of the community and begins to adumbrate, though scarcely to state clearly its preeminence; but it is still far from John, where the supernaturally privileged position of the Church is acknowledged. The Christians are the "branches of the vine"; they have a special relationship to Christ as Christ has to the Father, and this idea pervades the Gospel, which implies the Church in every line.

It is noteworthy that xx.21-23 represents the disciples as being given, by literal inspiration, the power of forgiving or retaining sins. This seems the Johannine analogue to the power conferred on Peter in Matt. xvi.17-19, but it is given to the disciples, not to Peter only. Moreover in Matthew the power given to Peter is that of "binding and loosing", which is a Jewish way of saying "forbidding and allowing", but in John the authority given to the disciples is that of forgiving or retaining sin. In the one case we are dealing with the regulation of conduct, in the other with the sacramental power of absolution.

[14] It is obvious that this feeling of continuity with the "chosen people" leads to the view that there were "Christians" before Christ, expressed, for instance, in the opening chapters of the Church history of Eusebius. On the other hand, the discourses of John led to the feeling that the Church was a new thing, and Christians a new race, expressed very vividly in the Apology of Aristides.

CHAPTER IV

Acts

THE Acts of the Apostles gives the continuation of the story of the Gospel of Luke. It is the only narrative which we possess of the way in which the disciples of Jesus became the foundation of the Christian Church. A few points concerning the book as a whole should be noted:

i. The title is either "Acts" or "Acts of the Apostles" with slight variations in different manuscripts.[1] It is probably not the title of the book as it was written by the author, as it is clearly the second volume of a completed whole, of which the Gospel of Luke is Volume I. The original book may have had some such title as "Luke to Theophilus," but this cannot be told with certainty. All that can be said is that the original title probably contained the name of Luke and the name of Theophilus. Unfortunately, nothing is known of this Theophilus. The Church separated the two volumes, accepted Volume I as the Gospel according to Luke and gave Volume II the title of "Acts." It is also quite likely that the end of the Gospel was slightly changed in order that it might more satisfactorily fit its new position.

ii. Tradition says that the author of this book and of the third Gospel was Luke,[2] the physician to whom Paul refers in Col. iv.14. The evidence for this, like that supporting most of the traditions about early Christian literature, has an unfortunate gap at the beginning. The author himself makes no statement; there is nothing on the subject until the end of the second century, and attempts to show by the evidence of the style that the author must have been a doctor have completely

[1] See *Beginnings,* Vol. IV, pp. 1 ff.

[2] There are also traces of an early tradition which identified Luke with Lucius of Cyrene; see Cadbury in *Beginnings,* Vol. V, pp. 489 ff.

failed,—there is no more medical language in Acts than in the writings of any educated man at any period.[3] Nevertheless, there is no evidence whatever in favour of any other authorship and the name of Luke may be retained for convenience if not by conviction.

The book is generally written in the third person, but some paragraphs are in the first person plural. These are usually called the 'We-sections.' Possibly the writer was once a companion of the Apostle Paul and adopts the first person in telling his story to indicate the time when he was an eye witness of the events described. But this is not certain, for whenever his statements can be compared with those in the Pauline Epistles there is so great a divergence in detail between the two, in spite of a general agreement, that many think that the author of Acts cannot have been a companion of Paul.[4] If the traditional theory be abandoned, the conjecture may be made that the We-sections are extracts from the diary of a companion of Paul.

iii. The text of Acts presents a very complicated problem.[5] The main facts are these:

a. There are two distinct texts discernible in the earliest period; one is usually called the "Western" text, but sometimes the β-text (not to be confused with the B-text). This existed in the second century. The other is sometimes called the "Neutral" text, following Westcott and Hort's system, sometimes the B-text (because it is found in Codex Vaticanus [B]) more rarely the α-text. This can be proved to have been in existence in the third, and probably in the second century.

b. Westcott and Hort held the Neutral text to be the original. F. Blass thought that Luke made two editions, the West-

[3] Cadbury, *Style and Literary Method of Luke*, in *Harvard Theological Studies*, VI, pp. 39 ff.

[4] See *Beginnings*, Vol. II, pp. 265 ff. (by C. W. Emmet) and pp. 298 ff. (by H. Windisch).

[5] Westcott and Hort, *The New Testament in the Original Greek*, Vol. II; F. Blass, *Acta Apostolorum*, 1895, and his two smaller editions of Luke and Acts, *Lucae ad Theophilum secundum formam quae videtur Romanam;* A. C. Clark, *Acts of the Apostles;* and J. H. Ropes in *Beginnings*, Vol. III.

ern being the earlier, and the Neutral a revision. J. H. Ropes thought that both are revisions of an earlier original, but that the Neutral text is much nearer to it than is the Western. We agree with Ropes as to both texts being revisions, but believe, —as against his view,—that in many cases the Western text is right.

c. The problem must not be confused with that in the gospels. The chief point is that the Western text of the gospels is quite different in Latin from what it is in Syriac, but in Acts is essentially the same.

iv. Though various motifs can be perceived in Acts, it is impossible to say precisely what was the purpose of the author in composing it. Among the more obvious are the following:

a. A desire to prove the supernatural inspiration and guidance given to the Church on the day of Pentecost and the continued guidance of the Spirit throughout its history.

b. A desire to show that the best Roman magistrates never decided against the Christians; all serious persecution was due either to the malignity of the Jews or to the ignorance of the mob.

c. A more purely historical desire to show how the Church ceased to be Jewish and became Greek, because the Jews rejected and the Greeks accepted the message of salvation.

No one of these motifs is so central as to justify us in calling it the "purpose" of the author. Moreover, his own words are unfortunately ambiguous. He tells Theophilus, to whom he addresses his preface, that he has written in order that he may know the truth of matters about which he has been informed. Usually "the matters about which he has been informed" is interpreted as meaning the stories he heard from Christians about Christianity, and it is assumed that he was a convert; but there is no evidence to this effect and the word rendered above as "has been informed" (κατηχέω) was perhaps more often used in the first century of defamatory stories.[6] Thus the

[6] Cf. Acts xxi.21 and 24; and see Cadbury's note in *Beginnings*, Vol. II, p. 508 f.

chances are about even whether Luke wrote to Theophilus to give a solid basis to the faith of a new convert or to correct the erroneous impression of a heathen to whom the Church had been slandered. It has even been suggested that Theophilus was the magistrate concerned with the trial of Paul. Some slight evidence for this may be found in the title given to Theophilus in Luke i.3, which may be rendered "Excellency," though this gives a rather exaggerated impression of his probable rank. The point of difficulty is that the Greek word κράτιστος was used to render the Latin *egregius,* a title reserved in the first century for very high officials, but it was also used to render *optimus,* which does not connote official rank.[7]

The value of ancient books, however, is not always to be identified with the purpose of their writers. Whatever Luke's purpose, the value of his book is that it affords us a unique series of glimpses into the beginnings of Christianity. It is not a complete nor a perfectly connected story, but our whole knowledge of the founding of the Greek-speaking Church depends on it. We can form hypotheses and make guesses as to other events which must have happened, but they are only hypotheses and guesses.

v. How far can Acts be assumed to give correctly the history of the early Church? Three conditions limit the use which can be made of it:

a. Acts is the story of the spread of the Apostolic message, that Jesus was the Messiah. In all the numerous sermons quoted there is no attempt to propagate the teaching of Jesus, —except, of course, that the Kingdom is at hand,—but merely to spread the teaching about Jesus which he himself had never given to the multitude, but only to the Apostles. He was the Lord and Messiah who would come from Heaven as God's appointed representative to judge the world at the last day, and the last day was very near at hand.

If we had only Acts,—or even Acts and the Pauline Epistles, —we might suppose that the teaching of Jesus himself had been

[7] For the use of the title, see A. Zehetmair, *De appelationibus honorificis* etc., Marburg, 1912, and the qualifying remarks of Cadbury in *Beginnings,* Vol. II, pp. 505 ff.

completely eclipsed by the teaching about him. It must be recognised that, according to Acts, it was this Apostolic message about Jesus, not the Sermon on the Mount, which conquered the Greek world. In this respect Acts is the legitimate sequel to Mark, rather than to Luke, for Mark—like Acts—deals almost exclusively with the things which Jesus did, but Luke is also concerned with what he said.

b. Acts itself assumes that the Church had penetrated into various cities such as Damascus and Ephesus, before Paul reached them, but the missionaries implied by this fact are unknown to us. *Vixere fortes ante Agamemnona*. Therefore, it is often necessary to remind ourselves, as was said above, that Acts is, after all, only a series of glimpses, not a complete view.

c. A comparison with the Epistles shows that Acts gives an unduly peaceful picture of the internal evolution of the Church. The Epistles show that the earliest days were marked by constant and violent controversy. Luke always omits this. Even the story of the Jewish controversy is represented as an attack from without or below, which never for a moment disrupted Apostolic agreement. Quite a different complexion is put on the story by Paul's account in Galatians, and we should never have guessed for a moment how stormy were the first five years of the Church in Corinth if we had not had the correspondence of St. Paul to guide us.

vi. What are the sources of Acts? No historical book was ever written without the use of sources by its author, but these may be written documents or merely local tradition. Many attempts have been made to discover the sources whicn are behind Acts. A full discussion of the subject is impossible,[8] but the following points should be kept in mind:

a. The paragraphs in which the first person plural is used (the We-sections) are probably extracts from a source, but it is open to question whether that source was a diary of the author or of someone else. A less probable alternative is that the first

[8] See especially Harnack's *Beiträge,* III and IV, and the discussion in *Beginnings,* Vol. II, pp. 121 ff. An admirable account of earlier work is given by W. Heitmüller in the *Theologische Rundschau,* 1899.

person is a purely literary device. It is also a question whether the narrative sections intervening between the We-sections should be regarded as drawn from the same source, or as "connective tissue" supplied by the editor.

b. Even a superficial reading shows that Luke was using various local traditions as his sources, especially the traditions of Jerusalem, Caesarea and Antioch, but it is not clear whether these were already in written form when he used them, still less whether they were in Greek or Aramaic. The Jerusalem tradition may be supposed to include i-v, and it is possible that in this section two forms may be distinguished,—commonly known as Jerusalem sources A (iii-iv.31) and B (i-ii and v.17-42). This was Harnack's view and though not certain it demands consideration. The attribution of the rest of iv and v is generally thought to be doubtful. It is also plausible to assign Acts xv-xvi.5 to a Jerusalem source tradition. The Caesarean tradition is clearly given in viii.26-40, ix.31-x.48, and possibly more. The Antiochian tradition may be claimed for xi.19-30 and xii.25-xiv.28. Finally, there is a certain amount which may be derived from more than one tradition. For instance the stories of Stephen and of the Antiochian mission to Jerusalem in the time of the Famine may have been told from the Jerusalem point of view as well as from that of Antioch.[9]

But traditions not only belong to places; they are necessarily derived from persons. Who told Luke the facts which he records? Obviously Paul himself may be the source of the Pauline tradition. The objection to this view is the difference between Acts and the Pauline Epistles at points where they can be directly compared. Similarly Peter may well be the main source of the Jerusalem tradition, either Peter or Philip of the Caesarean, Barnabas or Paul of the Antiochian. But it is sometimes forgotten that Mark, an inhabitant of Jerusalem, and a companion of Peter, Paul and Barnabas, is a possible source for all the facts in Acts up to the point where Barnabas and Paul parted company and that Mark's gospel is demonstrably one of the sources of Luke's first volume.

[9] See pp. 79-82.

Acts gives the story of the years immediately following the Resurrection in a series of scenes which the editor of the book has united by connective tissue which is usually readily distinguishable. Set into many of the scenes are speeches attributed to the main characters. The problems presented by the speeches differ from those in the narrative and can best be handled separately. The remainder of this chapter, therefore, deals first with the narrative and its chief problems, and then with the speeches.

NARRATIVE

i. Acts i-v gives a number of glimpses into the life of the first Christian community during the first year, or at most, the first two years after the crucifixion. The opening chapters, i and ii, strike the three notes which henceforward dominate the whole story and make it intelligible. These are *a.* the glorification of the risen Lord, who has become a heavenly being; *b.* the gift of the Holy Spirit, sent by the risen Lord to the Apostles; *c.* the universality of the Apostolic message about Jesus.

a. The risen Jesus ascended to heaven after he had promised to inspire the Apostles with the Holy Spirit, so that they could testify to him throughout the world; and the angels promised that he would return "in the same way as he had gone," that is in the clouds of heaven.

b. The gift of the Spirit to the Apostles, on the day of Pentecost, fulfilled the promise of the risen Lord and also afforded evidence that the End was at hand, for it made good the promise of the prophet Joel that in the last days men should "speak with tongues,"—as the Apostles did. It is also possible that the author intended this day to be regarded as the beginning of preaching to the Gentiles, but this depends on rather complicated questions of textual criticism and interpretation, for it is not clear whether the writer thought of the multitude which listened to the Apostles as composed of Gentiles or of Jews, since the word "Jews" in ii.5 is doubtful.

Moreover, the 'speaking with tongues' on the day of Pentecost and on other occasions presents a curious problem. The traditional view (and the text as it stands can mean nothing else) is that although the crowd was made up of many nationalities, each heard the message in his own language. The difficulties are that in the Epistles of Paul, especially in I Corinthians, there are many references to "speaking with tongues" where it clearly means ecstatic and unintelligible language such as is not infrequent under conditions of great emotion, and the accusation in Acts ii.13 that the Apostles were drunk suggests the Pauline unintelligible speaking with tongues, rather than a remarkable clearness in foreign languages; Peter's reply to the accusation does not deny the superficial appearance of drunkenness, but says that it was too early in the day for it to be true.[10]

These difficulties have led to the opinion, now widely held, that Luke, who had himself perhaps never heard "speaking with tongues," misinterpreted the phrase and "wrote up" the story in the light of this interpretation. It is certain that if Acts ii.6-11 is omitted, the text becomes a clear account of "speaking with tongues" similar to that described in I Corinthians.

c. The section is closed by a speech of Peter, giving the Apostolic testimony to Jesus and calling on his hearers to repent and be baptised.

The next chapters (iii-v) are a series of episodes in Jerusalem,—miracles performed by the Apostles, clashes with the Jewish authorities, and consequent speeches illustrating the relation of the Church to the outside world. Its internal life is portrayed in a summary account of an effort to deal with the problem of pooling all the property of the Christians and dividing it up according to individual needs.[11] These summaries may be generalisations from the two instances of Barnabas, who honestly lived up to this experiment, and of Ananias and Sapphira who tried to exploit it and were killed in conse-

[10] For glossolalia see the notes in J. Weiss' commentary on I Cor. xiv; E. Mossiman, *Das Zungenreden,* and *Earlier Epistles,* pp. 241 ff.

[11] See Troeltsch's *Soziallehren der christlichen Kirchen,* and R. von Pöhlmann's *Geschichte der sozialen Frage in der antiken Welt.*

quence. Or possibly these two stories are told in order to illustrate the summaries.

This ends the first part of Acts. It is obviously Jerusalem tradition; some critics think that it is a translation from an Aramaic source, others that it is a combination of more than one document, and yet others combine all or parts of all of these possibilities.

ii. Acts vi-viii.3 gives the story of the breakdown of the economic experiment, owing to the fact that even among Christians "economic desire" increases more rapidly than economic means. Hence the Apostles retired from its administration and left it to a committee of seven, whose preaching led the Jews to more active opposition. The leader of the Seven,—Stephen,—was killed, and most of the Christians had to leave Jerusalem.

No detailed reason is given why the Seven were persecuted and the Twelve were not, but the accusation against Stephen and the tenor of his speech in Acts vii (a speech against the Jews, not a defence) suggest that the Seven were Hellenistic Jews, belonging to the reforming school.[12] If so, and though there is not much evidence in support of this theory, there is also none against it, the next step,—the persecution of the Hellenists—is natural.

iii. Acts viii.4-xi.26 is a confused section in which Luke tells the story, certainly derived from more than one source, of how the Hellenistic members of the Church, driven from Jerusalem, began the conversion of the Greek-speaking world, and were helped by the miraculous conversion of one of their persecutors,—Saul of Tarsus. The friends of Stephen had been scattered into the Greek parts of Palestine and Syria and in every case Luke stresses the fact that Gentiles were converted under circumstances which showed that it was the will of God that the message of Christianity should not be confined to the Jews.

In discussing this story it seems better to vary Luke's order and to bring together the bits which really belong to three

[12] Philo in the *de Migratione Abrahami*, M. I 450, Cohn and Wendland, II, 285, speaks strongly against Jews who accept the allegorical and not also the literal meaning of the Law. See also pp. 222 ff.

separate traditions, though Luke did not necessarily derive these from three separate sources.

It would appear that Philip, one of the Seven, took up the preaching of Christianity in two definitely Greek districts of Palestine,–in Samaria [13] and in the Greek cities of the coast, including Caesarea, the capital of the country under the Romans. He was followed up by Peter, who went to Samaria to supplement his work, and Peter also finally went to Caesarea. Thus we have a complex of episodes which might be called the "Philip-Peter" or the "Jerusalem-Samaria-Caesarea" tradition.

The three important events in this tradition are *a.* the conversion of Simon Magus,[14] *b.* the conversion of the Ethiopian eunuch, and *c.* the conversion of the centurion Cornelius.

a. Simon was a popular preacher of a new sect in an unnamed city of Samaria. He was converted by Philip, but was later excommunicated by Peter for trying to purchase Apostolic powers. According to tradition, he became the leader of the first heretical sect.

The most difficult problems connected with this story con-

[13] There has always been a tendency to confuse the district of Samaria with its capital city. But Herod had renamed the city as Sebaste; would Luke have reverted to the old name any more than he used Stratonis Turris for Caesarea? See also p. 190.

[14] For Simon Magus, there is a mass of literature. The ancient sources are: Acts viii.9 ff.; Justin, *Apol.*, i.26, 56; *Dial. c. Tryph.*, 120; Irenaeus, *Adv. haer.*, i.16 (H), i.20 (G): Tertullian, *de anima*, 34, *Adv. omn. haer.*, 1; Clemens Alex., *Strom.*, ii.52.2, vii.107.1 (Stählin, iii, p. 75, Sylburg, p. 325); Hippolytus, *Ref.*, vi.7.20, x.12; Philastrius, *Div. haer. liber*, 29; Epiphanius, *Panarion, haer.* 21; Theodoret, *Haer. fabl.* i.1; Ps.–Augustine, *De haeresibus*, 1; Cyril of Jerusalem, *Catechesis*, vi.13 (P.G. xxxiii. 561); *Acta Pauli*, 7 (Schmidt pp. 73-75); *Acta Petri cum Simone*, 4 ff. (and allied documents, cf. M. R. James, *The Apocryphal New Testament*, Oxford, 1924, pp. 471-472); *Epistola Apostolorum*, 1 (Schmidt, pp. 25, 33); *Clementine Recognitions* and *Homilies*, passim; *Apost. Const.*, vi.8-9. On Oriental sources cf. F. Haase, *Altchristliche Kirchengeschichte nach orientalischen Quellen*, Leipzig, 1925, pp. 322-327; *Apostel und Evangelisten in den orientalischen Uberlieferungen*, Munster, 1922, passim. From these sources amazing combinations have been made by modern writers. For a sober statement, see especially the articles by A. C. Headlam in Hastings *Dictionary of the Bible*, and by R. P. Casey in *Beginnings*, Vol. V.

cern baptism and the gift of the Spirit.[15] Philip baptised his Samaritan converts when they believed him "preaching the things concerning the Kingdom of God and the name of Jesus Christ." But when Peter and John arrived they "prayed for them, that they might receive the Holy Ghost, for as yet he was fallen upon none of them, only they were baptised in the name of the Lord Jesus." The Apostles then laid their hands on the converts, who immediately received the Spirit. It seems clear that the baptism administered by Philip in Samaria resembled the baptism which was one of the less important requirements for a Jewish proselyte; it did not confer the Spirit, in distinction from the laying-on of Apostolic hands which did so.

The matter, however, is complicated by the fact that Acts seems not to be consistent with itself on this subject. In xix.1-7 it relates that in Ephesus Paul found Christians who had not received the Holy Spirit and the author explains that this is because they had not been baptised in the name of the Lord Jesus, but only with John's baptism. On the other hand, in i.4 f. the gift of the Spirit is represented as the baptism foretold by John the Baptist [16] and the Spirit in the one takes the place of the water in the other. The story of Philip in Samaria seems to agree with neither of these two, but, as was said above, to imply a theory that not baptism but the laying-on of hands conveyed the Spirit. This view would correspond with the story of Paul at Ephesus, but only if we assume that baptism in the name of the Lord Jesus was in some way identified with the baptism of John. It is, in any case, interesting to note that the close relationship between baptism and the laying-on of hands, and of one or both with the gift of the Spirit, is perpetuated in the history of the Catholic doctrines as to baptism and confirmation.

[15] See H. Gunkel, *Die Wirkungen des heiligen Geistes;* W. Heitmüller, *Taufe und Abendmahl bei Paulus,* and *Beginnings,* Vol. V, pp. 121 ff. (by S. New); Strack-Billerbeck, I, pp. 110 ff. and II, pp. 647 ff. R. Reitzenstein's *Die Vorgeschichte des christliche Taufe* should be read with caution and compared with the magistral review by H. H. Schaeder in *Gnomon,* V, pp. 353 ff.

[16] Cf. Mark i.8.

b. When Philip left Samaria he was inspired to go from Jerusalem toward Gaza and on the road he met and converted an Ethiopian eunuch, who was on a pilgrimage to Jerusalem, though it is not certain whether he was or was not a proselyte. In any case, Philip baptised him, and, if he was not a proselyte, he is the first clear instance of the baptism of an uncircumcised Gentile.

Perhaps the chief importance of this story is that it introduces for the first time in the New Testament the identification of Jesus with the "suffering servant" of Isaiah liii. This figure is central in all later Christian exposition and is made into a prophecy of the Passion. Oddly enough, however, though Ps. xxii appears in the gospels in connection with the Passion, Isaiah liii is not used.

After this episode, Philip went to Azotus and thence to Caesarea, where he appears to have settled down permanently. Traditionally, he is the first bishop of Caesarea and in Acts xxi.8 it is mentioned that Paul and his company, which possibly included Luke (as this is one of the We-sections) stayed in the house of Philip at Caesarea and noted that he had four unmarried daughters who were prophetesses. It is obvious that this point of contact between Philip and Luke gives a very clear hint as to the origin of the Caesarean tradition in Acts.

c. A centurion, Cornelius, living in Caesarea, was told by an angel to send to Jaffa and summon Peter,—who had gone there on leaving Samaria. While the messengers of Cornelius were on their way to him, Peter also had a vision warning him not to call "unclean" food which God had cleansed. As he was pondering this command, Cornelius' men arrived with their master's request and a voice from heaven told Peter to accede to it. He therefore set out to Caesarea, and when Cornelius, on hearing Peter, was converted and received the Holy Spirit, Peter baptised him. The Church in Jerusalem was shocked by this incident when it was reported, but was persuaded by Peter's account of the gift of the Spirit to Cornelius and accepted the view that Gentiles might become Christians without circumcision.

The most difficult point in the story is why Peter ever baptised Cornelius. He recognised in the gift of the Spirit to the centurion the fulfillment of the prophecy attributed by Luke to Jesus, "John baptised with water, but ye shall be baptised with the Holy Spirit," but then went on to baptise Cornelius *with water*. Why did he? Or did he not do so, and is this merely a reflexion of Church practice? Is there any importance in the fact that Luke in his narrative relates the baptism of Cornelius, but omits it in his account of Peter's report to the Church in Jerusalem?

While Philip and Peter were thus preaching in Samaria and Judaea, others who had been the adherents of Stephen went to Antioch,[17] the great Greco-Syrian city of Syria, and preached to the Gentiles with marked success, without requiring circumcision. This disturbed the Church in Jerusalem, which sent Barnabas to investigate, but he was persuaded by what he saw and became a leader of the Antiochian Church.

In xi.26 Luke gives the very interesting information that the name 'Christian' was first used in Antioch. It is, however, even more interesting that we do not know anything about the history of the word, or about another earlier name,—'the Way.' Both 'Christian' and 'Way' may have been phrases invented by the followers of Jesus, or by their opponents.[18] Certainly 'Way' was used by Jews to describe heresy and 'Christian' is a Greco-Latin Word which may have been made up in scorn of those who were the party of the derided 'Christ,' whose claims had been disposed of by crucifixion. It would not be the only time in history that sneering nicknames of contempt have been accepted as honourable titles,—for instance, 'Whig,' 'Methodist' and 'Quaker.'

At this point it is necessary to go back to Jerusalem at the time of Stephen's martyrdom. Among those who had been present at his death was a young man named Saul, who was afterwards a leader in the "pogrom" against the Christians. He was

[17] There is no outstanding book on Antioch, but doubtless the Princeton excavations will supply one. See E. S. Bouchier, *A Short History of Antioch,* and the articles in various Bible dictionaries, especially in Chabrol's *Dictionnaire d'archéologie chrétienne.*

[18] See Cadbury in *Beginnings,* Vol. V, pp. 375 ff.

given a special commission to go to Damascus and arrest any Christians whom he could find. It is noteworthy that this statement seems to imply that there was already a Christian Church in Damascus. On his way Saul had an overwhelming vision of the risen Jesus, and was immediately converted into as ardent a disciple as he had been persecutor. There are three accounts of his conversion in Acts and they are essentially the same, though they differ in some details: Saul, after his vision, staggered into Damascus, blinded and sick, and was entertained by a Christian named Ananias, who had been warned in a vision to expect him and to give him instruction. Saul stayed in Damascus for a short time and then, being in danger from the Jews, escaped in a basket over the wall. He went to Jerusalem and stayed there for a short time, finding natural hostility from the Jews and some equally natural suspicion from the Christians. Then he went, perhaps in accordance with another vision, to his original home in Cilicia, the famous university town of Tarsus.[19] He was there when Barnabas went to Antioch, and thence Barnabas sent and fetched him. Barnabas and Paul at once became leaders in the Church at Antioch, and Paul is henceforth the central figure in Acts, except in chapter xii.

The real difficulty in these narratives is not their slight inconsistencies, such as that in the one Saul's companion saw a light but heard nothing, while in the other he heard a voice but saw nothing. These are natural flaws, to be paralleled in all narratives, but there is a serious discrepancy between the accounts in Acts and Paul's own story, both as to the source of the commission which he received and as to his own actions immediately afterwards.

According to Acts, this divine commission for Paul to preach to the Gentiles was given not to him but to Ananias, who passed it on and baptised him. Is it not possible that Paul knew this account and is refuting it in his own story of the events in Gal. i.11-21, where he emphasises the statement that he received his Apostolic commission "neither from men nor through man" but directly from Jesus Christ? Ananias evi-

[19] For Tarsus, see especially H. Böhlig, *Geisteskultur von Tarsus.*

dently played a larger part in the story current in Damascus and Jerusalem than he did in Paul's own consciousness.

Moreover, Luke's account of Saul's movements after his conversion differs from that given in Galatians.[20] According to Acts, Paul went to Damascus immediately after his conversion, then straight to Jerusalem, then to Tarsus, where he stayed until Barnabas summoned him to Antioch. But according to Galatians, Paul immediately after his conversion consulted no one, but went to Arabia,—not, of course, the desert, but the prosperous district now called Transjordania, which at that time was at least as important as Palestine. He then returned to Damascus, and not until after three years did he go to Jerusalem, whence,—as in Acts,—he retired to Cilicia, that is to Tarsus.

These differences may not be vital, but they cannot be explained without a surgical operation on one or both narratives. It is far better to recognise them as the sort of inaccuracies found in all historical narratives written many years after the events. Of the two accounts, doubtless Paul's own is to be preferred, but even Galatians was written, according to the ordinary chronology, fifteen or twenty years after the conversion.

iv. At the end of Acts xi, Luke starts to tell the next episode, the relation of Paul, Barnabas and the Church at Antioch to the Apostles in Jerusalem, which is again taken up in the last verse of chapter xii and continued in chapter xv. But he interpolates, for the last time, an episode from the history of Jerusalem (xii.1-24) and the "first missionary journey" (xiii-xiv). For the sake of clarity it is simpler first to deal with this interpolation and then return to the main narrative.

According to Acts xii.1-3, Herod Agrippa in his last year (i.e. A.D. 44) began to persecute the Christians.[21] He beheaded James, the son of Zebedee, and put Peter in prison, intending

[20] See J. B. Lightfoot, *Galatians*, W. M. Ramsay, *Historical Commentary on Galatians*, and *Beginnings*, Vol. V, pp. 188 ff.

[21] See E. Schwartz, *Zur Chronologie des Paulus* in the Göttingen *Nachrichten* for 1907. This is one of the most important contributions of the last half-century to the understanding of the chronology of the New Testament.

to enliven the coming Passover with his execution. Peter, however, was rescued by an angel and left Jerusalem for "another place," possibly Antioch or possibly Rome, according to ecclesiastical tradition. Herod then left Jerusalem and went to Caesarea, where he suddenly died in the midst of festivities. His death is similarly, though not identically, described by Josephus.

v. The relations of Paul, Barnabas and Antioch to Jerusalem are described in Acts xi.28-30; xii.25-xiii.1; xv.1-35. This is an extremely important but very difficult section. As it stands in Acts it tells how in a few years a vigorous Church was built up out of "liberal" Jews and Gentile "God-fearers." It gives the names of the leaders, who are for the most part unknown, but include Barnabas and Paul. Their relation to the mother-Church at Jerusalem was made closer by the coming of the great famine in Palestine which, according to Josephus as well as to Luke,[22] was severe in A.D. 45. Antioch was the richer community and it sent help to Jerusalem by Barnabas and Paul.

At the end of chapter xii, we are told of the return of Barnabas and Paul to Antioch and this is followed in chapters xiii and xiv by the description of the "first missionary journey." From this journey Barnabas and Paul return to Antioch and immediately there ensues a controversy [23] between Antioch and Jerusalem as to the legitimacy of the Antiochian missionaries in making converts to Christianity without circumcising them.

It was decided that Paul and Barnabas should go to Jerusalem as the representatives of Antioch and discuss the matter with the leaders there. On their arrival a meeting, generally called the Apostolic Council, was held, presided over by James,

[22] The odd way in which the death of Herod (A.D. 44) is sandwiched in between the beginning and end of the story of the famine is perhaps a chronological indication. For the date of this event see p. 248.

[23] Out of many books dealing with this subject, a representative list would be: J. B. Lightfoot, *Galatians,* W. M. Ramsay, *The Church in the Roman Empire, St. Paul, the Traveler and Roman Citizen,* C. W. Emmet, *The Epistle to the Galatians,* E. H. Askwith, *The Epistle to the Galatians, Beginnings,* Vol. V, pp. 195 ff., and, in German, Zahn's *Apostelgeschichte* and the commentaries in Meyer and in Lietzmann's *Handbuch.*

the Lord's brother. Peter made a speech reminding the Church of his conversion of Cornelius,—although Cornelius' name is not mentioned,—and advocating the admission of the Gentiles without inflicting on them "a yoke which neither we nor our fathers were able to bear." Then Paul and Barnabas described the success of their mission and finally James summed up the sense of the meeting by proposing that no further burden be put on Gentile Christians, other than that they should abstain from "things offered to idols, from blood [24] and from fornication." The decision was embodied in a letter to the Gentiles in Antioch and other cities in Syria and Cilicia, and sent back by Paul and Barnabas, with whom also went Silas and Jude of Jerusalem.

The main difficulty is that if the words be given their ordinary sense in the context of the story, they state that the Church agreed to give up the requirement of circumcision for Gentile converts and substitute for it the three (or four) rules of conduct prescribed in the decrees which they formulated. Obviously, a decision of this kind was intended to have general force,—it would hardly be intended for one province and not for others. If so, it must have become obsolete at once, for there is no trace of this substitution of the decrees for circumcision in the Pauline Epistles. Paul never alludes to the decree, even when he is discussing circumcision, things offered to idols and fornication.

Moreover, it is probable that in Gal. ii we have Paul's own account of the controversy. According to this, on Paul's second visit to Jerusalem (and he is peculiarly positive that it was on his *second* visit [25] after his conversion), he found himself engaged in a dispute with Jewish Christians about circumcision. He refused to yield, even though as a temporary concession he probably circumcised Titus, and ultimately James, Peter and John yielded the point. Afterwards, when he returned to Antioch, Peter came to that city. At first Peter lived as Paul

[24] "Blood" meant meat from which the blood had not been removed by the method of slaughter, and some texts, probably later ones, add "things strangled," originally as a gloss on "blood" and afterwards as a fourth decree (see J. H. Ropes in *Beginnings,* Vol. III).

[25] Cf. Gal i.20.

did, on terms of free social intercourse with the Gentiles, but James sent down emissaries to object to this laxity and Peter withdrew. So also did Barnabas, and Paul was left alone in his opposition. It will be observed that this short account in Galatians clearly speaks of two controversies; the first, about circumcision, taking place in Jerusalem, and the second, about social intercourse, in Antioch.

Comparing this passage with Acts xv raises the preliminary question whether they are really referring to the same Jerusalem visit even though the controversy was similar. Galatians says that this was Paul's second visit; Acts makes it his third. Two ways of dealing with this difficulty are current:

On the one hand, it is supposed that Galatians refers to a controversy which took place on the occasion of Paul's visit at the time of the Famine,—his second visit, which Luke mentions in xi.30,—and that Acts xv. refers to a third visit which took place after Galatians was written.

The alternative solution, which is perhaps preferable, is that Luke had heard two stories about the early relations of the churches of Jerusalem and Antioch,—one the tradition of Antioch, the other that of Jerusalem. Possibly Antioch thought more of the help it had sent to Jerusalem and Jerusalem more about the controversy between the churches. If so, it is quite likely that Luke treated the two stories of one event as one continuous story. That would mean, of course, that Paul's second and third visits to Jerusalem (according to Acts) are both really his second visit (according to his own account).

Adopting this view, which seems the easiest solution of the contradiction between Acts and Paul as to the number of his visits to Jerusalem, two corollaries may follow, though with rather different degrees of probability:

a. It seems quite likely that Luke, writing at least twenty years after the events, confused two almost simultaneous controversies. The first was that about circumcision. That ended (so far as the party of Antioch, Paul and Barnabas were concerned) in the abandonment of circumcision as a requirement for converts of Christianity. The second controversy was on social intercourse with Jews and was settled by a compromise such as is embodied in the Apostolic Decrees. But it will always remain open to discussion whether Paul was really a party to the compromise, as Luke thinks, or not, as his letter suggests. Was he even present in Jerusalem when the compromise was made? Did Luke crystallise into the form of decrees the general custom of the Church at the time when he was writing?

b. If we assume that the famine relief visit in xi and xii and the discussion visit in xv are really the same, what is to be said of the episodes which follow? According to Acts, after the "famine visit" Paul went on a missionary journey and he did the same after the "discussion visit." If the "famine visit" be the same as the "discussion visit" are the two missionary journeys two accounts, or rather two halves of one account of the same? Perhaps they are, and possibly Luke divided up this story into two parts, using the Barnabas information for the earlier and the Pauline for the later part and merely adding "connective tissue." In any case, it is probable that the circumcision controversy came during Paul's second (the famine relief) visit to Jerusalem and his missionary journey followed immediately after it. He may have returned to Antioch from Lystra and Derbe, and the social intercourse controversy may have taken place then. Once more, we are never likely to settle the question, but it certainly exists.

It is now necessary to return to the decrees themselves.[26] In the text which is probably oldest, they enjoin on Christians (i.e. Gentile Christians) to abstain from three things,—things offered to idols, blood and fornication. The first two clearly refer to food, and it is well known how much community of custom in food affects social intercourse. Moreover, the Talmud refers to the similar rules traditionally given to Noah for the guidance of all his descendants, and both it and the Sibylline Oracles rather obscurely imply that compliance with some form of the Noachian precepts was demanded from such Gentiles as wished to be on friendly terms with Jews.

[26] See especially G. Resch, *Das Aposteldecret,* Harnack's chapter on *Das Aposteldecret* in his *Apostelgeschichte* (in the *Beiträge*) and Ropes' discussion of the text in *Beginnings,* Vol. III, pp. 265 ff.

The history of the decrees in the early Church is also a curious problem. In Alexandria, and probably in the East generally, the relation of the decrees to food was usually recognised, and a gloss was generally adopted in the Greek text, and is therefore in the English version.

In the West, the meaning of the decrees seems to have been completely forgotten and "blood" was taken to mean "murder," so that the gloss "things strangled" is not found in the West. Instead of it an interpretation was adopted which made the decrees refer to the three deadly sins of idolatry, murder and fornication, and an addition was made to the text at this point which reads "and whatsoever you do not wish to be done to you, do not do to others." This negative form of the "Golden Rule" is well known in both Jewish and Gentile literature and is found also in the *Didache*. The very marked difference between the East and the West in the interpretation of this passage probably reflects the fact that social relations with Jewish Christians was a living question in the East but not in the West.

vi. After their return to Antioch from Jerusalem, Barnabas and Paul decided to go on a missionary journey.[27] This is known as the "first missionary journey" and is described in Acts xiii.2-xiv.26. With them, as their assistant, they took John Mark, a nephew of Barnabas. The road they followed and the places in which they stopped can be satisfactorily traced on map 2 in App. B and that at the end of the book. On their return they retraced their steps, except that they did not stop at Cyprus. The narrative as given in Acts is quite clear and it is unnecessary to paraphrase it, but the following points should be noted:

a. In Cyprus[28] the name of the governor of the island was Sergius Paulus and it has been thought that the narrative means that he became a Christian and that Saul changed his

[27] See especially W. M. Ramsay, *St. Paul, the Traveler and Roman Citizen,* and for some details his *Church in the Roman Empire* and his *Historical Geography of Asia Minor.*

[28] See Hogarth's *Devia Cypria,* and the criticism of it in *Beginnings,* Vol. V, pp. 455 ff.

name to Paul in honour of so distinguished a convert. It has also been believed that this Sergius Paulus is mentioned in an inscription in Cyprus, but unfortunately the date given in it does not fit that of Paul's visit by about forty years.

In the same episode the name [29] of the sorcerer "Elymas or Bar-Jesus" is an insoluble puzzle, for in no way can "Elymas" be a rendering of "Bar-Jesus." Perhaps the most probable solution is that the Greek word meaning "translated" was also used to mean "the equivalent of,"—so that, for example, a Jew named Menahem who called himself Menelaus in Greek circles might refer to "Menelaus" as the "translation" of "Menahem," although in point of fact it was only the name which he adopted when talking Greek and did not translate the etymological meaning of his Hebrew name Menahem.

b. At Perga [30] John Mark decided to return, and left Paul and Barnabas to go on alone.

c. In Pisidian Antioch Paul made an address to the Jews in the synagogue, proving from Scripture and the fact of the Resurrection that the Christian belief was sound. But the Jews rejected his message and he turned to the Gentiles, probably at first especially to the God-fearers.[31] This is characteristic of Luke's account. He consistently emphasises that Paul's custom was always to preach to the Jews first and to go to the Gentiles only when the Jews refused to hear him.

d. In Iconium the same story is told, and once more Jewish opposition drove Paul and Barnabas out of the city.

e. In Lystra Paul and Barnabas are for the first time in a city without a synagogue. A miraculous cure persuaded the inhabitants that they were gods, and the priest of the temple outside the city wished to offer sacrifice to them. The speech in which Paul refused this honour raised resentment: he was stoned and, with Barnabas, barely escaped to Derbe.

In reading this story it should be remembered that it brings

[29] See Deissmann, *Zeitschrift für neutestamentliche Wissenschaft,* VII, pp. 91 ff. and A. Klostermann, *Probleme,* pp. 21 ff.

[30] For these cities, the most convenient summary of evidence is the series of articles by W. M. Ramsay in Hastings *Dictionary of the Bible.*

[31] See pp. 224 f.

us into a district with a very mixed and confused population and political constitution. The population was in the main Lycaonian and spoke that language, which is now not only extinct but entirely unknown, although it lingered on into the sixth century. But there were certainly some who spoke Greek, and,—since it was a Roman colony,—a few who knew Latin. Paul, of course, did not know Lycaonian and spoke Greek and it may be seriously doubted whether the gods whom Luke describes as Zeus and Hermes were not local divinities, who underwent a still further transformation in the English Bible where they were called Jupiter and Mercurius.

No details are told of the story in Derbe where the Apostles went after leaving Lystra. They returned through the cities which they had already visited, except those on Cyprus, appointing Presbyters and encouraging the converts, and so reached Syrian Antioch, thus ending the first missionary journey. But no details as to the events of the return journey are related.

vii. Acts xv.36-xviii.22 describes the "second missionary journey." After the Apostolic Council Paul and Barnabas returned to Antioch, and at once decided to repeat their missionary travel. But they could not agree about John Mark who had started with them on their first journey and had left them at Perga. Barnabas wanted to try him again, but Paul refused. In the end Paul took Silas and went to Asia Minor and Barnabas took Mark and went to Cyprus, and at this point Barnabas and Mark pass out of the pages of Acts.

On this journey Paul traveled across Asia Minor to Troas and then to Europe. His European journey is described in detail and very clearly, but his route across Asia Minor is summarised and hopelessly obscure.[32] Apparently he went by land from Antioch (see the map at the end of the book), through the Cilician Gates, the only practicable route, to Derbe, Lystra and Iconium.

Iconium was ethnologically a Phrygian city, Derbe and Lystra were Lycaonian, but all three were at this time included

[32] See especially Lightfoot's *Galatians*, W. M. Ramsay's *Church in the Roman Empire*, *Beginnings*, V, pp. 224 ff., and *Earlier Epistles*, pp. 309 ff.

in the Roman province of Galatia. This was an enormous tract of land which had been built up a generation earlier and called the Kingdom of Galatia because the centre of it was the territory of the Galatians, or Gauls, who spoke a language closely related to Welsh or Erse. Three centuries earlier they had occupied ground which marched on the south and west with that of the Phrygians.

At Iconium Paul wished to enter Asia,—a vague and difficult term. It is often thought that it means the Roman province of that name, but this is almost impossible, for the narrative goes on to say that he went through the Phrygian-Galatian countryside because he was prevented from preaching in 'Asia,' and came opposite Mysia. But to come opposite Mysia is only possible by going through the province of 'Asia.'

Among the less unsatisfactory solutions of this difficulty is to emphasise the phrase "speak the word" and suppose that Paul went through Asia, but silently. This is a popular interpretation and it is normally combined with the view that the "Phrygian and Galatian district" means the district[33] of the province of Galatia containing Antioch in Pisidia. It was expounded and advocated in the *Earlier Epistles of St. Paul,* as well as elsewhere, but the writer was led to abandon it, first because of the improbability that "prevented from speaking the word" was intended to mean 'could not preach, but did pass through'; secondly because the word rendered 'district' seems really to mean countryside, not 'provincial district,' and thirdly because even if 'district' did mean this, there is no evidence that "Phrygian and Galatian" was the official title of a subdivision of the province of Galatia.

A better view is that "Phrygian and Galatian countryside" refers to languages spoken. There must have been a district on the edge of the old Kingdom of Galatia where one village talked Galatian and the next Phrygian. This mixed population extended until "opposite Mysia." So far, therefore, there is no special difficulty. But there is still the problem of the meaning

33 That it was so is the opinion of Sir W. M. Ramsay, but there is no satisfactory evidence that the phrase was used in this province, though similar phrases were used elsewhere.

of 'Asia.' It cannot mean the province, but it might mean the Greek cities which dominated the western end of Asia Minor. Such a use of the word is implied in the κοινὸν τῆς 'Ασίας,—the federation of Greek cities in Asia,—for whether the phrase itself is found earlier or not it implies an organisation older than the Roman province and not coterminous with it.

However this may be, and certainty as to Paul's route is unattainable, it is clear that Paul's desire was to reach cities[34] where he could understand and be understood. This would have been the case in the Greek cities of Asia, but much less so in the country district north or north-west of Iconium. Doubtless there were some Greeks everywhere, but many fewer in this country. As soon, however, as Paul was opposite Mysia he was also close to Bithynia and another group of Greek cities. Nicomedia and others seemed to give him his chance, but once more he was unable to take it. This time we are told the "spirit hindered him," but, since no one knows, there have been many guesses as to what form this inspired hindrance may have taken. He swung around to the west and reached Troas where he had a vision of a Macedonian asking him to "come over and help." He took a boat at once and sailed past Samothrace to Neapolis, the modern Cavalla.

Immediately the narrative becomes as clear and full of details as it has up to this point been obscure.

Paul went from Neapolis, the end of the still visible Roman Via Egnatia, to Philippi and thence, keeping to the main road through Apollonia and Amphipolis, to Thessalonica and from it to Beroea, the modern Verria. Here comes the only point where there is difficulty.

From Beroea he went to Athens but his route is obscure, partly because the text is doubtful. There are two possibilities. The text may mean that he went from Beroea around Olympus to some small port on the coast, and thence by boat to Athens; or the statement that he was accompanied to the sea may mean that he was accompanied all the way to Athens.

[34] Christianity was a Greek religion,—as soon, at all events, as it left Jerusalem. Therefore it was a city religion and the heathen were "pagan" which means "country-folk."

In Macedonia he had been moderately successful, especially in Philippi and Thessalonica. In each case, he was driven out of the city, but Luke seems to emphasise that the opposition came from disreputable persons. In Philippi the owner of a "medium" who was being exploited commercially objected to Paul's exorcism and, although Paul was beaten by the local magistrates, they afterwards apologised for ill-treating a Roman citizen. In Thessalonica the case was only brought up through the hostility of the Jews, who employed low-class lawyers to frame an accusation. Moreover, it was never fully heard and Paul left the city because of the danger which his presence would have caused to Jason who had "given security."

These two Macedonian episodes are certainly told in such a way as to support the view that at least one of Luke's motives in writing was to show that Paul had never really offended against Roman law, and had never been in trouble except through Jewish malice, attacks by disreputable Gentiles, or the misunderstandings of inferior magistrates.

It should be noted that the We-sections begin in Troas (xvi.10) and stop in Philippi (xvi.17), begin again in Philippi (xx.5) and go on to Jerusalem and thence to Rome. At this point, too, we reach the first certain connection with the Pauline Epistles, for the two Epistles to the Thessalonians and that to the Philippians imply the visit of Paul to Macedonia described in Acts xvi.

Somewhere between Beroea and Athens Paul crossed from Macedonia into Achaea, governed by a Proconsul, the capital of which was Corinth.

Paul had little success in Athens.[35] Apparently there was no great number of Jews or "God-fearers" and he began to preach in the Agora, which was not so much the "Market place" as the great square of the city, surrounded by and containing buildings for public purposes. The control of this square and

[35] See Curtius, *Paulus in Athen* in his *Gesammelte Abhändlungen,* II, pp. 527-543; E. Norden, *Agnostos Theos;* Ramsay, *St. Paul, the Traveler and Roman Citizen,* and *Beginnings,* Vol. V, pp. 240 ff.

of the public life of the city generally, was in the hands of the Council of the Areopagus, or, as it was often called, "the Areopagus"—the "Field of Mars" of the English version—with an ellipse of "the Council." Its name went back to the almost legendary period when trials for murder were held on a small hill at a little distance from the Agora, and as Acts used the ordinary elliptic form of reference, saying "Areopagus," instead of "Council of the Areopagus," the improbable theory was formerly adopted that Paul was actually taken to the Hill of the Areopagus, and tourists in Athens are still shown where he stood. This is wholly unlikely, and Paul was surely taken into the office of the committee of the Areopagus in one of the buildings in the Agora. He had to show cause why he should be allowed to lecture and after he had spoken the case was adjourned, so that for the time at least Paul's public activity in Athens was stopped.

He went on to Corinth [36] and there met with his first great success. In Corinth there was an abundance of Jews, "God-fearers" and synagogues. Did he also find Christians in Corinth? This problem is stated but not answered in Acts xviii.2. According to this, Paul first lodged in Corinth with Aquila and Priscilla, Jews who had been expelled from Rome by Claudius. It is nowhere stated that Paul converted them, and since Luke elsewhere is careful to record all important conversions, there is considerable probability that they were Christians before they came to Corinth. This probability is strengthened by the fact that Claudius seems to have expelled the Jews because of riots between Jews and Christians.[37]

The Jews soon turned against Paul but, with more sense of opportunity than of tact, he established himself in a house next door to the synagogue. Of course this made a clash inevitable, but for eighteen months the Christian mission con-

[36] See pp. 109 ff. for the more important books on Paul in Corinth, and for a discussion of the Epistles.

[37] Suetonius says that in Rome there were constant riots "impulsore Christo." What other explanation approaches the probability of that adopted above? This was about the year 50 A.D. But, if so, who brought Christianity to Rome? Why not St. Peter?

tinued and the church grew. Acts tells us very little of the story, but I and II Corinthians give much information, and the whole account is better adapted for discussion in connection with them.

Ultimately the clash came and the matter was brought before the Proconsul himself.[38] This was Gallio, the brother of Seneca, who "cared for none of these things" and dismissed the case ignominiously. Luke obviously intends this decision to support the contention, which he implies throughout the book, that the decisions of responsible Roman magistrates were always in favour of the right of Christians to practise their religion.

While Paul was in Corinth, or possibly even while he was in Athens,[39] he wrote I and II Thessalonians.

After the Gallio episode,—and Acts is very vague as to the time which elapsed,—Paul decided to pay a flying visit to Antioch. He crossed to Ephesus together with Aquila and Priscilla, and spoke at least once in the synagogue, but he refused to stay longer and went on by boat to Caesarea and thence to Antioch.[40]

viii. Paul stayed a short time in Antioch and then returned to his missionary work in the Greek cities of Europe and Asia. It is customary to call this the "third missionary journey" (Acts xviii.23-xx.3), but in Paul's own mind the visit to Antioch was probably only an episode in his work and marked no special period in it.

This time he came by land through Galatia and Phrygia, whatever that means, and so to Ephesus,[41] where he stopped for three years. Luke tells us very little about this period. In Acts we have simply the story of the Christians who had received only the baptism of John, the story of Apollos, the story

[38] It is possible that there had been encounters before some lower magistrates before the case reached the Proconsul, and that Acts, as so often, "telescopes" the narrative.

[39] See pp. 131 ff.

[40] It is often said that he went to Jerusalem. This is possible, for in xviii.21 he expresses a desire to go there, but the statement in xviii.22 most naturally means that he "saluted the Church in Caesarea."

[41] See pp. 137 ff.

of Sceva, and the story of the disturbance raised by Demetrius. But the Epistles enable us to fill in some of the gaps.

From these it appears that Paul paid one more visit to Corinth and then returned to Ephesus. This was because of a long dispute [42] which is the subject of I and II Corinthians. It also appears probable that during this time he was in prison.[43] None of this is, however, related in Acts.

ix. Acts xx.4-xxi.26 describes Paul's last journey to Jerusalem. At the end of his three years in Ephesus, Paul went back for three months to Corinth, for purposes explained in II Corinthians but not in Acts, and then decided to go on to Jerusalem. He had induced the churches which he had founded to make contributions for the necessities of the Christians in Jerusalem,[44] and he decided to go to Jerusalem in order to present personally the alms which he had collected, taking with him a representative of each of the contributing churches.

Luke describes the voyage from Corinth to Jerusalem in considerable detail,—which is curious, for it is difficult to see that it was really important for his purpose. He mentions almost every place at which Paul stopped until he finally reached Tyre and then Caesarea, from which he went up to Jerusalem, where he was well received by James.

James persuaded him that he ought to do his best to show the Jews in Jerusalem how thoroughly orthodox he was. The purpose of this slightly disingenuous process is obvious, but it was not unnaturally a complete failure. No one who had been preaching in Europe that circumcision and the Law generally were unnecessary would have much hope of convincing the Jews in Jerusalem that his orthodoxy was unstained, though Paul did his best by paying the fees for some men who had had a vow [45] in Jerusalem.

[42] See pp. 107 ff.

[43] See pp. 139 ff.

[44] Or possibly for the Jews as well as for Christians.

[45] For a discussion of the details of this procedure and the Jewish Law, see Strack-Billerbeck, II, pp. 754-755; also D. Kittel, *Paulus im Talmud* in *Arbeiten zur Religionsgeschichte des Urchristentum,* I, 3.

x. The story of Paul's arrest, imprisonment and voyage to Rome is told in Acts xxi.27-xxviii.31. Before he had been long in Jerusalem he was falsely accused of defiling the Temple by introducing Gentiles into it,—a capital offence.[46] A riot ensued and the Roman soldiers intervened and saved his life by arresting him. After an abortive hearing before the Sanhedrin, he was sent by night to Caesarea, because it was understood that there was a plot to kill him and that he could not be taken publicly in safety. The governor, Felix, postponed a decision and kept him in prison and his case finally came before Festus, Felix' successor. This is referred to in Acts as "after two years," but it is not clear [47] whether the "two years" refers to the appointment of Festus or to the imprisonment of Paul.

Paul refused to go to Jerusalem for trial and appealed to Caesar. The meaning of this appeal is not clear.[48] Possibly he meant no more by it than to claim that, as a Roman citizen, he was entitled to be tried by Romans, not by a Jewish court. Luke clearly thought that he meant to exercise the right of asking to be sent to Rome, the *ius provocationis ad Caesarem,* that he did so in order to further the design of Providence which required his presence in Rome, and that the Governor allowed his appeal in order to pass on to others the responsibility for a difficult case.

So, in the autumn, Paul was sent off to Rome,[49] ran into a storm off Crete, was shipwrecked on Malta, but arrived the following spring.

What happened to him in Rome? Luke does not tell us, except that the Jews there refused to interfere at all, and that he lived two years in "his own hired house" or, to adopt a more probable translation, "on his own earnings." Did the case

46 Deissmann, *Light from the Ancient East,* p. 80. The regulation is referred to by Josephus, who says that the Jews had the right themselves to put to death transgressors, even if they were Romans (cf. Josephus, *B.J.* vi. 2.4.).

47 See further on p. 249.

48 See Cadbury's long discussion in *Beginnings,* Vol. V, pp. 312 ff.

49 For Paul's voyage, James Smith's *The Voyage and Shipwreck of St. Paul* is still of great value; cf. also A. Breusing, *Die Nautik der Alten,* and Ch. Voight, *Der Romfahrt des Apostel Paulus* in Hansa, Vol. LIII (1916), pp. 726 ff., *Beginnings,* Vol. IV, pp. 327 ff., V, Add. Note 27.

drop? Was he condemned? Luke does not say and possibly intended to write a third volume containing the story.[50] The tradition is that he was acquitted and made other journeys to the East and to Spain, and that after this he was brought back to Rome and executed by Nero in A.D. 64 at Tre Fontane.

SPEECHES

Interspersed throughout the narrative of Acts are a number of speeches.[51] It is open to question whether these represent the actual sayings of the speakers, or—as was common with writers of the period—were written in order to show what, in the author's opinion, was the tenor of Apostolic preaching. The latter view is widely held at present, and is supported by the marked similarity of all the speeches; the former is the traditional view.

Sub iudice lis est, but it should be noted that most older books, accepting the view that, for instance, the speech of Paul in Acts xiii and the speech of Peter in Acts iv are an accurate account of what was said, use them to supplement the Epistles and to prove the identity of Pauline and Petrine teaching. This use is excluded if the view be accepted that they were composed by Luke in the same way as Thucydides composed the speeches of Greek statesmen. A popular argument against the view that they are accurate reports of actual speeches is that they all say so nearly the same things. To this there is a possible counter in the question, why should not Paul and Peter have preached much the same message?

More important is the extreme similarity in language and general structure between the various speeches. It is not unlikely that the Apostles had the same message,—on the contrary

[50] See *Beginnings,* Vol. V, pp. 319 ff. and J. de Zwaan's *Was the Book of Acts a Posthumous Edition?* in the *Harvard Theological Review,* 1924, p. 95.

[51] See H. J. Cadbury, *The Making of Luke-Acts,* pp. 58 ff., and *Beginnings,* Vol. V, p. 402; Percy Gardner in *Cambridge Biblical Essays* (1909), pp. 379 ff., and B. W. Bacon in *Biblical and Semitic Studies,* 1902, pp. 213 ff. Cadbury gives a long list of the superabundant literature on the subject.

it is extremely probable that they had,—but it is very unlikely that they all had the same style. Therefore, while there has been a growing tendency in recent years to accept the speeches as a good representation of Apostolic Christianity, there has also been a tendency to think that their actual form is Luke's rather than Peter's or Paul's.

On the other hand, if the speeches be the composition of Luke, they have a unique importance as the opinion of a careful and instructed observer as to the main outlines of that Apostolic teaching, which in the first century was accepted by the Gentiles and rejected by the Jews. There is no other evidence on this subject which can be compared with Acts in importance. Thus, the speeches in Acts should be looked on as the best, and indeed our only records of the general topics of Apostolic preaching, which can be summarised thus:

i. The proof from prophecy that Jesus is the appointed Messiah who will come as the Judge sent from heaven. This is found in the speeches of Peter in Jerusalem in chapters ii-v, and of Paul in Pisidian Antioch in chapter xiii.

ii. The case against the Jews, who had throughout their history disregarded the teachings of God, sent through the prophets, and had filled up the cup of their sin by rejecting Jesus. This is found especially in Stephen's speech in chapter vii—which is an attack on the Jews, not a defence of himself—and in Paul's final speech in Rome; but the same characteristic can be seen in Peter's speeches in Acts ii-v.

iii. The message to the Gentiles to turn from the worship of idols and false gods to that of the true God, the creator and sustainer, whose existence and nature is proved by a consideration of the world and by references to Greek literature (Aratus and Epimenides), just as the argument in the speeches in synagogues is supported by quotations from the Old Testament. This is found in the speeches of Paul in Lystra (Acts xiv) and in Athens (Acts xvii).

The general accuracy of this presentation is confirmed by Paul's own summary of his message to the Gentiles in I Thess.

i.9 f., "to turn from vain idols to the living and true god, and to wait for his son from heaven."

Thus the speeches in Acts serve as a summary of Apostolic teaching which fits admirably with the view that the Gospel of Mark is a faithful representation of the way that the Apostles told the story of Jesus so as to prove their message.

There are two remarkable omissions:

If we trust Acts, the Apostles did little to perpetuate the teaching *of* Jesus as distinct from the teaching *about* Jesus. This, again, is corroborated by the Gospel of Mark, which gives so little information about what Jesus said, as distinct from what he did. But the question arises, how then did the teaching *of* Jesus come to be preserved and incorporated in the Gospels of Matthew and Luke? The answer depends largely on imagination, for we have no documents to tell us, but probably the memory of Jesus' teaching remained among Galileans and others who had heard him. One can see a picture of Greeks in Antioch or Ephesus asking for more information about this wonderful Jesus, and someone telling them how he had heard Jesus tell the parable of the Good Samaritan or of the Prodigal Son. One can be sure that a demand was heard for more stories of the same kind.

Similarly, if we trust Acts, the Apostles, including Paul himself, said nothing about "Paulinism." There is nothing about the characteristic Pauline teaching as to "Faith and Works" and nothing about the need for regeneration. The speeches in Acts are in this respect definitely nearer to the general ideas of the synoptic gospels than to the Epistles. Why is this if Luke was a pupil of Paul? A partial, but only a partial answer is that "Paulinismus" owes more to Pfleiderer than to Paul. The Epistles are in the main letters, not treatises. They were sent to Paul's converts who accepted his main teaching, but were doubtful as to points on the periphery of it. His letters deal with these peripheral points, not with the central ones. A picture based on the Epistles only would be as one-sided as one derived only from Acts.

CHAPTER V

The Canonical Collection of the Pauline Epistles

THOUGH the Epistles of Paul refer to a period later than that described by the gospels or the first chapters of Acts, they were written earlier. They are, moreover, a collection, a *Corpus Paulinum.* By whom, or when and where this collection was made is quite unknown,[1] but it is clear that someone at an early date put together all the Pauline material which he could find.

The first person clearly known to have used such a collection is Marcion [2]; it is, however, rather improbable that he made the Corpus, for the Church would hardly have accepted the work of a heretic. In the case of the gospels, Marcion's selection of one book as "The Gospel" certainly affected the Church by way of reaction and lent strength to, if it did not create, a desire to retain the fourfold Gospel. Similarly it may have led to a revision of the text of the Epistles, but hardly to the acceptance of a collection made by Marcion.

The main features of the problem which a recognition of the Corpus produces are as follows:

The first Epistle of Clement [3] shows that the author was ac-

[1] See A. Harnack, *Die Briefsammlung des Apostels Paulus,* 1926, E. J. Goodspeed, *New Solutions of New Testament Problems,* 1927, both of which are extremely interesting and valuable. We are especially inclined to accept Goodspeed's view that the publication of Acts may have led to the collection of the Epistles. Whether this was made in Ephesus, as Streeter suggests (*The Primitive Church,* p. 160), is perhaps more doubtful but not improbable, and seems to us more probable than Harnack's suggestion of Corinth. Cf. also P. N. Harrison, Polycarp's *Two Epistles to the Philippians,* p. 236.

[2] See Harnack, *Marcion,* and Th. Zahn, *Geschichte des Neutestamentlichen Kanons.*

[3] The evidence for the use of the New Testament in the Apostolic Fathers is collected and discussed most conveniently in *The New Testament in the Apostolic Fathers,* Oxford, 1906.

quainted with I Corinthians, Hebrews, and possibly Romans; but except in I Corinthians, the quotations and allusions are not assigned to Paul. Thus, in the first half of the second century, Pauline Epistles were known, but it is not clear whether the collection of Epistles had yet been made.

By the year 140 the scene had changed. Marcion, adjudged a heretic, but in his own opinion a devoted follower of Jesus and Paul, rejected the Jewish element in Christianity altogether, and substituted for the Old Testament two Christian books, "The Gospel" and "The Apostle." The Gospel was a more or less modified edition of Luke, and The Apostle was a collection [4] of Pauline Epistles, in the order Galatians, Corinthians, Romans, Thessalonians, Laodiceans (Ephesians), Colossians, Philippians, Philemon. It is a matter of dispute if this is the first New Testament, or if there were gospels and Epistles recognised as Scripture in non-Marcionite Catholic circles. It should be remembered that the point in dispute is not whether the individual gospels or Epistles existed, but only whether they had yet been recognised as Scripture.

In later writers of the end of the second and of the third centuries, signs appear of the same collection of Pauline Epistles in a somewhat varying order. Tertullian seems to have had the order Corinthians, Galatians, Philippians, Thessalonians, Ephesians and Romans. That Tertullian also knew Colossians and the Pastoral Epistles is probable, but their position in his list is doubtful. In the *Testimonia* of Cyprian it also appears that in his Bible Corinthians was the first and Romans the last of the Pauline Epistles. Similarly, Origen had Corinthians first and Romans last, but there is the variation that he seems to have had the order Corinthians, Ephesians, Colossians, Thessalonians, Philippians, Romans. Doubtless he knew the other Epistles, but their position cannot be established.

Thus there is some reason for thinking that in the original Corpus, Romans was the last Epistle. This may be combined

[4] See Zahn's *Geschichte des Neutestamentlichen Kanons,* II, pp. 344 ff., and the *Earlier Epistles of St. Paul,* p. 356, for a discussion of the order of the Epistles.

with the very reasonable doubts thrown by Corssen[5] and others on the authority of the Doxology in Romans xvi.25-27 by the theory that this Doxology was written either by the maker of the Corpus, as a fitting conclusion to it, or possibly by a Catholic redactor. The latter is perhaps more probable as Marcion did not have the Doxology.

In the third century, we have the earliest evidence of manuscripts: the Chester Beatty Papyrus[6] (P46) has the order Romans, Hebrews, I Corinthians, II Corinthians, Ephesians, Galatians, Philippians, Colossians, I Thessalonians, (II Thessalonians, Philemon). It probably did not contain the Pastoral Epistles.

Finally, in the fourth century, Athanasius[7] insists on the order found in Westcott and Hort's text and this with minor variations became the accepted sequence. It is apparently a revision of the Egyptian order found in P46 and roughly an arrangement by length.

Obviously, we have here to deal with one Corpus of letters, in which the contents were fixed though the arrangement varied; but certain problems remain:

i. Assuming the correctness of the view that II Corinthians is made up of fragments of two letters[8] and that Romans is extant in two forms,[9] both Pauline, what is the relation of these facts to the making of the Corpus? Similarly, assuming the correctness of the view that we have three forms of address for Ephesians[10] what is the relation of these to the Corpus? Clearly, existing theories need revision, but it is hard to see the right way to go about it.

[5] See Corssen, *Zur Uberlieferungsgeschichte des Römerbriefes* in the *Z.N.T.W.* 1909, 1 and 2, and *Earlier Epistles*, pp. 359 ff.

[6] The final edition, up to the present, is by F. G. Kenyon, *The Chester Beatty Papyrus,* III, 1936. See also the valuable introduction of H. A. Sanders in *A Third Century Papyrus Codex of the Epistles of Paul,* 1935. In the interval between their publication new leaves were found; hence the necessity for so speedy a republication.

[7] In his Paschal letter 39. It was the custom for the Patriarchs of Alexandria to issue annually a "Paschal" letter fixing the date and using the opportunity to express their opinion on matters of importance.

[8] See pp. 121 ff.

[9] See pp. 107 f.

[10] See pp. 146 ff.

ii. Is it significant that the earliest manuscript of the Corpus (P46) probably (not certainly) omitted the Pastoral Epistles, and that the earliest known user of the Corpus (Marcion) also did so, especially in view of the probability that these Epistles are not usually thought to be genuine?

iii. The whole problem of the original text of the Pauline Corpus may need reconsideration. It is generally argued that Marcion revised the text to suit his own ideas of the truth, but it is not certain that the Catholic text does not contain changes made in opposition to Marcion, and possibly to other heretics, and this question has never yet been adequately studied. The nature of a Catholic and of a heretic in those days was not so different that the one may be supposed to have emended the text often and the other never. This is not due to dishonesty, but to the character of minds and manuscripts. Every mind, Catholic or heretic, was convinced *a.* that he knew the truth, *b.* that the truth was contained in Scripture. But it was conceded that every manuscript was written by a scribe prone to error, for though the Holy Spirit guided the authors of the New Testament, it did not protect the scribes who copied it. Therefore, when anyone, Catholic or heretic, found a statement in the New Testament which appeared to be wrong, it would seem to him a moral duty to correct an obvious scribal error into a true statement. But who can say what are the limits of "scribal errors?"

The usual method of dealing with the text is therefore open to criticism. Marcion's text can be partially reconstructed from Tertullian's treatises and similar polemical works. These give a long list of passages in which it differed noticeably from that used by Tertullian. When Tertullian does not mention any variant it is assumed that Marcion had the same text as Tertullian, and that Tertullian had the same text as the Old Latin. Clearly this method needs more consideration. Tertullian's silence probably means that Marcion and he had the same text, but the tacit assumption that this was the same as the Old Latin, except when the contrary can be shown, is liable to make Marcion accept verses which contradict his views. The time is ripe for an investigation of the possibility that the current Greek text of the Epistles shows traces of an anti-Marcionite and possibly anti-Gnostic revision.

Thus, though the fact that a Corpus was collected early in the second century cannot be gainsaid, it is unknown who made it or where or exactly what it contained.

Turning to the individual Epistles, the place from which they were written can in some cases be deduced from the contents; in others it is extremely doubtful. It would also seem that the Christians of the second and later centuries knew no more about it than we do, for the short prefaces to the Epistles found in some Greek and Latin manuscripts are merely deductions from the context.

Of these prefaces there are two relatively early sets:

i. The Marcionite [11] prologues, found by an extraordinary accident in most Latin manuscripts. That they come from the Marcionite *Apostolos* is generally conceded, though the question may well be reopened.

ii. The Euthalian apparatus,[12] published in full by Zaccagni in 1698 and reprinted in Migne's *Patrologia Graeca,* Vol. 85, 609-700. It is not known with certainty who Euthalius was, nor when or where he lived. His prologues, though interesting, contain nothing valuable for the Epistles, as they are clearly based on internal evidence possibly supplemented by the Apocryphal Acts of Paul.

Turning, therefore, to the internal evidence of the Epistles, the following results seem probable; the bases for these conclusions are summarised in the sections of the next chapters dealing with the individual letters.

I and II Thessalonians were sent from Athens or Corinth, c. A.D. 49.

I Corinthians was sent from Ephesus, c. A.D. 50.

II Corinthians x-xiii was sent from Ephesus, c. A.D. 51.

II Corinthians i-ix was sent from Macedonia c. A.D. 51.

[11] Published by Dom de Bruyne, *Prologues Bibliques d'origine Marcionite,* in the *Revue Bénédictine,* 1907, pp. 1 ff.

[12] See also J. A. Robinson, *Euthaliana* in *Texts and Studies.*

Romans (in its present "long" form) was sent from Corinth *c.* A.D. 52. The short recension cannot be dated.

Galatians: place and date of writing doubtful.

Philippians, written from prison either in Ephesus, Caesarea or Rome between 51 and 64.

Colossians, Ephesians and Philemon,–if authentic,–were sent from prison in Ephesus, Caesarea or Rome between 51 and 64.

I and II Timothy and Titus are probably not Pauline, but, if they are, were presumably written after the events described in Acts, i.e. between 56 and 64.

CHAPTER VI

The Epistle to the Romans

THE Epistle to the Romans consists of four parts: i-viii which is concerned with the problem of righteousness; ix-xi which is concerned with the problem of the chosen people; xii-xv which is concerned with practical questions; xvi a letter of introduction for Phoebe.

The theme of the first part is that righteousness can be obtained through faith in Jesus Christ and not through the works of the Law. This is set out in orderly fashion, at considerable length, and the writer endeavours to show that the Old Testament taught that righteousness is obtained by faith, not works, the crucial evidence being that of Abraham, who was justified by faith.

Problems of exegesis which are crucial in this section are the meaning of righteousness and the meaning of faith. These points will be found discussed in any commentary on the Epistle to the Romans.[1]

With regard to righteousness, the question of most importance is not so much what Paul thought the word meant as the psychology which conditioned his thoughts. Probably (as is often said) Paul regarded righteousness as the relation towards God which man ought to occupy. The righteous man is the man who is in this right relation to God. That position will lead to a verdict of acquittal at the final Judgement and the righteous will pass on into the Life of the Age to Come. Moreover, Paul certainly argued that righteousness cannot be obtained by the Law, but is the gift of God to those who have faith in Jesus.

But the important question is whether Paul equates right-

[1] For example those of Sanday and Headlam, Denney, Gifford, and H. Lietzmann.

eousness and salvation. This is important because of its bearing on the problem of whether Paul was fair towards Jewish theology.[2] The point is this; no Jewish Rabbi then or at any other time ever maintained that the Life of the Age to Come could be obtained only by an unfailing following of the Law, because the Law obviously cannot be kept in this way. That would have been recognised universally. The answer of the Rabbi was that although righteousness cannot be obtained by the works of the Law, salvation is guaranteed to those who endeavour to fulfill the Law and repent of their errors. Repentance and effort, rather than perfect performance, was the requirement for salvation in Rabbinical theology.

It is said that Paul overlooks this point altogether. But, as a matter of fact, he is discussing righteousness, not salvation. If chapter vii be read, it is difficult to reject the hypothesis that it is autobiography. The Apostle seems to say that he was extremely wretched because he was a sinner, although he wished to be righteous. He had, however, found a means,—faith in Jesus,—which enabled him to become righteous, not with a righteousness which he has earned with his own acts, but which has been given him by God, who is able to give moral and spiritual qualities just as well as he is able to give riches or strength.

The picture of righteousness, or rather of the distress experienced by the man who wishes to be righteous and feels that he is not,[3] will be recognised at once, by readers of William James' *Varieties of Religious Experience,* as a typical picture of the "sick soul," and the joy that Paul expresses at obtaining righteousness through faith in Jesus Christ is an exact and beautiful portrayal of the point of view of the "twice-born" man. Psychologically, the picture presents no difficulties at all. The problems which are difficult are the forms in which Paul expresses this psychological experience. It is impossible here to

[2] See C. G. Montefiore, *Judaism and Paul,* and Lake, *Paul, His Heritage and Legacy.*

[3] The technical terminology of the psychologist usually calls this "sense of guilt." It does not mean that the sufferer has really been especially wicked, or that he has really become especially good, but he has felt so.

discuss the details, but the student will do well to consider the relation of the Epistle to at least four points.

In the first place, the explanation which Paul gives of the righteousness which he obtained is that it is God's gift to him because he has accepted Jesus as the Messiah. It should be noted that in this connection "Messiah" has become the giver of private salvation, rather than the King of Israel, or the Judge who will appear at the End. It fits into the scheme of the evolution of the denationalised cults which became religions of private salvation.

Secondly, this gift of God came in the form of inspiration, or, perhaps one should say, obsession.[4] The man who obtains this supernatural righteousness, which is the gift of God, does so because he lives in Christ and Christ in him. The language is clearly reminiscent of that form of thought which believes that ill health and good health are due to obsessions by good and bad spirits.

Thirdly, the gift of righteousness is equated with what is quite obviously the same mystical experience[5] that can be traced in many forms in every age,—a feeling that a way has somehow been found into a higher and better reality, which in this case is described as life in Christ.

Finally, the problem is raised of the extent to which the belief in the acquisition of righteousness is connected with eschatological expectations.[6] There is a good deal of evidence that the Jewish belief was that in the last days the gift of righteousness would be given by God to his chosen people. It is a question how far early Christians of Paul's type held that they had received the gift of righteousness because it was the last day, and how far they reversed the argument and maintained that it must be the last day because they had received the gift.

It must be observed in any case that Paul and others felt convinced, as a matter of direct experience, that they were

[4] See Lake's *Paul, His Heritage and Legacy.*
[5] See Inge's *Mysticism.*
[6] See H. Windisch, *Taufe and Sünde.*

righteous. Righteousness is not a verdict on their current conduct, but a description of their conscious nature.

One of the intellectual difficulties of early Christians was to explain to themselves or to others how it could be that the Old Testament, which they accepted as God's infallible word, announced that the Jews were the chosen people,[7] whereas their own experience seemed to show that they, Gentiles by birth, were really God's chosen people and that the Jews were their worst enemies. Had God changed his mind, or were the promises wrong or what explanation could be suggested?

Paul's answer to this problem is given in chapters ix-xi. It cannot be said that it is easy to follow or clearly expressed. The details, discussed in all the commentaries, will always remain obscure, but the general outline can be understood. Paul is anxious to support the following propositions:

First, God has not cast off his people. There has, however, been some mistake in thinking that "his people" means all the Jews by race, independent of spiritual experience. On the contrary, the true seed of Abraham is not according to the flesh but, like Isaac, according to the promise.

Secondly, if God had chosen to create the Jews for a special damnation, there is no one who has any right to complain; he is the creator and has the same right to predestine men to one fate or another as a potter has when he makes vessels for different purposes out of the same clay. In this connection, Paul enunciates in the clearest terms a doctrine which produced terrible results in later centuries, to the effect that God is capable of deliberately hardening men's hearts in order to make them deserve the damnation to which he has predestined them.

Finally, the apparent rejection of the Jews is not final. The Gentiles have been called in with a view to the ultimate inclusion of the Jews in one great family of the chosen,—Jews and Gentiles alike.

This part of the Epistle is particularly important, because

[7] See Hamilton's *The People of God.*

it is to a large extent the scriptural basis of the doctrine of predestination, developed first by Augustine and afterwards by Calvin. That the greater part of the Epistle up to the end of chapter xi is controversial is easy to see. More difficult is the question of whether it was controversy with Jews, with Gentiles, or with Hellenistic Jews. As the problem used to be formulated, it was held to be a choice between Jews and Gentiles as the opponents of Paul. Most of the earlier commentators thought that it was with Jews; the later ones inclined to the view that it was with Gentiles. Others took refuge in the belief, extremely probable in itself, that the church at Rome was from the beginning a mixed church of Jews and Gentiles. But the situation has been changed to some extent by the wider recognition that Judaism in the Roman Empire was already much more Hellenistic than had been supposed, so that the problem cannot be enunciated quite so clearly.

Chapters xii-xv are given up to a consideration of practical problems. The first part, in chapter xii, deals in the main with general ethical precepts, some of which strikingly resemble the teaching of Jesus in the Sermon on the Mount, but the remarkable fact is that Paul supports them not by a reference to the teaching of Jesus, but to that of the Old Testament.

In chapter xii Paul begins with a statement which has probably caused as much controversy in political fields as the rest of his Epistle in theological: "The powers that be are ordained by God." He goes on to say that the duty of Christians is to obey the government and yield to its commands. The Divine Right of Kings and Passive Obedience were deduced,—not quite illogically,—from this view.

In chapter xiv there is a very obscure treatment of the question of food. It would seem that there was some controversy in Rome about the eating of meat as opposed to vegetables, but it is open to doubt whether this was the point of view of a group of Jews, comparable perhaps to the Essenes in Palestine, or of Gentiles who are to be identified with, or compared with, the vegetarians mentioned by Seneca. To us it seems that the arguments for the latter view are somewhat better than for the former.

Chapter xvi belongs to a different category. Many critics think that it did not originally belong to the Epistle to the Romans at all.[8] It is a short letter of introduction for a certain Phoebe who was going from Corinth to some other city and Paul sends greetings to all his friends in the place to which she was going. Can this be Rome? There is a very long list of greetings to friends, and Paul never went to Rome until the end of his life. How, then, did he have so many friends in that city that he included more greetings in the Epistle to the Romans than in any other that he wrote. Moreover, how did it happen that he greets Aquila and Priscilla, who we know had left Rome and gone first to Corinth and afterwards to Ephesus? Or that in Rome there was someone called the "first fruits of Asia?" None of these things are quite impossible, but taken together, they are improbable, and many scholars think that chapter xvi is really a short letter to Ephesus.

The problem of chapter xvi is not, however, the only critical difficulty in connection with this Epistle. The references to Rome, in i.7 and i.15, are omitted by an early text still preserved in Codex G and in quotations from Origen and Ambrosiaster, and mentioned in notes in two related Greek manuscripts.[9] Obviously this means that at one time there were two recensions of the text—one which wished it to appear that the letter was sent to Rome, the other which wished it to be regarded as a general letter to all Christians rather than as an Epistle to Rome.

At the end of the letter, there is a similar phenomenon. The Doxology, printed at the end of chapter xvi in the King James' Version, is not found in this position in all manuscripts. In many it is given at the end of chapter xiv, in others both at

[8] See Sanday and Headlam, *Epistle to the Romans, ad loc.*, J. B. Lightfoot, *Philippians*, pp. 171-178 and *Earlier Epistles*, pp. 325 ff.

[9] For the details of this very complicated problem see *Earlier Epistles*, pp. 335-370, and see E. van der Goltz, *Eine textkritische Arbeit des zehnten bzw. sechsten Jahrhundert*, and *Six Collations*, pp. 141-219, in *Harvard Theological Studies* XVII.

the end of xiv and xvi and in the famous Chester Beatty papyrus,—the oldest of all,—at the end of xv. It seems obvious that the Doxology ought to be at the end of the Epistle. It is quite possible that it originally belonged at the end of a short recension which finished either with chapter xiv or chapter xv and was moved to the end of chapter xvi when this was added. If so, chapter xv and chapter xvi are under suspicion. Moreover, we know that just such a short text did once exist. Origen states that Marcion left out chapter xv and chapter xvi and there is evidence, though mostly from silence, that the African church fathers also used a short recension of this kind. Finally, the earliest paragraph-marking [10] in the Latin tradition does not continue beyond the end of chapter xiv.

Thus we have considerable evidence for the existence of the Epistle in a form which left out all reference to Rome at the beginning and ended with chapter xiv. On the other hand, it seems impossible to deny that chapters xv and xvi are Pauline, and the continuation of chapter xiv by chapter xv is so good and natural that if the letter once ended with chapter xiv it must have been Paul himself who added chapter xv to it, so that it circulated in both forms.

The matter is, of course, open to discussion and always will be, but there are two main theories.[11] One is that Paul first wrote the short recension to some other church and added the rest when he wrote to Rome. The other is that Paul first wrote the long recension and that Marcion cut it down, so that evidence for the short recension is really all Marcion's. The latter theory is widely held but we find it less satisfactory, because there seems no reason in the world why Marcion should have left out the reference to Rome, nor indeed is it easy to see why, if he included chapter xiv, he should object to chapter xv.

[10] See Berger, *Histoire de la Vulgate,* p. 257; Zahn, *Einleitung,* 3rd ed. I, p. 250 f. and *Earlier Epistles,* pp. 355 ff.

[11] See *Earlier Epistles,* pp. 350-370.

CHAPTER VII

I AND II CORINTHIANS

THE two Epistles to the Corinthians [1] are the remnants of the story of a great quarrel which lasted over many months, and was finally resolved in a manner agreeable to Paul. Curiously enough, there is not a trace of this in Acts, though the framework is provided by its account of the foundation of the church in Corinth. The whole story is quite complicated and it is by no means easy to fit together the references in I and II Corinthians. Probably the most lucid method of describing the situation is to give the results first and afterwards discuss them and the difficulties which they present.

The probable story appears to be this. The church was founded by Paul and developed by Aquila, Priscilla and others. A little later Apollos [2] came to Corinth, and at some period for which Acts gives us no help it is probable that Peter also paid a visit to Corinth. In the meantime, Paul had gone to Ephesus and Apollos also came there. Soon after this Paul, while in Ephesus, wrote a letter to Corinth. This letter is not in existence, unless it is possible that a fragment of it has been inserted into the middle of II Corinthians.[3] Still a little later, Paul received disquieting information from the household of Chloe and immediately afterwards three Corinthians [4] arrived in Ephesus bringing him a letter from the

[1] The outstanding commentaries are those of Lietzmann (in his *Handbuch*) and J. Weiss in Meyer's *Commentary*. There is no satisfactory commentary known to us in English.

[2] Apollos is a very difficult problem. Acts xviii.24 ff. says that he had been instructed in the way of the Lord and taught accurately the 'things concerning Jesus' but knew only the baptism of John. Aquila and Priscilla gave him more accurate information about "the way of God," after which he taught that the Messiah was Jesus. What is meant by the "Way of the Lord?" What is the baptism of John? Is it the baptism of Jesus by John, or John's baptism in distinction to Christian baptism.

[3] See p. 111.

[4] See I Cor. xvi.17.

church. He answered this letter in what we now call I Corinthians, which, however, as is obvious, was really the second letter which he sent. At the same time, and possibly with this letter, he sent Timothy to Corinth to help straighten out the difficulties which had arisen, but Timothy's mission was a failure and Paul himself went to Corinth as he had promised to do. His own visit was as much a failure as Timothy's had been, and he was in great distress about the situation. He went back to Ephesus, wrote a severe letter to Corinth and sent it with Titus, threatening to come himself and if he came not to spare, though it is by no means clear what form of coercion he proposed to adopt. Meanwhile he stayed on in Ephesus in order to see what the results of his severe letter and of the mission of Titus would be. After a time he decided to go by the long land route through Macedonia to Corinth. While he was still in Macedonia he received a message from Titus and learned that his letter and the persuasion of Titus had been entirely successful. He therefore wrote a letter to Corinth, rejoicing over the change of heart and urging gentleness to defeated opponents, saying that when he came he would again take up the question of the collection which he was making for the Christians in Jerusalem.

Such is a very brief summary of the conclusions which have been very laboriously reached by some generations of enquirers into the Epistles. It remains to discuss the problems which are under the surface of this summary, to show how it is reached, and to treat further Paul's answers to the Corinthians. The points to be discussed are:

i. The previous letter.

ii. Paul's sources of information.

iii. Paul's answer to the Corinthian letter.

iv. The mission of Timothy.

v. Paul's flying visit to Corinth.

vi. The severe letter and the partition of II Corinthians.

vii. The mission of Titus and Paul's letter from Macedonia.

i. The evidence that Paul wrote a letter to Corinth before he sent I Corinthians is the reference in I Cor. v.9 ff. and it is often thought that a fragment of this Epistle can be recognised in II Cor. vi.14-vii.1. A glance at these verses will show that they would fit very well into the context of the "previous letter" and do not seem to have much connection with the context in which they are at present, but of course this kind of reconstruction is always open to doubt, and from the nature of the case can never be proved to demonstration.

ii. The evidence as to the basis on which Paul wrote I Corinthians is contained entirely in the Epistle itself. This shows that while Paul was in Ephesus he was informed of the condition of the church at Corinth from at least three sources: *a.* the household of Chloe (I Cor. i.11); *b.* the verbal communication of Stephanas, Fortunatus and Achaicus (I Cor. xvi.17); and *c.* a letter from the church asking Paul for his judgement on various questions.

The information given by "those of Chloe" was primarily that the church of Corinth was in danger of completely breaking up into parties,—"of Paul," "of Peter," "of Apollos" and possibly "of Christ." Paul insists that all Christians should feel that they are one brotherhood.[5] Incidentally he argues that Christianity is a divine revelation and a divine miracle, not a new philosophy.[6]

Besides this, "those of Chloe" seem to have told Paul that there was some kind of matrimonial scandal in Corinth, and that, possibly in this connection, Christians were taking their quarrels before the Roman courts instead of leaving them to the church to settle.[7] In I Cor. xvi.17 Paul mentions that he has received information from Stephanas, Fortunatus and Achaicus and in vii.1 he also mentions that he has received a letter from the Corinthians. It is an easy guess that the letter had been brought by Stephanas, Fortunatus and Achaicus.

[5] For the problem of the Christ party, see *Earlier Epistles,* pp. 125 ff.; Räbiger, *Kritische Untersuchungen,* 1886.

[6] See I Cor. i.18 ff.

[7] I Cor. v.1-5 and vi.1-7.

The letter contained a series of questions. Doubtless Paul used freely the information afforded by Stephanas, Fortunatus and Achaicus, but the only section of I Corinthians in which their conversation can be presumed to have supplemented the information in the letter is that dealing with the question of worship.

iii. Paul's answer begins in vii.1. As he takes up the Corinthian letter, question by question, it is almost possible to reconstruct the Epistle which he received. Apparently it dealt with five main problems: *a.* questions dealing with sex and marriage; *b.* questions relating to "things offered to idols"; *c.* questions relating to inspired persons and their gifts; *d.* Christian worship; *e.* the hope of a resurrection.

a. Sex and Marriage (I Cor. vii.1-40). The Corinthians were doubtful whether any sexual intercourse was permissible for Christians. Paul answered that marriage was not sin, though he esteemed celibacy the higher life. He then dealt with marriage, divorce, and a peculiar class of "virgins." Presumably the Corinthians had raised these points.

Marriage, he decreed, was to be a true marriage, for physical satisfaction, not merely for the generation of children. Indeed, one of the curious features of this discussion is that the problem of the procreation and education of children is not mentioned. Probably this was partly, at least, due to the expectation of the speedy coming of the End.

Divorce Paul did not permit at all. It is to be noted that on this point he diverges both from Roman and from Jewish Law, but follows and possibly quotes Jesus as the basis of his position.

The problem [8] of "virgins" is more difficult. The English translators adopt the view that 'virgins' means 'unmarried daughters' and that the Corinthians and Paul were discussing the duty of a father to his daughters. It is, however, more probable that the background of the question is the custom which prevailed among Christians, at least until the third century, of men and women living together but remaining vir-

[8] I Cor. vii.25.40. See H. Achelis, *Virginies Christi* and F. C. Conybeare, *Myth, Magic and Morality*, and *Earlier Epistles*, pp. 184 ff.

gin. This attempt to lead a rather unnatural life was not always successful and was finally forbidden by the Church. Apparently its difficulty was perceived in Corinth and Paul's advice was that where this kind of union proved too difficult it should be abandoned in favour of marriage, though he adds that this is the inferior alternative.

b. Things offered to idols (I Cor. viii.1-13, x.14-xi.1). No Christian in Corinth or elsewhere doubted that he was pledged to worship only the one true God. Therefore, he certainly could not sacrifice to the heathen deities. But the food which was sacrificed [9] in the temples was afterwards sold, and, moreover, there was no perfectly clear line between a sacrifice, a sacrificial feast and a dinner-party in which food was used that had been sacrificed.

What was to be the Christian theory and practice? One line of logical approach was to say that the heathen gods are a fiction, and the nature of the food cannot be changed by being sacrificed or consecrated to a fiction. Therefore, it would make no difference whether a Christian ate consecrated meat or not. Paul admits this, but advises abstention in order to avoid causing scandal or misunderstanding.

But he seems not to have been quite clear on the point, for he also advances the view, so common in later Christianity [10] that the heathen gods are not mere fictions. They are not gods, but they are not non-existent; they are demons pretending to be gods. Therefore, there was danger that those who partook of a meal where food was used which had been consecrated to idols, might gain a share in the demons, just as in the Eucharist the Christian gained a share in Christ. It will be seen that this position shows more common sense than logic, and some critics have doubted whether Paul can have held both the view advanced in I Cor. x and that in I Cor. viii. This is quite unnecessary scepticism. Common sense is often more valuable than logic in dealing with the practical difficulties of others

[9] See *Earlier Epistles*, pp. 198 ff.

[10] Especially in the first Apology of Justin and in Tatian, but it was a common belief in the first century and is found in Plutarch, *De Iside et Osiride*. See Glover, *The Conflict of Religions*, pp. 94 ff.

and Paul was faced with a practical problem. After all, though he seems to follow two theories, his practical solution is clear: —have as little to do with idols as possible, do not shock others and do not raise unnecessary questions.

c. Inspired persons and their gifts (I Cor. xii.1-xiv.40). It was generally held in Corinth, and doubtless in all other Pauline churches, that Christians were men who had received the gift of the Spirit. Whether the Spirit was given by the risen Jesus or was identical with him is open to discussion, but there was no doubt as to the fact of inspiration.[11] Therefore, several questions arose: What is the test of inspiration? What is its most significant symptom? What is the relative value of various forms of spiritual gifts? Paul wrestles with these questions for three whole chapters, and from them the background of Corinthian problems becomes clear.

How can you distinguish a man inspired by the Holy Spirit from a man inspired by a demon, who is imitating the symptoms of genuine inspiration? Paul lays down the rule that no one who is not genuinely inspired can repeat the formula "Jesus is Lord." It will be seen that this is the beginning of a long chapter of Christian practice which uses subscription to a creed as a criterion of genuine Christianity.[12]

The Corinthians appear to have suffered from a desire to estimate the value of individual members of the church by a nice appreciation of the relative merits of the various gifts which they attributed to inspiration. Being unable to agree on the subject, they asked Paul to settle it, but they expressed their opinion that those who "spoke with tongues" should stand very high. Paul did not agree; he regarded "speaking with tongues" as unintelligible speech which, he felt, may create emotion, but has no other value. He laid down the rule that ability to serve the community is the true test of value. Of course, both the Corinthians and he were speaking of gifts attributed to supernatural inspiration, though he at least

[11] Not only in the New Testament, but in actual experience it is important to distinguish the psychological fact from the name given to it, and the theory which that name implies. "Inspiration" is sometimes used in one sense, sometimes in the other; hence confusion.

[12] See further pp. 169 f.

paved the way for the view that all ability should be regarded as a gift, even if he did not quite hold this view. The difficulty as to the distinction between natural and supernatural is perhaps plainer to us than it was in the first century, but two points should be noted:

Paul saw and explained that Society is not a collection of persons brought together by similarity of desires and abilities, but of those who contribute diverse and divergent abilities to a common effort to reach a common object.

No gift is so important as the right attitude to others, and after, as it seems, agonising in I Cor. xii to say this in calm prose Paul, completely changing his style, inserts in I Cor. xiii his magnificent rhapsody [13] on "Charity" or "Love."

d. Worship. (I Cor. xi.2-34). From I Cor. xi.17 f. it would seem that this section is based partly on the verbal information given by Stephanas and his companions, partly on the letter which they brought.[14]

It deals with two subjects: worship in general and the Eucharist in particular.

Apparently the church doubted whether women should be allowed to speak in the assembly. Possibly some thought that if in Christ Jesus there is neither male nor female, there should be no such distinction in the assembly of Christians. Paul, however, felt that in public women should practise si-

[13] "Charity" is the traditional English rendering, because the Vulgate writes *Caritas*. The Revisers, recognising that "Charity" usually means "Alms" emended this to "Love,"–improving the meaning, but spoiling the music. But "Love" is only a little better than "Charity" for in modern English it implies some degree of emotional affection. Perhaps "Sympathy" is a useful paraphrase, but it is not a translation and is open to valid criticism.

[14] Perhaps the Corinthians took over the general outline of a service in a Hellenistic synagogue. This was a combination of Prayer, Lections, Homilies and probably the singing of Psalms. The investigations of Bousset (*Gött. Nachr.*, 1915, pp. 435 ff.) and others have shown that the earliest extant Christian prayers are based on Jewish ones. The earliest Christian "Prophetologion" may be connected with the Jewish, but the possibility has not been finally discussed; the earliest extant Greek Church music seems cognate to Jewish. See Duchesne, *Christian Worship;* G. H. Box, *The Synagogue,* and *Monumenta Musicae Byzantinae,* published by the Danish Academy.

lence, offer no remarks and, if they desired information, obtain it from their husbands at home.

A more difficult point is the question of dress and the length of hair. In favour of long hair for women, and no hats for men, Paul appeals to common sentiment. He also says that women should have their heads covered, "because of the angels," but no one knows certainly what this means—it may refer to Genesis vi.2.

The obvious difficulty is that the present Jewish habit is for men to be covered in the synagogue, but this custom is apparently of later growth, and Paul is clearly ignorant of it.[15] Probably Jews in the Empire followed Greco-Roman custom in dress, and it is human to regard the customary as the correct.

It would seem from I Cor. xi that the Corinthians did not consult Paul on the subject of the Eucharist, but that Stephanas etc. spoke to him about it. Among much that is obscure the following points seem to be clear and provide the foundation for further study. First, the "Lord's Supper" was a meal; and secondly, each brought his own food with him—some took too much, while others had too little (I Cor. xi.21).

Inasmuch as the Eucharist soon became merely a symbolical eating, there has been a tendency to distinguish from the Eucharist an *agape*,—a religious meal which existed in the early Church.[16] If so, Paul's advice might apply to the *agape*, but xi.23-26, containing the words which have always been the centre of the Eucharist, points very strongly in the other direction. It is therefore more probable that the *agape* of the third century and the Eucharist of that date are two descendants of the original practice, the *agape* inheriting the characteristics of the actual meal, the Eucharist the sacramental nature. That the Pauline Eucharist was a sacrament and not merely a religious meal seems proved by I Cor. x.16-21.

It is obvious that these passages in I Corinthians raise one of the most controversial questions in the New Testament.

[15] See Strack-Billerbeck *ad loc.*

[16] See Battifol's very important essay in his *Étude d'histoire et de Théologie positive*, pp. 277 ff., M. Goguel's *L'Eucharistie*, and H. Lietzmann's *Messe.*

Clearly Paul implies the existence in Corinth of a sacrament differing from the Catholic Eucharist little if at all in the significance attached to it. Moreover, Paul says that he "received" the story of its institution. From whom did he receive it? The question is complicated by the fact that the narrative of the Last Supper in Mark and Matthew does not appear to imply the institution of the Eucharist, though Luke gives, roughly speaking, the Pauline account, and John seems to imply a knowledge of a sacramental Eucharist in John vi, though he does not relate its institution.

Two theories are defensible and widely held:

On the one hand is the traditional view that Jesus instituted the Eucharist, with the addendum that Mark implies this, though he does not state it. A subordinate problem is, whether, granting this, the original Eucharist, as established by Jesus, had a sacramental meaning or was merely a commemoration.

On the other hand, it is contended that the Last Supper was not a Eucharist. The meaning of Jesus' words is that the Kingdom of God will be present before the next common meal of commemoration,[17] which, under the influence of Greek thought was transformed into a sacrament. The discussion of these alternatives is obviously outside the range of this book, but it is perhaps well to point out that whichever is adopted the attack is easier than the defense and that the problem is parallel to that of Baptism; the evidence in Mark for the institution of Baptism by Jesus is non-existent, and for the Eucharist is weak, but the evidence in the Epistles for both the Baptism and Eucharist as sacramental is very strong and, at least for Baptism, is corroborated by Acts.

e. The hope of resurrection. Paul, and Jewish Christians generally, believed in a future resurrection.[18] Greeks, if they believed in any existence after death, believed in immortality. The difference is often overlooked. Belief in immortality means the belief that life (and usually individual life) sur-

[17] See p. 236.

[18] For the Greek point of view, see Rohde's *Psyche;* for the Jewish, Gressmann's *Der Ursprung der Israelitische- jüdische Eschatologie,* Volz's *Jüdische Eschatologie* and R. H. Charles' *Eschatology.*

vives the death of the body. Belief in resurrection means that the dead body will come to life again.

It is essential to realise that the point at issue in Corinth was this distinction, and it is difficult to do so because at present many who believe in immortality think that they hold the early Christian faith, which was the resurrection of the flesh. The Corinthians appear to have been divided on the subject and appealed to Paul.

His answer is given in I Cor. xv. He begins by reciting the evidence for the resurrection of Jesus: that many witnesses had seen Jesus alive after his death. That, he argued, proves that resurrection does take place, and that the resurrection of Jesus is the first example of what is in store for Christians. Then he makes a concession to the Greek point of view. "Now this I say, (or almost "this I admit") that flesh and blood cannot inherit the Kingdom of God." This, of course, is hard to reconcile, if the words be given their natural meaning, with that belief in a resurrection of the flesh which was current among the Jews, and was afterwards taken up in the creed of the Church; for this speaks of a *resurrectio carnis* (not *corporis*). Paul's explanation probably satisfied the Greeks of Corinth, and he went on to explain that the resurrection which he preached was a resurrection of "the body," not of "the flesh," and that the body which would be raised was a body "of spirit." It must be remembered that until the end of the second century 'spirit' did not mean 'immaterial,' but the 'finest form of matter' according to Stoic categories. The Stoics were materialists [19] who denied the existence of any immaterial reality, but analysed all existence into four or five divisions,—earth, water, air, fire, and sometimes spirit.

Paul's theory is that there will be a transmutation of both the living and the dead at the resurrection, converting flesh into spirit. It is hard to see how, if this be so, he can have thought of the risen Lord as other than spirit, and one of the major problems of New Testament interpretation is to reconcile (or contrast) this with the fact that Luke and John both

[19] See pp. 214 f.

emphasise their belief that the risen Lord had a body of flesh and blood, identical with that which was crucified and buried.

Thus I Cor. vii.1-40, viii.1-13, x.14-xi.1, xi.2-34, xii.1-xiv.40 and xv.1.54, are answers to the Corinthians. I Cor. ix.1-33 is an extension of his answer about things offered to idols, in which he emphasises his recommendation not to offend other persons' consciences by quoting his own refusal to make use of the privileges claimed by other Apostles. He is, however, in this section, obviously thinking more of criticisms passed on him than of the subject of the Corinthians' question, and it would seem that some of his opponents had argued that his self-abnegation was a confession of inferiority. I Cor. xi has even less obvious connection with its context than has I Cor. ix. It is possible that it is really a separate answer to a separate question, dealing with the organisation of Christian worship and the conduct of worshippers.[20]

There remains one other passage which may be an answer to queries from Corinth, whether by letter or through its emissaries. Chapter xvi is taken up with a few short directions about practical affairs. In the first place, there is a collection for the saints, and this collection is being taken up not only in Achaea, but also in Galatia. Paul is proposing to send this collection to Jerusalem in charge of persons whom he will appoint and give a commendatory letter. He hopes that he will be able to spend the next winter in Corinth, and proposes to come from Asia overland through Macedonia, but he will stay at Ephesus until Pentecost. He hopes that they will receive Timothy properly and also Apollos. The Epistle ends with a few personal greetings.

iv. From I Corinthians xvi, it is clear that Timothy was sent over to Corinth, as well as the answer to their letter. Whether the letter was entrusted to Timothy or to Stephanas and his companions is not stated. The mission of Timothy is not mentioned in II Corinthians though it is certain that he had left Corinth or never reached it, for he is joined with Paul in the opening salutation in II Cor. i.1. Therefore,

[20] See pp. 115 ff.

though there is no definite proof that he had ever reached Corinth and still less any evidence as to his reception there, if his visit had been a success the whole situation implied by II Corinthians would have been impossible, and there is no reason to suppose that it was cancelled.

Thus, apparently Timothy's mission was unsuccessful, and whatever may have been the original source of trouble, it soon developed into a definite refusal to accept Paul's authority. The premonitory signs of this can be seen in I Cor. i.14 ff. and iv.1-21, and though the exact point of controversy is not quite clear it is very clear indeed in II Cor. x-xiii where it is the main subject.

v. That Paul himself went to Corinth is proved by II Corinthians xii.14: "Behold, this is the third time I am ready to come to you"; and II Corinthians xiii.1-2: "This is the third time that I am coming to you." No straightforward interpretation can explain these passages except as implying that Paul paid a visit after the first Epistle to the Corinthians and before II Corinthians, and that it was a failure.

vi. There is no doubt on the basis of the Epistles themselves that Paul wrote a severe letter to Corinth after he had failed to bring the church into agreement with him either by I Corinthians, by Timothy's visit, or even by a visit of his own. The writing of the severe letter to the Corinthians is proved by II Cor. ii.4 and by II Cor. vii.8. That II Cor. x-xiii is a fragment of this letter is indicated by the following argument [21]:

It is obvious that there is not only no connection between II Corinthians i-ix and II Corinthians x-xiii, but that there is an absolute break between them. The whole tone of the two

[21] See *Earlier Epistles,* pp. 154 ff., and for Paul's opponents, see W. Lütgert, *Freiheitspredigt und Schwarmgeister in Korinth,* the commentaries of Lietzmann and J. Weiss, and the *Earlier Epistles,* pp. 219 ff. These generally hold the view that Paul's opponents were Hellenisers rather than Judaisers and emphasised the gift of inspiration, especially in its more spectacular forms. Probably, this is right, but there is much to be learnt from the older books, cf. F. C. Baur, *Die Christuspartei* (in the *Tübingen Zeitschrift,* 1831, Part 4, pp. 61 ff.) and his *Paulus,* pp. 260 ff.; also C. Weizsäcker, *Apostolische Zeitalter* (2nd ed.). pp. 299 ff.

parts is entirely different. II Corinthians x-xiii is an anxious and rather angry letter in which the writer defends his own position and threatens severe action against the disobedient church. There has never been any doubt on this point, but a great many of the older interpreters spent a great deal of time imagining how these two things could be combined in one letter and trying to show that it was directed first to one party and then to another.

Internal evidence, however, also shows that x-xiii is earlier than i-ix. This is proved by a series of cross-references. In II Cor. i-ix there are general descriptions of the severe letter, to which II Cor. x-xiii answers perfectly, and there are also some special allusions to the contents of the severe letter, corresponding to definite passages in II Cor. x-xiii.

The general descriptions of the severe letter are found in the following four passages:

a. In II Cor. ii.4 Paul says that he has written the "severe" letter "out of much affliction and anguish of heart, beset with many tears."

b. In II Cor. vii.8 he says "though I made you sorry with my letter I do not regret it,"—that is to say, the letter was so severe that after sending it he wondered whether it was not, after all, excessive.

c. In II Cor. iii.1 he says "Do we begin again to commend ourselves?"—implying that in the previous letter there had been a marked element of self-commendation.

d. In II Cor. i.23 he says "I call God for a witness upon my soul that to spare you I did not come again to Corinth," which statement is repeated in II Corinthians ii.1: "I determined this for myself, that I would not come to you again with sorrow."

These passages all imply that a severe letter had been written and, moreover, that before it there had been an unsuccessful visit to Corinth. They obviously would admirably fit II Cor. x-xiii. Besides these general allusions, there is a series of three cross-references which can best be shown in parallel columns.

1. "For this cause I write these things from a distance, that I may not when I come deal sharply"—II Cor. xiii.10.	"And I wrote this same thing, that when I came I might not have sorrow"—II Cor. ii.3.
2. "If I come again I will not spare"—II Cor. xiii.2.	"To spare you I came not again to Corinth"—II Cor. i.23.
3. "Being in readiness to avenge all disobedience when your obedience shall be fulfilled"—II Cor. x.6.	"For this end also did I write that I might know the proof of you, whether ye are obedient in all things"—II Cor. ii.9.

These three pairs of passages are very striking and lose nothing if read in their context. It seems impossible to deny that in each pair the same thing is referred to twice; in II Cor. x-xiii in the present or future tense and in II Cor. i-ix in the past.

Thus, there is overwhelming reason for believing that II Cor. x-xiii is part of the severe letter and that II Cor. i-ix is a later letter which was written after Paul had seen Titus in Macedonia.

Apparently the scribe who first copied the Epistles found in the archives at Corinth one complete letter,—I Corinthians,—and parts of two letters, a beginning and an ending. Not unnaturally, though not very intelligently, he added the ending to the beginning and thus made II Corinthians. Possibly he also found a small fragment of the "previous letter" [22] and incorporated it in II Cor. vi.14-vii.1.

vii. Paul had sent a severe letter of rebuke to Corinth (II Cor. x-xiii) and also sent Titus directly to Corinth to see what he could do. He proposed to come again himself, but, to give Titus time, he came by the much longer way by land. While he was half-way, in Macedonia, he heard that Titus, supported by his letter, had been successful. He therefore wrote again urging that his friends should be lenient to their discomfited opponents.

[22] See p. 111.

Part of this letter is preserved in II Cor. i-ix. In it he also urges them to contribute liberally to a collection which he was making from all the Gentile churches for the benefit of the Christians in Jerusalem.[23] He suggested that he would accompany the representatives of Corinth who would convey this contribution to Jerusalem and this seems to link up the story with Acts, which tells how he went from Macedonia to Achaea, and then, in company with various Gentile Christians to Jerusalem. Acts, however, makes no mention of this collection and, curiously enough, Paul never mentions the one [24] which is described in Acts xi.29.

[23] See especially V. Weber, *Die Antiochenische Kollekte.*

[24] In Acts xxiv.17 Paul mentions "alms", but does not say that they were the result of collection. See *Beginnings,* IV, p. 303.

CHAPTER VIII

Galatians

THERE are two subjects of importance discussed in this Epistle.

In the first place, Paul is on the defensive.[1] His claim to be a true Apostle, with a divine commission, was being disputed among the Galatians. To establish his position that he is "an Apostle neither from men, nor through a human being," he tells the story of his career from his conversion down to his return to Antioch after his second visit to Jerusalem.

In the second place, he is combating Judaisers who wish the Law, including circumcision, to be enforced on Christian converts. He argues against them, in much the same way as in Romans, that righteousness is obtained by faith not by works, and proves this[2] by the example of Abraham. The general meaning of the Epistle is not difficult, but the exact interpretation of individual verses is often obscure.

It is tantalising that no certain answer can be given to any of the obvious questions as to Paul's opponents.[3] They were Judaisers, but were they Jews or Jewish Christians? The point is this: we know that the first Christians were Jews, who converted Gentiles, especially God-fearers, and these became the foundation of Greek-speaking Christianity, cutting loose from the Law and Circumcision. Obviously these Gentile converts stood closer to the synagogue than did the heathen, for they claimed to worship the same God, to use the same Scripture

[1] The best commentaries are by J. B. Lightfoot, Ramsay's *Historical Commentary* which is, however, apt to compensate by emphasis for the deficiencies of evidence, C. W. Emmet's *Galatians,* the commentary of Zahn and those in Lietzmann's *Handbuch* and in Meyer's *Commentary.*

[2] Cf. Rom. iv.1-25.

[3] See especially J. H. Ropes, *The Singular Problem of the Epistle to the Galatians* in *Harvard Theological Studies,* XIV.

and to be more truly the people of God than the Jews; but for just these reasons, they must have been fiercely controverted by Jews, and by such primitive Christians as had remained adherents of the Law. The question both in Romans and Galatians is whether Paul's opponents were Jews or Jewish Christians. The point may be expressed differently by asking whether the Judaisers were the same as those who denied Paul's authority, or were a separate party. Obviously there is here an opening for many imaginative reconstructions of the situation, but no evidence to prove any. The most perplexing point is that in I and II Corinthians there is also strong evidence for a party which refused to accept Paul's authority, but very little that it Judaised. The problems in Corinth were Greek, not Jewish. In Romans and Galatians they are Jewish, not Greek. The common element is doubt as to Paul's Apostolic claims. We have, as it were, fragments of a jig-saw puzzle, of which too many pieces are lost to enable us to reconstruct the whole with any certainty.

But this is not all. It is impossible to fix the time when Galatians was written, or the persons to whom it was addressed.[4]

The main cause for these difficulties is the ambiguity of the words "Galatia" and "Galatians." They have one meaning if interpreted ethnologically, another if taken politically.

In the third century before Christ, Phrygia, which was, roughly speaking, the centre of Asia Minor, was invaded by the Gauls. This was a Nordic tribe that had started from some unknown spot on the northern side of the great mountain-ridge (Pyrenees, Alps, Carpathians, Balkans, Caucasus, Altai Mountains, Hindu Kush, Himalayas) which stretches across Europe and Asia. This tribe had penetrated the passes, and in the end they occupied part of Italy, all Gaul and Britain in the west and a great part of Phrygia in the east. In Britain they were called Britons, and later Welsh, Irish or Gaels. In France and Italy they were called Gauls, and in Greek-

[4] See Mommsen's *Provinces*, W. H. Ramsay, *The Church in the Roman Empire*, and *St. Paul, the Traveler and Roman Citizen*, E. H. Askwith, *The Epistle to the Galatians*, Lightfoot's commentary, pp. 1 ff., and *Earlier Epistles*, pp. 309 ff.

speaking countries Galatians. Their language still survives in Welsh, Erse, Gaelic, Cornish and Breton. In Asia Minor it has died out, but in the first century it was still widely used.

After a century of fighting the Galatians were forced to settle down in a restricted area in the north-east of central Asia Minor, Ancyra (the modern Ankara) being more or less their centre.

In the first century before Christ the Romans were gradually organising Asia Minor as part of the Empire. Their method was to establish what would now be called "protectorates," having local kings in nominal charge of the outlying districts on condition that they were friendly to Rome and followed its orders. As soon, however, as a monarch died or failed to be satisfactory, his kingdom was reorganised as an imperial province under the rule of a Legate Propraetor or a Procurator. This side of the Roman Empire is admirably illustrated in the history of Galatia.

In 189 B.C. the Galatians had joined Antiochus of Phrygia, whose most dangerous rival was Mithridates of Pontus, and were defeated by the Romans at the battle of Magnesia. Nevertheless, even after this, the power of Galatia was considerable in the south, though in the north it was inferior to that of Pontus. In 121 the Romans declared Galatia to be "free,"—that is from Pontus,—but the Mithridatic wars followed and Galatia was not really safe until 73. In 64, when Pompey reorganised the East, the tetrarchy of Lycaonia (including Iconium and Lystra) was taken away and the rest divided among three chiefs. The ablest of these was Deiotarus who died in 40 B.C. and Antony appointed Castor to succeed him. At the same time, Antony made Amyntas, formerly secretary to Deiotarus, king of Pisidia and Pisidian Phrygia, and appointed Polemon king of Lycaonia, with Iconium as his capital. In 36 B.C. Castor died, Polemon was moved northwards to administer Pontus, and his kingdom and Galatia were both given to Amyntas who took the title of King of Galatia. After the fall of Antony, Augustus added Pamphylia to the kingdom of Galatia, but when Amyntas died in 25 B.C. his kingdom was made into the province of Galatia, with Derbe as its frontier, Lycaonia being thus divided.

Thus, in the time of Paul, the province of Galatia included not only the original kingdom of Galatia, but also large parts of Phrygia and Lycaonia. There is no doubt that this large district was officially called the Province of Galatia; but were its inhabitants called Galatians, especially by non-officials? [5]

There seems to be no evidence to settle this question.

It is not any easier to deal with three other problems: First, when, according to Acts, did Paul go into the province of Galatia? Secondly, when did he meet with Galatians in the racial sense? Thirdly, to whom is the Epistle addressed? The answers appear to be as follows:

He probably entered Galatia (the Province) three times: *a.* after he reached Pisidian Antioch on the first journey he was in the province, in Iconium, Lystra and Derbe, for the rest of the journey; *b.* when he went through this district on his second journey (Acts xvi.6), but of course if Schwartz' theory [6] be accepted, these two are really the same visit; and *c.* on the third journey (Acts. xviii.23), for he could not have reached Ephesus by land without passing through Galatia.

He probably met no 'Galatians' in the ethnological sense on the first journey. But he must have done so on the occasion described in Acts xvi.6 if the doubtful phrase "the Phrygian and Galatian country" means, as we believe, the country which was partly Phrygian-speaking and partly Galatian-speaking.[7] This mixed population would be found on the road between Iconium and Troas. Moreover, in such cities as Dorylaion or Kotiaion there was perhaps a sufficient number of Greek-speaking Gauls or Galatians to account for their being converted by the Greek-speaking Paul and receiving an Epistle in Greek.

The grave objection to this view is that it makes the conversion of the Galatians take place after the visit to Jerusalem

[5] See the many books of W. M. Ramsay, and pp. 86 ff.

[6] See pp. 81 f.

[7] See *Beginnings*, Vol. V, pp. 224 ff.

described in Acts xv. Surely, this visit can hardly have been omitted from a letter dealing with the same subject as that discussed at the meeting. If both Paul and Acts are to be believed, the visit in Galatians was the second which Paul made after his conversion and is that mentioned in Acts xi. If he is writing before the time of the visit described in Acts xv, obviously he could not mention it. And conversely, the fact that he does not mention it seems to prove that it had not yet taken place. But this is impossible if the conversion of the Galatians was not on the first journey and the second came after Acts xv.

One (perhaps the best) way of eliminating this difficulty is to emphasise the fact that there were really two controversies between the church at Antioch and Jerusalem, the first dealing with the question of the Law and circumcision, the second with that of social intercourse.[8] The Decrees dealt only with the second point, and therefore had no importance for the Galatians. This implies that Luke confused two controversies, but inasmuch as they were simultaneous this is not improbable.

If this be accepted, the Galatian church may have been founded on Paul's "second journey," during that curiously obscure passage [9] from Iconium to Troas, of which Luke says so little.

If so, it can be supposed .hat Galatians was written from Corinth or Ephesus, at about the same time as Romans, but the matter is complicated by the disturbing element introduced by our inability to say whether the short or the long recension of Romans is the earlier. If the short form be the earlier, it may have been sent to Antioch rather than to Rome, at the same time as Galatians was sent to whatever city was the centre of the Galatian church, and at any time during the first or second journey.

Nevertheless, we are inclined to doubt this view for two reasons: first, these cities (Dorylaion, Kotiaion etc.) may have had Galatian-speaking citizens, but they were not in any sense

[8] See *Beginnings,* Vol. V, pp. 213 ff.
[9] See pp. 85 f.

in Galatia; and secondly, the implication of Acts is that Paul did *not* preach (i.e. find an audience that understood Greek) between Iconium and Troas.

Two other theories must be mentioned:

Lightfoot[10] thought that Paul on the occasion described in Acts xvi.6 went to Ancyra, and that this was the occasion of the conversion of the Galatians. The difficulty of accepting this view, generally called 'the north Galatian theory,' is that it does not fit the description given in Acts xvi. According to this, Paul went northward until he was "Mysia-ward" (Κατὰ τὴν Μυσίαν), which is an impossible description of Ancyra, though it would fit the head waters of the Rhyndakos near Kotiaion or Dorylaion. Nevertheless the possibility that Paul did go to Ancyra, and that Acts suggests this visit, is not to be rejected wholly. Luke omits a great deal; perhaps he omitted this.

Ramsay[11] thought that the "Phrygian and Galatian country" in Acts xvi means a regular division (a *regio*) of that part of the province known as *Phrygia Galatica.* The serious objections to this view are that there is no evidence that this was the name of a division of Galatia and the fact that the Greek rendered "district" (χῶρα) seems rather to mean country-side as distinguished from cities. Ramsay also thought that 'Galatia' in Gal. i.2 means the province and that 'Galatians' in Gal. iii.1 means inhabitants of the province.

It seems to us that Ramsay's interpretation of Acts xvi.6 ought probably to be rejected, though like all his theories it calls for the attention due to a scholar who for fifty years has done so much to inspire the historical study of the New Testament. The case is different if the question be limited to the identity of the churches to which Paul wrote. Clearly, Galatia may mean the province, which includes Pisidian Antioch, Iconium, Lystra and Derbe. These therefore might be the "churches of Galatia." But Paul also addresses his readers as "Galatians," and that is exactly what the inhabitants of Iconium etc. were not. Can Paul have used "Galatians" to mean

[10] See Lightfoot, *Galatians,* p. 20.
[11] Cf. his *Paul the Traveler and Roman Citizen,* pp. 103 f.

persons of whatever race living in the province? Ramsay thinks that he did. It seems to us that there is a nice balance of improbability between this, the possibility of an unrecorded visit to Ancyra, and the view that the Galatians were racially Galatians living in Dorylaion and other places which ethnologically were on the border between Phrygia and Galatia. But we incline to accept Ramsay's view because the implication of Acts is that Paul did not preach between Iconium and Troas. The point which seems too often overlooked is that the identification of the churches of Galatia is not the same problem as the exegesis of Acts xvi.6. Ramsay seems to us clearly wrong as to Acts xvi.6, but he may be right as to the locality to which the Epistle to the Galatians was addressed.

CHAPTER IX

THE EPISTLES TO THE THESSALONIANS

THE church in Thessalonica[1] was founded when Paul visited it on his first trip to Europe. He appears, according to Acts xvii, to have preached for three weeks in the synagogue. He converted a few Jews and many Gentiles. That he stayed more than three weeks is not excluded, but is certainly not implied by the text. According to I Thessalonians ii.9 Paul supported himself by working, but according to Philippians iv.16 he also received help from Philippi.

No reason can be seen for the sudden outburst of hostility recorded in Acts xvii.5-10 except that given by the writer,—Jewish hostility. Certainly if Paul detached a number of God-fearers,—potential converts,—from the synagogue, the irritation of the Jews is intelligible. The only reason for doubting this is the probability that Luke is inclined to emphasise the iniquity of the Jews under all circumstances and in all places.

Apparently Paul and Silas were accused of being agitators who wished to start rebellion, and, though the magistrates did not condemn them, they were deported,—a friend, Jason, going bail for some unmentioned purpose, perhaps that Paul would not return. Possibly I Thessalonians implies this.

From Thessalonica Paul, Silas and Timothy went to Beroea, but again Jewish opposition drove them out. Paul was taken "to the sea" but Silas and Timothy stayed behind.[2] Paul went to Athens, which is possibly a synonym for "to the sea" and sent back a message to Silas and Timothy to join him as soon as possible.[3] The question is whether they joined Paul in

[1] See especially J. E. Frame's commentary in the *International Critical Commentary,* which should also be studied as a model of what a commentary ought to be, E. von Dobschütz in the Meyer commentary, and M. Dibelius in Lietzmann's *Handbuch.*

[2] See below p. 87 and *Beginnings,* Vol. IV, note on Acts xvii.14.

[3] Acts xvii.15.

Athens, whence Paul wrote to Thessalonica, or in Corinth, which Paul had already reached,—in which case, of course, he wrote from Corinth.

The latter alternative is suggested by Acts, which says in xviii.5 that "Silas and Timothy came down from Macedonia." If there were no contradictory evidence, this would doubtless be accepted as final. But the evidence of I Thessalonians is equally strong in favour of the other view. In I Thessalonians iii.1 Paul (or Paul and Silas) says that he preferred to be left alone in Athens in order that Timothy might go to Thessalonica, and it is clearly implied that at the moment of writing Paul had been rejoined by Timothy. There is no suggestion that this was not in Athens and, without Acts, it would never be doubted.

The most popular attempt to reconcile the two pieces of evidence is still that of Paley's *Horae Paulinae,* which suggests that Silas and Timothy came from Beroea to Athens, that Timothy was sent back immediately to Thessalonica and possibly Silas to Philippi, and that Acts xviii.5 recounts their return to Paul in Corinth. This is not impossible, but no one could have guessed it from Acts or I Thessalonians. Moreover, the easiest, if not the shortest way from Beroea to Athens (or Corinth) is through Thessalonica. The land route from Beroea to Athens (except by train) is to be avoided.

It is not impossible that all that happened is that Paul sent back a message by the Beroean friends who went with him on the way to Athens, instructing Timothy to get news of the church in Thessalonica on his way southwards. Paul's notoriety prevented him from going to Athens by the natural route, but Timothy was not so well known. If so, it is quite possible that Timothy did in fact come to Corinth. But the question can never be settled and is not important.

The important part is plain; I Thessalonians was written by Paul when he was in Greece, either in Athens or Corinth, about the year 50,[4] when Timothy had come down from Macedonia and joined him and Silas.

Thus it is clear that I Thessalonians was written in reply to

[4] See p. 249.

a report which Timothy brought down from Macedonia. Possibly II Thessalonians was a second letter sent at the same time, but this raises the much disputed question whether this letter is genuine.

There has always been some doubt about the authenticity of this Epistle.[5] It is not that it is unlike I Thessalonians, but rather that, on the contrary, it is too like it, so that it may be an imitation, and the main argument which has carried weight with critics is that it contains an Apocalyptic section which refers in a way without parallel in the New Testament to the belief in the coming of Antichrist. This belief is very interesting and difficult to place. At one time it was thought that *Nero redivivus* was the origin of the theory of an Antichrist. If this were so II Thessalonians could not be Pauline, for in that case it must have been written after Nero's death.

The main points of the story about Nero are these:—when the Emperor died in A.D. 68, the first feeling of the populace was joy at their deliverance from the tyrant, but in a short time doubts began to arise as to whether the report of his death was not a piece of news too good to be true. The result was that pretenders appeared who gave themselves out as Nero. The first of these appeared in 69 and was speedily destroyed. Another, eleven years later, in the reign of Titus, was, according to Zonaras, recognised as Nero by Artabanus, the king of the Parthians; and still later, in 88, another impostor almost succeeded in raising the Parthians in revolt against Domitian. After 88 the fact of Nero's death was recognised, but a belief arose that he would return from the dead and lead the armies of the East against Rome. Finally, the figure of Nero himself became obscure, and there remained that of a partly human, partly diabolic Antichrist.

But Gunkel and Bousset[6] have showed that, as a matter of fact, the belief in Antichrist is the survival of an old myth earlier than the Nero Saga. The history of the Antichrist legend

[5] See W. Wrede, *Die Echtheit des zweiten Thessalonicherbriefs* in *T U* xxiv.2.

[6] H. Gunkel, *Schöpfung und Chaos,* and W. Bousset, *Der Antichrist Legende,* translated by A. H. Keane. See also *Antichrist,* in the *Encyclopedia Biblica.*

is far too complicated to be dealt with here; the main outlines alone can be given. There seems to have been current among the Jews and among other Eastern peoples the belief that the "end shall be as the beginning." The sign that the New Age is near at hand will be the repetition of the events preceding the Creation. Now, these events comprised a struggle between God and a daemonic being who strove to take the place of God. This is the old Babylonian myth of the strife between Marduk and Tiamat, of which there are many traces in the Old Testament. It was believed that at the end of this Age the struggle would again be renewed and the victory of God would be the inauguration of a New Age, as it had formerly been of the Creation. Thus we find in Jewish and early Christian sources a certain amount of confusion of thought as to whether the Antichrist would be a human or a daemonic figure, and sometimes even a duplication in which a human Antichrist is accompanied or followed by a still more terrible supernatural apparition.

But assuming the belief, though not without hesitation, that II Thessalonians is genuine, the problem is to establish its true relationship to I Thessalonians. F. C. Burkitt used to think that the best solution was to suppose that this Epistle is really the Epistle of Silas, rather than of Paul. This view, though presented by him with great ingenuity, has failed to meet with much acceptance, and Harnack's view,[7] possibly with some modification, is more likely to be true. He thinks that the split between the Jews and the Greeks in Thessalonica was of so serious a nature that Paul wrote I Thessalonians in the main to the Greeks and II Thessalonians exclusively to the Jews. Obviously this theory can be stated either so as to make the two letters contemporary, or II Thessalonians somewhat later than the other, when it was realised that the first letter would not satisfy the Jewish Christians. To us the latter view seems more likely, and that Paul had received some communication which made him realise that I Thessalonians was not quite satisfactory. Paul thus finds it necessary to write im-

[7] A. Harnack, *Das Problem der zweiten Thessalonicher Briefs* in S.A.B. 1910.

mediately to explain that the day of the Lord has not yet come,[8]—or, to translate the word perhaps more accurately, has not yet "set in,"—and that it will not come until the great apostasy and the coming of Antichrist. That would seem to be the probable explanation of II Thessalonians.

It is now possible to reconstruct the sequence of events.

When Paul left Thessalonica, the Christians whom he had converted either from Judaism or heathenism, were in a difficult position. The Jews had brought an accusation against Paul. The matter had not been fully heard, Paul had left the city, and Jason had given "security." Presumably after he had gone the case was continued, and the Jews, who claimed that Christianity was a treasonable association, were in a very superior position, because they could claim that Paul had, in effect, "jumped his bail." It was extremely likely that persecution would follow, and Paul would want to know what had happened to his converts under those circumstances. It was to strengthen their courage and to bring Paul news that Timothy had gone to Thessalonica. He reported that there had indeed been persecutions,[9] but that the Christians had stood firm and their courage was famous among all the brethren in Macedonia and Achaea.

The rest of the news that Timothy brought was perhaps less satisfactory. There would appear to have been a cleavage between those of Greek and those of Jewish origin. Paul has to insist that his letter must be read to everyone. A second point which Timothy appears to have reported suggests the appearance in Thessalonica of the same attempt to discredit Paul by throwing doubt on his motives as exists in Romans, Galatians and Corinthians. It is clear that in the early days of the Church the device of discrediting the teachings of a prominent man by throwing doubt on his motives and conduct was perfectly understood and efficiently practised.

Timothy also appears to have reported a tendency to immoral life and idleness; the latter may have been due to the

[8] See *Earlier Epistles*, p. 94, for a discussion of II Thess. ii.1 f.
[9] Cf. I Thess. ii.14 ff. and i.8.

expectation of the speedy coming of the Lord, which would appear to render any further work quite unnecessary. The immorality is probably the result, which has so often been noticed, of an unduly enthusiastic type of religion. Finally, it is clear that the Thessalonians were greatly interested in eschatological questions. These are dealt with in I Thess. iv.13 ff. Apparently the first converts believed that Paul had assured them that the coming of the Lord was close at hand, and that they would live to see it. When, therefore, some had died before the coming of the Lord, they were distressed and Paul answers their difficulties by telling them that those who are already dead will be raised up at the coming of the Lord and rejoice with those who survive in the joys of the Kingdom. A further treatment of this point, to satisfy the Jewish Christians, was the chief purpose of II Thessalonians. Apparently Paul's teaching had been misunderstood or misrepresented,[10] so as to mean that the "Day of the Lord" had come. To remedy this Paul expounds the doctrine of the "Apostasy" and "Man of Sin" or Antichrist.

[10] Cf. II Thess. ii.2.

CHAPTER X

The Epistles of the Imprisonment

THE Epistles to the Philippians, Ephesians, Colossians and Philemon seem to have been written from prison. The evidence is:

> "Even as it is meet for me to think this of you all because I have you in my heart; inasmuch as both in my bonds and in the defence and confirmation of the Gospel ye all are partakers of my grace" (Philipp. i.7).
>
> "So that my bonds in Christ are manifest in all the palace and in all other places; and many of my brethren in the Lord, waxing confident by my bonds, are much more bold to speak the word without fear" (Philipp. i.13-14).
>
> "The salutation by the hand of me Paul. Remember my bonds. Grace be with you" (Col. iv.18).
>
> "For this cause I Paul, the prisoner of Jesus Christ for you Gentiles" (Eph. iii.1).
>
> "I therefore, the prisoner of the Lord, beseech you that ye walk worthy of the vocation wherewith ye are called" (Eph. iv.1).
>
> "For which I am an ambassador in bonds; that therein I may speak boldly, as I ought to speak" (Eph. vi.20).
>
> "Paul, a prisoner of Jesus Christ, and Timothy our brother, unto Philemon, our dearly beloved and fellow-labourer" (Philemon 1).
>
> "Yet for love's sake I rather beseech thee, believing such an one as Paul the aged, and now also a prisoner of Jesus Christ" (Philemon 9).

These verses clearly indicate that Paul was a prisoner at the time he wrote, but unfortunately nothing in these passages shows where he was.

Three theories have found wide acceptance:

i. Paul was in Rome. This view is best stated in Lightfoot's commentary on Philippians [1] and is now widely held. It rests on the hypothesis that the mention of the Praetorium in Philipp. 1.13 and of "those of the household of Caesar" in iv.22 most naturally refer to Rome.

ii. Paul was in Caesarea. This view interprets the Praetorium and "the household of Caesar" as referring to the Governor's palace in Caesarea. This theory is now rarely held, though it was once dominant.

iii. Paul was in Ephesus,[2] though the fact is not mentioned in Acts. It is deduced from:

"And why stand we in jeopardy every hour? I protest by your rejoicing which I have in Christ Jesus our Lord, I die daily. If, after the manner of men, I have fought with beasts at Ephesus, what advantageth it me if the dead rise not? let us eat and drink for tomorrow we die" (I Cor. xv.30-32).

"Are they ministers of Christ? (I speak as a fool) I am more; in labours more abundant, in stripes above measure, in prisons more frequent, in deaths more oft" (II Cor. xi.23).

"For we would not, brethren, have you ignorant of our trouble which came to us in Asia, that we were pressed out of measure, above strength, insomuch that we despaired even of life; but we had the sentence of death in ourselves, that we should not trust in ourselves, but in God which raiseth the dead: who delivereth us from so great a death, and doth deliver; in whom we trust that he will yet deliver us" (II Cor. i.8-10).

These three passages taken together seem to imply an imprisonment or imprisonments which might end in death, and even in "fighting with beasts" in the arena.

The probability of this deduction is now widely accepted and seems to us to be incontrovertible; but it does not neces-

[1] J. B. Lightfoot, *Philippians,* pp. 1-46. This view is also taken by most German scholars, though O. Holtzmann and Spitta are exceptions.

[2] See especially G. S. Duncan, *St. Paul's Ephesian Ministry.*

sarily follow that the Epistles of the Imprisonment were written from Ephesus.

For Philemon, however, a far better case can be made for Ephesus than for Rome, because a runaway slave from Colossae, such as Onesimus, would be vastly more likely to be in Ephesus than in Rome or even in Caesarea. Moreover, if this be conceded, Philemon seems to carry with it Colossians and Ephesians, provided that their authenticity be granted.[3]

Philippians is on a different level, but a most attractive case has been made out by Professor Duncan for thinking that it was written from Ephesus, possibly before I Corinthians. The latter point is not essential; all that is necessary is that Paul should be in prison and Timothy[4] be with him, but the most natural view certainly is that such an imprisonment was over before I Corinthians xv was written, as Paul seems to imply that the danger of his being given to the beasts is now past. Therefore there is much to be said for the view that Philippians was written while Paul was in prison in Ephesus and I Corinthians after he had been released. The main difficulty is to decide whether the affliction referred to in II Corinthians i.8-10 and xi.23 is the same as this imprisonment, or is a second one. The latter view is extremely attractive, and if so, Colossians, Ephesians, Philemon and Philippians may have been written during either the first or second Ephesian imprisonment, and either before or after I Corinthians.

It should be noted that the main reason for the increased support given to the theory that the "Epistles of the Imprisonment," or some of them, were written from Ephesus is the realisation that 'Praetorium' was the customary Latin word for 'Government House' in the Roman provinces, and that the 'household of Caesar' means those who were attached to the personal service of the Emperor, whether in Rome or elsewhere, so that these two phrases are as applicable to any great city, such as Ephesus or Caesarea, as to Rome.

The main objection to accepting the Ephesian hypothesis is

[3] See pp. 140 ff.

[4] Cf. Philipp. i.1 and 7.

that it makes these Epistles almost contemporary with Corinthians, while their Christology[5] insists that they—or at least Ephesians and Colossians—are later.

The usually accepted explanation is that Paul's Christology developed in his later years. Obviously, this explanation serves best if the imprisonment implied by Colossians be put as late in his career as possible. It is a choice of difficulties. Philemon fits much better into an Ephesian framework; Colossians is closely associated with Philemon, but Colossians seems to imply a development, not to say a change of thought, which fits better into a late Roman framework than into an early Ephesian one.

The authenticity of Philippians and of Philemon is rarely questioned; Ephesians and Colossians on the other hand, have always been doubted.[6] At present, indeed, the majority of critics accept both as genuine, but not without some hesitation, and the problem really remains unsolved. It has merely been changed from a question of literary criticism to one of history and psychology.

The point is this. There is an essential difference between Ephesians-Colossians and the earlier Epistles.

The earlier Epistles represent the work of Christ as the redemption of man from the consequences of the sin of the first man. This work is not yet complete, but will culminate in the reign of Christ who will return and conquer all enemies, ending with Death. After this Christ will surrender the kingdom to God "that God may be all in all."

In Ephesians-Colossians the work of Christ is the redemption of the Universe; it is complete, and Christ has and will have eternally the preëminence in all things. It has culminated already in the conquest of all hostile beings and in the Church.

Obviously there is here a difference not only in language but in thought.

[5] See pp. 165 f.

[6] See, for instance, J. Moffatt,—with much hesitation—in a very judicial discussion in his *Historical New Testament.*

Moreover, Ephesians and Colossians have the closest literary similarity to each other. This extends to whole sentences, and the linguistic argument for community of origin, directly or indirectly, is as strong as in the Gospels of Matthew and Luke. Nevertheless, this similarity does not extend to ideas. Colossians and Ephesians agree in general in a "cosmic" Christology, but whereas Colossians is Christological and polemical, Ephesians is Ecclesiological and hortatory.

This problem has been dealt with in three ways:

i. Paul's thought developed deeply during his imprisonment. Obviously if the "Ephesian" imprisonment be accepted this view is much more difficult than otherwise,[7] but in any case it calls for a remarkably rapid change.

ii. Both Colossians and Ephesians are the work of a "Paulinist" school of the second generation, just as are Hebrews and the Pastoral Epistles. A modification of this view is that Colossians is a genuine Pauline Epistle and that Ephesians is not. This was popular about thirty years ago, but since then has faded out. It fails to explain the close similarity between Colossians and Ephesians. Both or neither of these Epistles may be genuine, but a 'straddle' which accepts one and not the other combines all the difficulties and solves none.

iii. A third theory was suggested in 1872 by H. Holtzmann.[8] He recognised the close similarity in language of the two Epistles but claimed that a double classification could be seen; in one list of passages Colossians seemed to be primary and Ephesians secondary, in the other list Ephesians was primary. The same phenomenon is found in the long recension of the Ignatian Epistles. In that case the explanation, triumphantly discovered by Lightfoot, is that a writer who knew the seven original letters wrote six more and added them to the original seven, which he modified by interpolation so as to agree with the new letters. Fortunately, though no manuscript of the original seven exists, some manuscripts of the thirteen have copied

[7] See p. 140.

[8] H. J. Holtzmann, *Kritik der Epheser und Kolosserbriefe*, 1872. This book is now difficult to obtain, but the main points of the argument are given in his *Einleitung*, pp. 261 ff.

an uninterpolated seven, and these are the basis of modern critical editions.

Holtzmann argued that this is just what happened to Colossians-Ephesians. There was an original—not very important—letter of Paul to the Colossians. A Paulinist of the second generation used this as a model and wrote Ephesians, and then revised the text of the original Colossians. The original Colossians was lost, but the revised form and Ephesians were taken into the Corpus Paulinum. Possibly—though Holtzmann did not suggest this—the theory might be rounded out by the corollary that the writer of Ephesians was the collector of the Corpus, though if so it would be hard to explain why he did not revise the other Epistles.

This theory of Holtzmann's has been almost forgotten, but those who have rather contemptuously put it aside seem to have forgotten the Ignatian parallel.

To choose finally between these three theories is perhaps impossible; but it is important for students to understand the facts on which they are based. The whole subject seems to us ripe for fresh study.

CHAPTER XI

The Epistle to the Philippians

THE Epistle to the Philippians[1] was sent to Philippi primarily in order to thank them for having sent help to Paul while he was a prisoner (whether in Rome, Caesarea or Ephesus is not stated), by the hand of Epaphroditus,[2] who was a member of their church. Epaphroditus, on reaching Paul, had been taken ill and now that he was going back to his home, Paul gave him this letter to carry with him, thanking the Philippians for all their kindness.

The letter is not comparable to the earlier ones in importance. Paul begins by telling the Philippians a little about his own affairs and expresses his sympathy for their present distress. He then promises that as soon as possible he will send Timothy and warmly commends Epaphroditus. That brings us down to the beginning of chap. iii, but at that point the letter completely changes its tone, and Paul speaks in the strongest terms of the enemies who are trying to undo his work. In conclusion he begs his readers not to forget the Gospel and again thanks them for their help.

Two interesting problems emerge from the Epistle:

i. Is it certain that this Epistle is a unit and not, like II Corinthians, a combination of two original documents?[3] The suggestion is that the passage beginning in iii.2 and going down to the end of the chapter, or possibly a little further, is a fragment of another Epistle. This can be seen best by reading the Epistle with the omission of this passage, and then reading it with this passage included.

1 See the commentaries of Lightfoot and of Dibelius in Lietzmann's *Handbuch*.

2 Philipp. ii.25 and iv.18.

3 See K. Lake, *The Critical Problems of the Epistle to the Philippians*, *Expositor*, June, 1914.

In the first place, we get "For the rest, my brethren, rejoice in the Lord! For me to write the same things to you is not wearisome and for you it is safe. So my beloved brethren, my joy and crown, stand fast in the Lord, beloved." That leaves out almost the whole of chap. iii except the first verse. On the other hand, if we read it as it is now it reads: "For the rest, brethren, rejoice in the Lord. For me to write the same things to you is not wearisome and for you it is safe. Beware of dogs!" What can be the connection? If it were not for the manuscript evidence, no one would think that this second piece, which begins with "Beware of dogs," is really part of the same letter as that which both before and after the advice about dogs recommends "rejoicing in the Lord."

ii. More important than the critical questions raised in the last paragraph is the interpretation of Philippians ii.5-11. Few passages have been more used (and none more abused) for theological purposes than has this one.[4] Two lines of interpretation are possible. The first is that which understands the beginning and its reference to the form of God as indicating the nature of Jesus. "He was in the form of God, but emptied himself, taking the form of a slave." This is regarded as a reference to the incarnation of the pre-existent Christ. This may be called the "classical" interpretation and the question of what is the exact meaning of "emptying himself" in verse 7 gave rise to the Kenotic theory of the Incarnation.[5]

The alternative interpretation of the passage takes the opening words of it as a reference to the account of Adam who was made in the form of God and by trying to obtain the fruit of the Tree of the Knowledge of Good and Evil fell from his estate through disobedience. With this is contrasted the life of Jesus who exactly reversed the proceeding of Adam.

It should, in any case, be noted, that whatever the interpretation of the first part of the passage be, the name which is above every name must almost certainly be understood as the Greek word for "Lord" (Kurios). That is the name which

[4] See Lightfoot's commentary *ad loc.*

[5] See especially C. Gore's Bampton Lectures on *The Incarnation* and the volume of essays called *Lux Mundi.*

is above every name, for it is, in the Old Testament, the name of God Himself. It may, however, be doubted whether, even if this be so, as it almost certainly is, the passage does not also mean that the words "Jesus Christ" to which "Lord" was applied, shall be the power to which everything will submit.

CHAPTER XII

Ephesians

THERE is nothing in the body of this epistle [1] to indicate its occasion and perhaps not even its recipient, but its similarity to Colossians, and the suggestion in iii.1, iv.1 and vi.20 that Paul was in prison, justify the traditional view that it was written at the same time.

An interesting possibility is raised by a textual variant in i.1. In most manuscripts this reads "to the saints in Ephesus," but ℵ B read merely "to the saints who are," which makes no more sense in Greek than it does in English. It would seem that the name of the place to which the letter was sent is deliberately omitted in the archetype of these manuscripts. For this two explanations have been offered:

a. One of the earliest lists of the Pauline Epistles is that of Marcion,[2] which omits Ephesians but inserts an otherwise unknown Epistle to the Laodiceans. What was this unknown letter? The early Church was aware of the problem, and some ingenious scribe forged a letter which is still preserved in Latin and cannot be that used by Marcion. The matter is complicated, but partly elucidated, by the reference in Colossians iv.16 to a letter "from Laodicea," which the Colossians are urged to read. Apparently this was a letter of Paul which was sent to Laodicea, and was to be forwarded to Colossae. It has therefore been held, especially by Harnack,[3] that Marcion's letter "to the Laodiceans" is the same as ours "to the Ephesians." This seems at least highly probable, but why was

[1] See the Lietzmann and Meyer commentaries. The edition of J. Armitage Robinson is excellent philologically. T. K. Abbott in the *I.C.C.* is disappointing. A new English commentary which will really deal with the critical problems of the Epistle is desirable.

[2] See pp. 96 ff.

[3] Harnack, *S.A.B.* 1910, pp. 696 ff.

Ephesus ever substituted for Laodicea? Harnack suggests that Laodicea suffered so much in general estimation owing to Rev. iii.14 ff. that it incurred a *damnatio memoriae* and its name was always omitted or erased. This custom of a *damnatio memoriae* was quite common, so that, for example, the text of Eusebius[4] has suffered in some manuscripts by the omission of the name of Licinius, the rival of Constantine.

b. A somewhat different theory was rendered popular, especially in England, by a suggestion of Hort and Lightfoot,[5] who thought that originally Paul wrote a circular letter to the churches of Asia, leaving a blank for the address. When a copy was sent to a church the blank was filled in. Marcion and others were acquainted with the copy sent to Laodicea, the traditional text goes back to a copy sent to Ephesus, and א B to a copy in which the blank for the address had never been filled up at all.

This theory is not impossible, but it is perhaps a little influenced by the modern habit of printing, or of using 'carbon copies.' In antiquity each copy had to be made separately, and the picture of an apostle traveling about with a packet of copies of a letter, with a blank for the address, is not quite convincing. It is true that this theory admirably explains the Laodicean tradition and the blank in א B, but not so satisfactorily the reference in Col. iv.16 which implies a single copy circulating from church to church, not the existence of many copies each sent to a separate address.

Like Colossians, the Epistle to the Ephesians was entrusted to Tychicus.[6] The Epistle is in many ways extremely like that to the Colossians, but in one respect it differs very markedly. Colossians is largely controversial; its object was to counteract the bad effect of teachings to which Paul objected. Ephesians, however, has extremely few, if any, controversial elements. It is the most constructive of all the Epistles which we possess.

[4] See the discussion in E. Schwartz, *Prolegomena* to the Berlin edition of the Ecclesiastical History of Eusebius and in Lawlor's *Eusebiana*.

[5] The two contributions were originally separate but are now most easily accessible in Lightfoot's *Biblical Essays*.

[6] Eph. vi.21; Col. iv.7.

So much is this the case, that much the most attractive argument in favour of its authenticity is that advocated by Prof. Scott[7] in his Introduction, that "Paul decided, while the theme of Colossians was still fresh in his mind, he would write another letter in which he would leave all controversial issues aside and set forth more fully in their positive significance the ideas which possessed him."

More than in any other Epistle, the theme of this letter or treatise, for it is hardly a letter, is the purpose and nature of the Church. Why did the Church exist? What was its function? And what were the duties of those who belonged to it?

The central note of the Epistle is struck in the first chapter: "God has revealed to us the mystery of his will, according to his good pleasure which he hath purposed in himself, that in his ordering of the fulness of time, he might reunite all things with Christ, things which are in heaven and things which are in earth." This passage is very similar to Colossians, but Paul in elaborating this 'cosmical' view of Christ in the first part of the Epistle does not enter into any of the controversies to which it might give rise, nor does he discuss the theory of the ultimate plan of God's government of the world.

In the second half of the Epistle, the same idea is taken up from a slightly different point of view. The main feature of this, one of the most important passages in the New Testament, is to regard the Church as the extension of the Incarnation. Christ is the agent and the embodiment of God's plan for the world. The Church is the society by which this plan is carried out, and is, as it were, the continuation not only of Christ's work, but of Christ himself. It is scarcely necessary to point out how extraordinarily important this view was for the development of Church history.

Moreover, this section of Ephesians is one of which the importance is obviously not yet lost. It would not be true to say that Paul regards Christ as the embodiment of 'values' in the world of immaterial reality, but certainly it is those values which are prominent in his mind. Opinion today as to the

[7] In his *Literature of the New Testament.*

historical phenomena with which Paul links up these values may be widely different from the Pauline, but there can be little doubt as to the importance of the 'values' themselves, and the Pauline picture of a society which is to be partly the embodiment of them, and partly the instrument for finding them out and expounding them is a grandiose and marvelous one.

Another point of great importance is the stress the Epistle places on knowledge. It would not be fair to say that in this Epistle knowledge takes the place held by faith in the Epistle to the Romans: it is, rather, true that the writer emphasises knowledge as the necessary result of faith. If one may use the word "Gnostic" in its true sense, such as that given to it by Clement of Alexandria and by Origen, who claim to be true Gnostics as opposed to the false Gnostics, one may fairly say that this Epistle is the primary statement of Christian Gnosticism. It makes Christianity consist of an understanding of the values set forth by Christ and by his Apostles, and the Church the society of those who have this knowledge, the result of which is the attainment by man of the 'fulness,' the *pleroma,* of God; "so that ye, being rooted and grounded in love, may be able to comprehend with all the saints, what is the length and breadth and depth and height and to know the love of Christ which passes knowledge, that ye may be filled with all the fulness of God."

The idea of the Church which is here presented goes far beyond anything in the Epistle to the Romans or Corinthians. It may be a legitimate development of them, but it certainly is not paralleled in the earlier Epistles. It leaves little room for the eschatological coming of the Lord which is so prominent in the earlier Epistles, and looks upon Christians as a society which will live in a continuing world, rather than as inheriting a new one. The difference is very great. Is it possible that the gulf between the two was crossed by one man within the course of a few months?

CHAPTER XIII

Philemon and Colossians

COLOSSAE[1] was a city of second-rate importance in the valley of the Lykos, which is a tributary of the larger river Maeander which flowed out near Ephesus. In the valley of the Lykos, there were three cities,–Laodicaea, Colossae and Hierapolis. It would appear, from allusions in the Epistle, that Paul himself, though he was living for three years at Ephesus, had never visited the Lykos valley; but churches had been established there by some of his followers, notably by Epaphras. At the time when Paul wrote from prison to the Colossians (whether he was in Ephesus or in Rome makes little difference [2]), he received communications from the Lykos valley, from Onesimus and from Epaphras.[3]

PHILEMON

Onesimus was the run-away slave of Philemon, who appears to have lived in Colossae. Paul apparently had persuaded Onesimus to go back to his master and wrote a letter for him to take with him, urging Philemon to treat the returning slave with kindness. It is a very short little note which has no special importance, particularly now that slavery has been abolished. At one time, it was used with considerable effect to show that Paul thought that slavery was a permanent institution of society.

[1] See J. B. Lightfoot's *Colossians and Philemon*, pp. 1-70.

[2] See pp. 138 ff.

[3] It is usually said that Epaphras was the founder of the Church. The rather forced conclusion that Paul himself had never visited Colossae is based on Col. i. 6.

COLOSSIANS

Epaphras was a visitor from Colossae, and probably the Epistle to the Colossians is based on the information which Epaphras brought with him. This seems to have been somewhat disturbing. Apparently the Colossians were being taught [4] that faith in Christ was not sufficient and in order to be set free from the evil powers which rule the world, men require the help of other supernatural, possibly angelic, beings; they must perform certain ceremonies and be initiated into secret wisdom. Nothing is known of this form of thought, except what has been gleaned from the Epistle to the Colossians itself.

It becomes, however, tolerably clear that the background of thought at Colossae was the syncretistic paganism described on p. 225. It probably contained Jewish and astral elements. It endeavoured to explain evil as due to matter,—food, drink and contact,—leading to precepts such as "Touch not, taste not, handle not." It also paid excessive veneration to angels and to astral powers, described in the Authorized Version as "elements."

Who were the advocates of this school of thought? The same problem arises, *mutatis mutandis,* in this connection in Romans and Galatians. In them there is room for doubt as to whether Paul is arguing against Jewish Christians or against Jews: in Colossians there is room for doubt as to whether Paul is arguing against Gentile Christians—in other words, against heresy—or against Gentiles who are endeavouring to convert Christians to their way of thinking. This point has, perhaps, not met with sufficient attention, and writers have spoken too lightly of the Colossian "heresy."

Paul's answer to the Colossian 'heresy' is, in the main, an appeal to soteriology of the type found in Romans, basing salvation on the faith connected with the death of Christ. There is, however, a real difference between the position assigned to Christ in I Corinthians and in Colossians. In I

[4] See M. Dibelius, in Lietzmann's commentary and in his *Die Geisterwelt im Glauben des Paulus,* and Lightfoot's commentary.

Corinthians, the triumph of Christ and the coming of his kingdom is foretold. He will come shortly, for Paul expects that he himself will be alive at the time, and will reign until all enemies are subdued to him, but no longer. The last enemy that will be destroyed is Death, and, when this is accomplished, Christ will deliver the kingdom to God, that God may be all in all. Thus, the triumph of Christ is not yet complete, and his kingdom will not be everlasting but will have an end. In Colossians, on the other hand, the triumph of Christ is already complete; there is no reference to any future parousia, and Christ has, and will have eternally, the pre-eminence in all things. "His kingdom has no end."

It should be noted that this is the main argument against the Pauline authorship of Colossians. It might be regarded as conclusive if Paul had sent this letter to Corinth, but the possibility exists that he expressed his belief in Corinthians in Corinthian terminology but did so in Colossians in syncretistic terminology. This is conceivable, but it does not seem to us a wholly convincing argument and perhaps a Paulinist of the second generation wrote this Epistle, just as another Paulinist wrote Hebrews and probably yet another the Pastoral Epistles. To us this seems actually more probable, but very few scholars seem to agree with us.

Paul—if it was Paul—strongly combated the tendency at Colossae to explain evil as due to matter—the influence of food, drink and contact—and he objected to the tendency derived from this attitude to produce precepts such as "Taste not, touch not, handle not" and to pay excessive veneration to angels and to astral powers. His argument is the very penetrating one that evil is due to will, not to matter, and—which is less convincing in this generation—that the angelic beings, dominations, powers, etc. were created through Christ and had been stripped of their power by him.

Also, it should be noted that the Christology of Colossians is essentially parallel to that of the Epistle to the Hebrews and to the Fourth Gospel. Like these other documents, it is strongly reminiscent of Philo. In explaining the nature of Christ one can almost feel that the word "Logos" is trembling at the end of the pen of the writer, but the word itself never comes until we reach the prologue to the Fourth Gospel. That accident has obscured the fact that in many ways the Christology of Colossians and Hebrews is more advanced, and certainly more explicit, even than the Fourth Gospel, if the prologue be excepted.

Finally, there is a connection between Colossians and the Valentinian Gnostics, who undoubtedly made use of Colossians in their teachings. This can be explained in more than one way. It is quite conceivable that Valentinianism and allied sects are a developement from the form of thought which is combated in Colossians; but, if so, it is odd that the Valentinians should have made so much use of a document which was written to refute their predecessors. The truth appears to be that we know just enough about the world of syncretistic religions to realise that it was a curious, amorphous phenomenon, covering many variations, but we do not know much more. We have only a few remnants of what was originally a wide-spread movement and we cannot, without a quite illegitimate amount of guess-work, explain exactly what is the connection between the various points which survived.

The most important thing to note is that the recognition of syncretistic religions under-cuts the older arguments, which talked about a Jewish element in the Colossian heresy. Doubtless there was a Jewish element, but this was merely part of the general nature of the syncretistic religions, which had taken freely from every source that lay ready to their hand.

CHAPTER XIV

The Pastoral Epistles

THE three Epistles, I Timothy, II Timothy and Titus, owe their name of 'Pastoral' to the general nature of their contents, which unites them and separates them from the other Epistles. They all deal, to a greater or a lesser extent, with the duties of the Pastor of a Christian community.[1]

I Timothy purports to be written to Paul's disciple Timothy,[2] who was in charge of the community at Ephesus. Timothy is warned against the heretics who are perverting the Gospel. He is told how worship should be carried out and this is followed by a rather long description of the duties of bishops and deacons,—more especially of the way in which a bishop should combat heresy. Finally, there is a series of special admonishments to various classes in the community: widows, virgins, elders, slaves and rich men. The Epistle concludes with further warnings against heresy.

II Timothy begins with more intimate communications to Timothy, of whom the writer speaks with great affection, reminding him of his youth and education. He then turns to his own life and exhorts Timothy to follow in his footsteps, holding the Faith and withstanding heresy. The preachers of heresy are denounced, Timothy is exhorted once more to be on his guard against them, and the Epistle ends with a short account of the circumstances in which Paul then found himself.[3]

[1] The commentary in the *I.C.C.*, by W. Lock is probably the best in English, but it hardly deals properly with the critical questions. See also P. N. Harrison, *The Problem of the Pastoral Epistles,* and the incidental treatment in Duncan's *St. Paul's Ephesian Ministry*. In German the commentaries in Meyer and Lietzmann are, as usual, the best.

[2] See Acts xvi.1 ff.

[3] He was apparently in prison and not expecting release, as he had previously. Cf. II Tim. iv.6 ff. and 16 ff.

The Epistle to Titus is little more than another version of I Timothy. Titus,[4] who is in charge of the community in Crete, is reminded of the duty of a bishop and warned against heresy. He is given much good counsel with regard to the various classes within the Church. Christian behaviour is compared with that found among heretics, and the Epistle ends with a few personal directions.

It is generally held that these Epistles are not genuine, that is to say, were not written by the author of the earlier Pauline Epistles. The evidence for this is to be found in part in their language and in part in the ideas which they express.

The language is quite different from that of the earlier Epistles and cannot have been used by the same author. It is, however, possible that Paul had a secretary and that the language is that of the secretary rather than of Paul himself.

The ideas expressed in these Epistles are also by no means those of the earlier Pauline Epistles. The most important difference is probably that Faith[5] is no longer the courageous and confident acceptance of Christ, but the holding of opinions. It is, in fact, exactly the kind of Faith which the Epistle of James found unsatisfactory, and if one could suppose that the writer of James knew the Pastoral Epistles and nothing else, his complaint would be entirely intelligible.

The kind of heresy against which the writer fulminates seems to be very much the same as that which is combated in the Epistle to the Colossians, and all that is said on pp. 151-153 will apply with very little change to the heresy of the Pastoral Epistles.

An added difficulty, though not an insuperable one, in connection with the authenticity of these Epistles is that there is certainly no room for them within the framework of the life of Paul as sketched in Acts. It is, however, not impossible that one of two things may have happened:

In the first place, it is by no means certain that Luke gives

[4] Titus is not mentioned in Acts, but is prominent in Corinthians and Galatians.

[5] Cf. p. 160.

at all a full account of the activities of Paul. To us, indeed, it seems that the chronological scheme implied by Acts shows that Paul did not undertake any other large missionary enterprise during the period which Acts covers. This would seem, for instance, to rule out a journey which took him to the island of Crete. But of course it is true that Acts does speak about Ephesus and there is nothing in I Timothy or II Timothy which could not be brought into the framework of the Ephesian ministry mentioned in Acts. Modern scholars are increasingly aware that a comparison of I Corinthians with Acts shows that Luke left out much which one would have thought he must have known concerning Paul's life, and his account of what happened to Paul in Ephesus is probably quite as sketchy as his picture of the Corinthian church.

It is also possible, and this is the traditional view, that Paul was released from his imprisonment in Rome and undertook a further missionary journey to the East, during which he visited Ephesus again and also preached in the island of Crete. For this, of course, there is no evidence whatever except the Pastoral Epistles. If they be accepted as authentic, it is admirable evidence that Paul did undertake this other missionary journey. But, in view of the doubt concerning their authorship, this theory has to be left rather doubtful.

It has often been suggested that some parts of II Timothy may well be genuine.[6] They certainly seem to have a character rather different from the rest of the Pastoral Epistles. It is by no means impossible that there were some Pauline fragments floating about, which were inserted by the writer of the Epistles into the framework of his teaching. The statement of Paul's circumstances during his last days in Rome is of course almost always accepted by those who hold this theory and it must be admitted that it is a very beautiful passage which one would like to accept. But it is not inconceivable that someone else wrote an imaginary picture of Paul in prison and attributed its beautiful words to him. Beautiful writing does not always prove authenticity.

The Pastoral Epistles are largely specimens of didactic lit-

[6] See especially Duncan's *St. Paul's Ephesian Ministry.*

erature, that is to say of the literature which told the Christians of the second generation how they ought to live. These include also such books as the *Teaching of the Twelve Apostles,* the *Didascalia,* the *Epistola Apostolorum,* the *Egyptian Church Orders* now known to be part of the writings of Hippolytus or a document taken over by him, and were finally concentrated into the *Apostolic Constitutions* and so passed into the imposing structure of Church Canon Law.[7]

The Pastoral Epistles imply an organisation which is not quite the same as that with which we become more intimately acquainted in the third and fourth centuries, but is obviously some distance toward reaching that goal. The Church is already governed by bishops and deacons, widows are an established order and many other details are hinted at. Whether the bishop is already the monarchical official which he became in the middle of the second century is not clear, and the study of this subject goes far beyond the limits of an introduction to the New Testament.

But two things are perfectly clear. The organisation implied by the Pastoral Epistles is far more advanced than anything found in the earlier Epistles or the Acts of the Apostles, and it has very little relation to what is implied by the Johannine Epistles. On the other hand, it is markedly close to what we find in the literature of the second century, and clearly belongs to the main stream of the evolution of Church organisation. It should be studied in this light.

[7] See especially A. von Harnack's *Kirchenverfassung,* pp. 49 ff. and the literature to which he refers on p. 1.

CHAPTER XV

Hebrews

THE Epistle to the Hebrews[1] was probably taken into the *Corpus Paulinum* at an early stage in the history of that Corpus, but not at the beginning. It comes second in the list of Epistles in the earliest papyrus[2] (Pap.46). The reason for believing that it was not included in the earliest stage is that, though known in the West, it was there attributed to Barnabas instead of to Paul. Therefore, from the beginning of Christian history its authorship has been disputed, and Origen in the third century was undoubtedly justified when he said that "only God knew" who wrote it.

In modern times various guesses have been made, and the Epistle has been attributed in turn to Apollos, Aquila, Priscilla, Luke, and Clement. Since we know nothing of the writings of Apollos, Aquila, or Priscilla, it is obviously impossible to prove or disprove their authorship. As to Luke, the linguistic evidence of his gospel and of Acts negatives the suggestion that their author wrote Hebrews. The problem of Clement is more complicated. He apparently quotes the Epistle to the Hebrews in his own First Epistle.[3] This might seem to show that he knew Hebrews, rather than that he was its author. But it is also possible that he was merely repeating himself, for the passage which appears to be a quotation from Hebrews is not quoted as such, but is part of the fabric of I Clement.

The form of the Epistle is another curious problem.[4] It

[1] The facts are admirably given in B. F. Westcott's commentary, which is also excellent for exact verbal exegesis. A. Nairne's commentary is perhaps the most penetrating in any language, but the writer saw deeply rather than expounded clearly. The chapter in E. F. Scott's *Literature of the New Testament* is very valuable; its only defect is its brevity.

[2] The Chester Beatty Papyrus, published by Sir F. G. Kenyon and classified as P. 46.

[3] See pp. 96 f.

[4] See especially W. Wrede, *Das Literarische Rätsel des Hebräerbriefs.*

begins as a treatise and ends as a letter. An epistle ought to open with some sort of salutation to its readers. Hebrews does not. On the other hand, a treatise ought not to end with greetings to a series of friends. Apparently, either the end or the beginning of Hebrews has been altered by some editor. Which of the two is the more probable has never yet been satisfactorily settled, but most critics argue that the greetings are an addition by a scribe or editor who wished to fit the Epistle into the *Corpus Paulinum* and produce an ending in the same style as that used by Paul. This theory is certainly not impossible and would account for the anomalous construction. If it be accepted, Hebrews should be regarded as a treatise turned into an epistle. It remains, however, curious that, if this be the case, the editor did not go one step further and write a proper epistolary introduction.

It is also doubtful whether the letter was written from Italy or to Italy, for it contains greetings from "those from Italy"; but this can be explained equally well as conveying greetings from persons living in Italy or as from those who had formerly lived there. The generally accepted view that the persons addressed were Hebrews, rather than Gentiles, depends mostly on the title; but there is nothing in the contents to contradict this, and the constant reference to ritual in the Temple and so on suggests that the title is correct. There is, however, nothing to show whether the Hebrews in question are in Palestine, or belonged to the Dispersion, perhaps in Egypt.

The references to the Temple raise an interesting point. If they imply an actual knowledge of the ritual in the Temple, the Epistle must have been written before the memory of the Temple, which was destroyed in A.D. 70, had died out; but it seems equally or even more likely that they are only based on a knowledge of the Septuagint.

The Epistle consists of a long argument to prove the superiority of Jesus, as "the Son," to all possible rivals:

i.2-ii.18. This section shows the superiority of the Son to angels, and ends by declaring that the Son had become human in order to be a "merciful and faithful high priest."

iii.1-x.18. This shows that the priesthood of Jesus is perfect and excels that of the Aaronic priesthood.

These main divisions are broken by homiletic sections, urging the Christian not to be slothful, or negligent to take advantage of their privileges. The dividing lines between the main body of the treatise and the homiletic sections is not always quite clear, but the chief homiletic passages are ii.1-4, iii.12-vi.20, x.19-xiii.21. It must be admitted that this division into theological and homiletical sections is not perfectly satisfactory. There is much theology in the homily, and the homiletic purpose is never far removed from the theology. Nevertheless, the division seems roughly justifiable.

In the homiletic passages two points stand out:

i. The "Faith" which is discussed in Heb. xii is not quite the same as the "Faith" either of James or Paul. For James, Faith is merely intellectual assent; for Paul, it is a confident acceptance of Jesus as the source of new life; for Hebrews it is the courageous following of the call of God, even through suffering and death, as it was followed by the heroes of ancient Israel, and, most perfectly of all, by Jesus, "the leader and completer of faith" (not *our* faith).

ii. In Heb. vi.4 ff. and x.26 ff. it appears that the writer thought that sin after baptism [5] was unforgiveable. It is noteworthy that once more it is the Shepherd of Hermas which takes up this question and introduces the "angel of penance" as a modification of this doctrine, and that there also is a modification of it in I John, which introduces the distinction between 'deadly' and 'venial' sins.[6]

The theological sections are concerned mainly with two controversies. The first section discusses the question of the true nature of Jesus. The earliest and most Jewish answer, that he was the Man who would judge the world, was proving insufficient. It was being replaced by a more "cosmological" view in the later Pauline Epistles. Apparently another answer

[5] See especially H. Windisch, *Taufe und Sünde.*

[6] See p. 172.

seems to have been that Jesus was an angel, a view which Hebrews rejects, and there are other traces of this controversy in early Christian literature. In the Shepherd of Hermas written in Rome about A.D. 140, the Lord is called "Son of God," but also is described as "the most glorious angel" and is perhaps identified with Michael.[7] Moreover, a possible interpretation of the last scene in the Apocalypse seems to identify Jesus with the Angel who is talking to John.[8]

The doctrine which Hebrews supports is a "cosmological" Christology which can be grouped with that of Colossians, Ephesians and the Fourth Gospel, and is markedly Philonic. It is almost a surprise to the reader that the word "Logos," used in John, is not used in Hebrews. But the idea is present,—it is only the word which is missing.

The second and longer theological section discusses the Priesthood of the Son. It invites comparison with Romans, for these two Epistles taken together give us a nearly complete summary of the early Christian position towards Judaism, partly as a system of approach to God through sacrifice, partly as a code of conduct.

This was in many ways the most serious problem which the Church had to meet. The Old Testament was accepted as Scripture, the word of God, the revelation of his will, which should be followed by men. But if that were so, it was difficult to explain why the Christians rejected part of it and why they were so hostile to the Jews who accepted the whole of it. Romans deals with the question of the Law as a code of conduct: Hebrews with it as an exposition of the sacrificial system. Neither seems interested in the problem discussed by the other, and though both are reminiscent of Hellenistic Judaism, Hebrews is far more so than Romans.

The problem of the Old Testament as the divinely ordained code of conduct was complicated. Marcion felt that Paul's teaching completely rejected the Law, a logical enough view but open to the fatal objection that it rejected history.[9] Bar-

[7] See Hermas, *Sim.* viii.3.3 and cf. Lueken, *Michael.*
[8] See Rev. xxii.8 ff.
[9] Cf. F. C. Burkitt, *The Gospel History and its Transmission.*

nabas accepted the Law as an allegory and stigmatised a literal interpretation as the device of the devil,[10] thus taking the position of those Hellenistic Jews whom Philo regarded as reprehensible extremists.[11] But the Church as a whole settled down to accept a distinction most clearly formulated in the Didascalia. According to this, all that part of the Old Testament legislation which comes after the sin of Israel in worshipping the Golden Calf on Sinai is to be regarded as Mishnah (δευτέρωσις, *secundatio*) and as punishment inflicted on the Jews. It does not apply to Christians, and laymen ought not even to read it, but the rest is really Law, and should be observed.

A glance at the Old Testament will show that this is plainly a "way out" and not a very happy one, but it "worked." The truth is that the actual meaning of the Old Testament was on the side of the Jews, with Marcion as the real alternative, but life was on the side of the Christians because the Law was out of date. History with its usual ruthlessness settled the point in agreement with facts rather than with literature and the solution given in the Didascalia has been commonly modified into the distinction between 'ceremonial' and 'moral' law.

The question of sacrifice had confronted Hellenistic Judaism in the Dispersion, before it was faced by the Church. Jews, such as Philo, remote from all possibility of sacrifice in the Temple, spiritualised the whole idea, making its importance lie in the attitude of the worshipper, not in the material object offered; they allegorised and spiritualised the whole idea of sacrifice, so that their religion grew to be independent of the Temple. None has a more grandiose view than the writer of Hebrews. His mysticism is far more Platonic than anything else in the New Testament. To him the invisible world of the immaterial was a very vivid reality, separated from us only by a veil through which Jesus had opened the way by his sacrificial life and death and by his faith, which affirmed the reality of things unseen.

10 See Barnabas, ix.4.

11 See p. 223.

CHAPTER XVI

The Catholic Epistles

THE seven Catholic Epistles or, according to the translation in the King James' Version "The Epistles General" are the two of Peter, the three of John and those of James and Jude. Some have thought that the fact that there are seven is connected with the seven letters to the seven churches in the Apocalypse, but it is probably a coincidence and 'Catholic' [1] or 'General' perhaps means that they are addressed to Christians as a whole rather than to one particular church. This view, however, is contradicted by the contents of the Epistles, some of which (e.g. I Peter) are directed to definite places. It is therefore possible that originally the title 'Catholic' was given to the First Epistle of John and passed to the others as they were added to the collection.

The growth of the collection cannot be traced accurately, but it would seem, from the scattered evidence which we possess, that I John and I Peter belonged to the earliest days and that the others were added at different times and in different places. II Peter is probably the latest and James was accepted in the Western church only at quite a late date.

JAMES

The Epistle of James [2] was recognised as a canonical Epistle in the East earlier than in the West. In its opening verse it is ascribed to James, a servant of God and of the Lord Jesus Christ. This is not distinctive, for the name James was about

1 The word is said to have been originally an astrological term,—that which affected every one, not only individuals.

2 The best editions are J. H. Ropes in the *I.C.C.*, H. Windisch in Lietzmann, and the very conservative but linguistically superb edition of J. B. Mayor, 1892.

as common in those days as it is today. But the tradition of the Church has generally been that the writer of the Epistle was the brother of the Lord and the first head of the Church at Jerusalem.

It is addressed to the twelve tribes of the Dispersion. Considering that the twelve tribes had disappeared many centuries earlier, this cannot have been meant literally; but the question has been raised, yet never solved, as to whether this is merely a symbolic way of referring to Christians as a whole or whether it means Christians who had been converted from Judaism.

It consists in the main of a series of moral instructions which are arranged with no special sequence. Three or four topics recur: patience in time of distress, the value of works as opposed to faith, respect for the poor, the danger of speaking evil and the need for humbleness. Of these, the two which are expressed with the greatest emphasis are the preference of the writer for works as a sign of religion, and his objection to the evil practices of the rich. It should also be noted that the writer is still looking forward to the speedy coming of the Lord and, like the First Epistle of John, he implies that the Church was much disturbed by internecine quarrels.

The point which stands out most clearly in the Epistle is that it regards salvation as due to works,[3] and implicitly rejects the Pauline or Johannine notion that Christians are persons who have attained an entirely new and different nature from other people. In this respect, it is completely Jewish, perhaps the most Jewish book in the New Testament, its only possible rival for that distinction being the Apocalypse.

It is quite impossible to fix any date for the letter. It is of such a nature that, so far as its contents go, it might, as has been said, have been written any time from the second century B.C. to the eighteenth century A.D. To us it would seem to imply a period when the teaching of Paul was not yet universally accepted by all Christians, and therefore cannot be placed at too late a date. On the other hand, the allusions to rich men in the Church are not very consistent with an extremely early

[3] James ii.14 ff.

date, so that there is a good deal to be said for the point of view of most critics, who think that it was probably written about the end of the first century.

The question has sometimes been raised whether it is a Christian document at all. Of course, in its present form it contains obvious allusions to Christianity, but they are extremely few and the Epistle is not much changed if they be excised. Thus, though it can never be proved, there is always something to be said for the theory of Spitta,[4] that we have here a Jewish document that has been Christianised by a few additions.

I PETER

According to the address, the author of this Epistle was St. Peter,[5] writing to Christians of Pontus, Galatia, Cappadocia, Asia and Bithynia, and the implication probably is that he intended the Roman provinces of those names. The Christians are described as "sojourners of the dispersion" which might suggest Jewish Christians, but more probably the word "dispersion" is used to describe all Christians, in the same way as "pilgrims who are seeking a city." [6] The general background of the Epistle is that Christians are subject to ever-increasing persecution, and that they must stand fast. The duties of various classes—parents, husbands, wives, masters, slaves—are enumerated, but always with the idea of persecution in the background. This point is essential in the attempt to fix the date and authorship of the Epistle. The most significant verses are iv.12-19, which say that Christians must be careful not to suffer as murderers or thieves or malefactors generally, but if they are attacked "for the sake of the name," that is as Christians, they must count it a privilege.

The natural date for an authentic Epistle of Peter referring to persecution would be in the days of the persecution of

[4] F. Spitta, *Der Brief des Jacobus,* 1896.

[5] The best edition is that of H. Windisch in Lietzmann's *Handbuch;* a modern English commentary is needed.

[6] Heb. xi.15 ff.

Nero,[7] in which tradition says that Peter was put to death (A.D. 64). Moreover, the language of these Epistles can be made to fit fairly well into the framework of what we know, and it is not very much, of the Neronic persecution.

According to Tacitus, who is our only source of solid information, Nero accused the Christians of having set fire to the city and afterwards it was regarded as sufficient to prove a man guilty of a capital offence if he were shown by his own confession, or otherwise, to be a Christian, because the church as a whole was responsible for arson. It is clear that this could be fitted into I Peter, or I Peter into it, because the Epistle is quite ambiguous as to whether Christians are already being persecuted "for the sake of the name," or whether that is only something that the writer sees coming. It must, however, be admitted that the more obvious meaning of the letter is that the writer knows that Christians can be indicted merely because they are Christians, but that this does not always happen.

The really serious objection to the Neronic date is that there is no reason to suppose that the persecution in the time of Nero was anything except a local one in Rome. That it had spread to Pontus, Asia, Bithynia, Cappadocia and Galatia is an unwarranted assumption. For this reason, it has often been suggested that the letter belongs to the beginning of the second century when, in the time of Trajan in the governorship of Pliny,[8] we know that Christians were indicted "for the sake of the name" and that to be, or to have been a Christian was regarded in Bithynia as a capital offence. Of course, if this be so, the letter cannot have been written by Peter. As a third alternative, it was suggested by Ramsay and others that the letter belongs to the time of Domitian and that Peter may have escaped, in spite of the tradition, from being put to death under Nero. This is extremely improbable; the date under Domitian seems to combine all the difficulties of the other

[7] See W. M. Ramsay, *The Church in the Roman Empire,* Th. Mommsen, *Römische Strafrecht* and his *Die Rechtsverhältnisse des Apostels Paulus, Z.N.T.W.*, II (1901), pp. 81 ff. and E. T. Merrill in his *Essays in Early Christian History,* 1924.

[8] Pliny's *Letters,* x.96-97.

views. Moreover, there is very little real evidence that there was a persecution in the time of Domitian.[9]

It seems that the real choice is between accepting the Petrine authorship, thus ascribing the Epistle to a date in the time of Nero, or putting it into the days of Trajan and Pliny. Of the two, we are inclined to accept the latter view as the more probable, because it appears to us that the letter as a whole implies a more developed Christianity than is probable in the time of Nero; but the matter is open to much doubt.

JUDE

These few verses attributed to Jude,[10] the brother of James, cannot be dated with any certainty, or ascribed to a known person. They are an attempt to encourage Christians to hold the faith delivered to them against those who, though appearing to be Christians, have in practice denied the Lord.

It is interesting that, in warning his hearers against the fate reserved for those who have done this, the author quotes Enoch. This is the most important direct evidence which we possess that the Book of Enoch was widely read in Christian circles.

There has been and always will be considerable controversy and discussion as to the identity of the heretics described in this Epistle. Obviously the writer regards them as immoral in life and erroneous in thought. But that is not sufficient to identify them with any known body of heretics, and to call them Gnostics is merely *obscurum per obscurius.*

II PETER

The popularity of Jude is best illustrated by the fact that at a later date some unknown writer took practically the whole of the Epistle and incorporated it into a larger whole which he attributed to the Apostle Peter. Very few scholars today think that there is any possibility that the letter was written

[9] See especially the excellent article by Merrill, op. cit. pp. 148 ff.
[10] See H. Windisch's commentary in Lietzmann's *Handbuch.*

by the Apostle.[11] Among other things, the way in which it refers to Paul's "Epistles" is almost sufficient to show that it belongs to a later date, and the most popular period for dating is the middle of the second century. The background of the Epistle is much the same as that implied by Jude, though it is remarkable that the writer leaves out the references to Enoch and particularly emphasises his opposition to those who do not believe in the coming of the Lord. He is himself convinced that the End is at hand, though it will come suddenly and unexpectedly.

THE EPISTLES OF JOHN

It is probable, according to modern scholars, that the three Epistles of John [12] are the work of the author of the Fourth Gospel. There is no absolute unanimity on this point, but a preponderance of opinion. It is, therefore, extremely important that the two shorter ones, the second and third, begin with an inscription of the Epistle to "the Elder who lived in Ephesus."

Assuming that the three Epistles belong together, it is probably better to begin with the shorter ones. They indicate that the Church is facing the difficult problem of how to deal with traveling Christians. Ought they to be entertained by the Church or not?

The most interesting sidelight on this question is provided by the treatise of Lucian on the death of Peregrinus.[13] This delightful essay describes the possibly imaginary, possibly partly actual career of a man whose chief object in life was to avoid doing any work,—a type which does not wholly belong to past centuries. He discovers that a very easy living can be made by one who pretends to be a Christian and goes from city to city explaining Christian doctrine to the churches. Ultimately he comes to grief. But, in the interval, Lucian has

11 See H. Windisch, op. cit.

12 See A. E. Brooke's commentary in *I.C.C.* and H. Windisch, op. cit.

13 Lucian, *De Morte Peregrini,* and cf. S. Dill, *Roman Society from Nero to Marcus Aurelius,* pp. 337 ff.

given us a most interesting proof that the travelling missionary had provided the lazy with a very easy means of livelihood. Especially important is the statement that Peregrinus not only lectured on early Christian literature, but also wrote some of it. Obviously, the Church had to do something to guard itself against impostors of this sort.

In the third Epistle of John we have a little letter which deals most illuminatingly with this problem. The Elder is writing to Gaius and commends him because he has entertained strangers who have visited the Church. At the same time he reprimands Diotrephes, who desires to have complete control over the community and refuses to entertain strangers. The Elder sides with Gaius and threatens to deal severely with Diotrephes.

Nevertheless, it must have been clear that the problem remained. If Christians were to entertain all travellers who shared their belief, it was obviously necessary to guard against impostors. In the second Epistle the rule is laid down that only those should be accepted who believed that Christ was coming in the flesh. The same advice is repeated, but with a remarkable variant, in I John iv.1 ff.: "Beloved, believe not every spirit, but prove the spirits whether they are of God, for many false prophets have gone out into the world. Hereby know ye the spirit of God. Every spirit that confesses that Jesus Christ is come in the flesh is of God, and every spirit that confesses not Jesus is not of God, and this is the spirit of Antichrist whereof ye have heard that it cometh, and now it is in the world already."[14] Obviously, this passage reflects a period in which the hatred of Christians was directed against heretics even more than against heathen or Jews.

In I John the doctrinal test is recognition that Christ was a

[14] There is a most interesting point in the text of this passage, for in some of the oldest Greek and Latin authorities, though not in any of the oldest extant manuscripts, the second paragraph, which says "who confesses not Jesus," is represented by "who destroys Jesus," and this reading appears to have been prevalent in the west and well known in the east down to the fifth century. It is by no means clear what it means, but it is generally supposed to refer to that early form of Docetic heresy which made a separation between the human Jesus and the divine Christ. Though this is not certain, it is the most probable view.

human being of flesh when he came; but in II John it is the recognition that Jesus will be a human being of flesh when he returns. This difference has often been discussed and even explained away, but it has hardly been dealt with satisfactorily.

The test from doctrine had already been adumbrated in I Corinthians, where Paul suggests that, in order to distinguish between a true and a false prophet, the best criterion was whether the alleged prophet would say "Jesus is Lord,"—the earliest form of creed used as a test.[15] In the Epistles of John, this view is merely carried a step further, and the test of a true Christian is whether he says that Jesus Christ has come or is coming in the flesh. This reflects controversy in the early Church as to the true humanity of Jesus, and possibly also as to the resurrection of the flesh, both points which we know from other sources were much disputed.

It is obvious that this method of test would present no difficulties to the clever impostor, and it must have proved quite useless to meet the exigencies of the situation, though it did serve later on to distinguish between the heresy or the orthodoxy of honest people.

An alternative method of solving the problem is indicated in the Gospel of Matthew, which says "Beware of false prophets: by their behaviour ye shall know them." This line of thought was developed a little later in the Shepherd[16] of Hermas and in the Didache by formulating the kind of things which true Christians or true prophets would or would not do. A traveling Christian who asked for lodging should be given it for one night; if he was very tired for two; but if he decided to stay for three days he was a false prophet. A similarly naïve code was worked out in other details in order to test the true or the false Christian by his behaviour. Once more, it is obvious that this method of distinguishing the true from the false would be powerless against any intelligent impostor and the guess may be ventured that in the end the Church naturally came to rely more on the individual judgement of the bishop of the community than on any set system of tests.

[15] Cf. p. 114.

[16] See Hermas, *Mand.* xi. and Did. xi-xiii.

The first Epistle of John is much longer than the other two, though shorter than most of the Pauline Epistles. It is quite impossible to make a scheme of connected reasoning out of it, but it is more important to note that the disjointed observations of which it consists do not sound especially disjointed if it be read aloud with no too intent notice of the connection. The talk slips, as it were, easily from one point to the other and the absence of logical construction is not so obvious as when an attempt is made to form an analysis.

Three motifs seem to run through the whole Epistle:

i. A warning against heresy, described as the "spirit of Antichrist" and the preachers of heresy as themselves Antichrists.[17] No particular explanation is given of what the Antichrists held, but it would appear that they denied that Jesus was the Christ. The sense, however, in which they meant "Christ" is not explained. Obviously, there was a ferment of controversy in the district to which the Epistles belonged and that district is almost certainly Asia Minor.

ii. Another motif in odd contrast to the rather ferocious denunciation of heresy, is that Christians should love one another.[18] Obviously, the writer had felt that Christian love was not sufficiently emphasised in the life of the community.

iii. A very important motif is the question of sin. It is hard to say what was the position of the writer. Did he think that Christians were sinners or not? The best way of proving the difficulty of this point is to read the Epistle through in two different ways, taking the paragraphs as they stand, and reversing the order. If, in this way, you start at the beginning it will appear in the first chapter perfectly obvious that the writer thinks of Christians as sinners who constantly needed forgiveness. But, as the end of the letter is approached, some doubt creeps in, because it sometimes seems that the Christian is regarded as possessed of the ability not to sin, and the Christian who does sin is treated as a sad exception. On the other hand, if the letter be begun at the end, the exact reverse is

[17] Cf. p. 169.
[18] Cf. p. 164.

felt. At first, it would seem clear that the Christian as distinct from other people could be set free from sin and does not sin; if by any chance he does sin, he can be helped by the prayer of other Christians intervening for him. But this prayer will be valid only for sins which are venial, not mortal. Moreover, Christians have an advocate with the Father, Jesus Christ, who is the propitiation for our sins. As the beginning of the Epistle is approached, in this backward reading, it becomes obvious that the exceptions to the rule that Christians do not sin were greater than the writer had admitted.

The whole question is obviously bound up with the problem of sin after Baptism.[19] The original theory was that after Baptism the Christian was set free from sin, and if he did sin there was no forgiveness for him. It was only later that experience showed that Christians did not, in point of fact, abstain from sin after Baptism. It seems to have been the *Shepherd of Hermas,* written in Rome, which opened the way for that subtle change in doctrine and modified the belief that the Church was a society of saints into the more obviously correct one that it was a society of penitents. Finally, in considering this question the difference between Matt. xvi.19 and John xx.22 f. noted on p. 63 should be taken into account. It cannot be accidental that in the Johannine writings, which pay so much attention to the problem of sin, the administrative control given to St. Peter in Matthew is changed to the power of absolution given to the disciples in John.

A part of the business of the Church historian is to estimate how far the survival of Christianity over other sacramental religions was due to the fact that Christians had introduced an educative element, missing in other religions, by their doctrine of penitence and the constant education which was given to the sinner who repented. He was not a saint, but he might become one in the course of time, either in this life or the life to come.

These three motifs,—heresy, Christian love and sin,—will be found interlaced throughout the Epistle and over them all is spread a certain web of mysticism which shows that the most

[19] See H. Windisch, *Taufe und Sünde.*

important thing to the writer was the conscious experience of union with God, which he expressed sometimes as the "life given by Christ," sometimes as the knowledge of God.

For the historian of religion the last point,—the mystic element,—is much the most important. The whole future of religion, both as a subject of speculation and as an approach to reality, depends on the investigation of mysticism. Is it a form of auto-intoxication or a revelation of the truth?

For the historian of the Church a different problem emerges —the evolution of Christianity in Ephesus,—and this is likely to be one of the major problems of future discussion. The foundation of the Ephesian church is obscure. It already existed when Paul reached it, and possibly there is significance in the fact that he gave the spirit to the twelve disciples whom he found.[20]

A little later the speech of Paul at Miletus [21] shows that he foresaw and that the writer of Acts recognised that the church in Ephesus was disturbed by factions.

The same conclusion is to be reached from the Epistles to the Colossians, Ephesians and II Timothy. Whether any of these Epistles, in their present form, were written by Paul himself is open to doubt. But in any case they show that Asian Christianity was soon invaded by a type of teaching which has analogies to "Gnostic" sects of the following century. It contained a doctrine of supernatural beings, good and evil, a Christology far more advanced than anything either proposed or controverted in the earlier Epistles and probably a theory of matter as evil. The latest of these Epistles, II Timothy, states that "all in Asia had deserted Paul," which at least suggests that, in the opinion of the writer, a great part of Asian Christianity had ceased to accept Paul as their leader. At the same time the Epistles are a proof that a Pauline party still existed.

The coming of Johannine Christianity to Ephesus cannot be dated much later than a few years after the Pastoral Epistles.

20 Acts xix.1 ff.
21 Acts xx.18 ff.

Whence did it come? Was it indigenous? Or did it come from Alexandria? Or from Palestine?

There is a tendency to assume that Johannine thought is an outgrowth of Pauline.[22] For this there is no proof. The evidence for distinctively Pauline influence in the Johannine books is as slight as it is in the synoptic gospels, in fact it simply does not exist. The Johannine literature is a monument of sacramental Hellenistic Christianity and of a tradition which there is no valid reason to doubt flourished in Ephesus. It is at least as likely to be a movement parallel to Pauline Christianity as a developement of it. Only the full discussion of this question, which has never yet been adequately faced, can settle the point; but the evidence seems to us to point to the view that it was parallel rather than derived.

Alongside of Johannine Christianity existed other forms. One of these was especially associated with the name of Cerinthus.[23] Its nature is obscure; it may represent the outcome of the heresies combatted in Colossians etc., but there is no clear evidence that this was the case.

Even more obscure is the circle from which came the Leucian Acts of John.[24] They are neither Pauline nor Cerinthian. To the mind of their writer, though not to that of the later church, they probably seemed a legitimate development of Johannine thought. They may represent the Docetic Christianity regarded by John as "Antichrist" and condemned in the Ignatian Epistles, but it must be remembered that when these letters were written, this Docetic Christianity was inside and not outside the Ephesian church. The matter was controversial, and "Ignatius" held strong views on the subject; but the Docetics, like the Judaisers, had not been expelled or discredited when he wrote, though he hoped that they would be.

[22] For instance in P. Gardner, *The Ephesian Gospel,* or in Pfleiderer's *Paulinismus.*

[23] See the excursus in C. Schmidt's *Epistola Apostolorum,* and his "auseinandersetzung" with E. Schwartz.

[24] See Lipsius and Bonnet's text in their *Acta apostolorum apocrypha,* and M. R. James in his *Apocrypha of the New Testament* and in *Texts and Studies,* II, 3 and V, 2.

The *Epistola Apostolorum* [25] has thrown a flood of light on the next step. This document is probably to be dated as written in the year 150 A.D. and shows the harmonisation of three elements in the church. *a.* Johannine, obviously the dominant factor. *b.* A "Twelve Apostles" element, which concedes the first place to John, but claims authority for the Twelve, whose names however are not the same as those in the synoptic tradition. Has the number 'Twelve' any significance in relation to the Christians whom Paul found in Ephesus? *c.* A Pauline element which the writer of the *Epistola* recognises, but only on the distinct understanding that its authority was derived from that of the Twelve. It is important to note that the *Epistola Apostolorum* is one of the earliest documents which shared in the development of the Didactic literature which, through the Didascalia and the Apostolic Constitutions, played so formative a part in ecclesiastical law, customs and institutions.[26] In that development the subordinate position attributed to Paul ultimately disappeared; but it is remarkable that it was present in an Ephesian document of the middle of the second century, which was not held to be heretical but was used as a basis for ecclesiastical teaching.

Finally, some thirty years later than the *Epistola,* the position of Paul was still under fire, for as Tertullian tells us, a "presbyter of Asia" wrote the *Acts of Paul* [27] in honour of the Apostle. These *Acts of Paul* narrowly missed being included in the Canon of Scripture, and seem to represent a victorious effort to exalt Paul above the position conceded to him in the *Epistola Apostolorum.*

To consider the full importance of these factors in the history of Ephesus between the years 50 and 180 A.D. would be obviously out of place here; but their existence cannot be questioned and it has seemed not inappropriate to emphasise

[25] The full title of C. Schmidt's edition is *Gespräche Jesu mit seinen Jüngern nach der Auferstehung,* in *T. U.* XLIII. There is a description of the book in *Beginnings,* Vol. V, pp. 43 ff.

[26] See F. X. Funk's edition of the Apostolic Constitutions, and consult Harnack's *Kirchenverfassung.*

[27] Tertullian, *de Baptismo,* 17. See C. Schmidt, *Acta Pauli.*

the importance of that dimly seen world from which emerged the conquering Logos-Christianity which turned from Paul who had prophesied the coming of the ravening wolves, and in which we vaguely see the figures of Philetus, Hymenaeus, Cerinthus, Leucius Charinus, and the authors of the *Epistola Apostolorum* and the *Acta Pauli*. If we only knew something certain about any of them! We can only read the Acts of John and the *Epistola Apostolorum* and wonder what can be the bridge between them and the Ephesians who sorrowed that they would see the face of Paul no more.

CHAPTER XVII

THE REVELATION

THE book of the Revelation of St. John the Divine[1] has a title which is frequently misquoted and even more frequently misunderstood. In ordinary speech, it is constantly referred to as "Revelations,"—in the plural,—which is a mistake, and the majority of readers probably think that 'divine' means 'god-like.' As a matter of fact, 'Revelation' is in the singular, and classes the book in its proper literary genre, rather than explains its contents. 'Divine' is the old English word for 'Theologian.'

The literary genre to which the Revelation, or, as it is sometimes called, the Apocalypse, belongs is that of Apocalyptic Jewish literature.[2] The ultimate source of Apocalyptic literature is unfulfilled prophecy, and it is probable that the cause of this Christian Apocalypse was the unfulfilled prophecy of the speedy coming of the Kingdom of God and the Judgement conducted by the Son of Man.

It is noticeable that this literature as a whole was pseudonymous,—Enoch, for example, obviously was not written by the man whose name it bears, but it has often been maintained that this Christian Apocalypse is the one exception to the rule. It is hard to see why this view should be held, though, of course it is not impossible.

The traditional view is that the writer is the same as the John who wrote the fourth Gospel and the Johannine Epistles. The improbability of this was perceived as far back as Dionysius of Alexandria. The style of Greek in the Apocalypse is wholly different from and, it may be said, much worse than that in any other book in the New Testament. It may be true

[1] See R. H. Charles in the *I.C.C.*, and Bousset in the Meyer commentary.
[2] See pp. 200 ff.

that it has a grammar of its own, but that grammar is certainly not that of conventional Greek writing. Nominatives following a preposition and similar eccentricities are far too frequent.

It has also been maintained, not without some reason, that the book has an Aramaic or Hebrew original behind the Greek text. Furthermore, many efforts have been made to analyse it into sources. Many of these have been extremely ingenious, none more so than the first, by Vischer.[3] But it cannot be said that any one effort of this kind has carried general conviction. The fact is that all such criticism is, to some extent, an illegitimate use of the fact that there is occasionally a change of topic in the book. It is, of course, possible that the change of topic means a change of source, but this is not necessarily so.

In the same way, by leaving out all the passages which have obviously Christian content, it is possible to arrive at an original Jewish source. But the question remains whether it is legitimate to excise those passages which are contrary to the hypothesis. Our own opinion is that it is not, and that the book was Christian from the beginning, though it is undoubtedly based on Jewish models.

The Book of the Revelation may be divided conveniently into three main portions.

i. First, the seven letters to the churches of Asia with an introduction to them. The *mise en scène* is that John was on the island of Patmos "for the word of God and the testimony of Jesus" and received a vision instructing him to write the letters which follow. The churches are the Greek cities in the province of Asia: Ephesus, Smyrna, Pergamum, Thyatira, Sardis, Philadelphia and Laodicea. These all belong to the Greek population of the province of Asia and the word Asia may be used here in the official sense.

[3] E. Vischer, *Die Offenbarung Johannis, eine jüdische Apokalypse in christliche Bearbeitung,* 1886. It also contains a very valuable "epilegomenon" by Harnack. Inasmuch as Vischer's work was constantly in the mind of later writers such as Charles and Bousset, it is very desirable to read him first,—even though this is a counsel of perfection.

How did John come to be on Patmos? The traditional story, told first by Tertullian,[4] is that the Apostle John, the son of Zebedee, was in Rome, that there the Emperor Domitian sent him to be boiled in oil, but the oil took no effect on him and he was banished to Patmos. Eusebius, telling the same story, says he was released after the time of Domitian and went to live in Ephesus. This is obviously not a story which commands whole-hearted belief.

The letters to the churches present no particular difficulty in content, but the exact meaning of the "angels" of the churches is always a matter for discussion. Perhaps they were the heads of the churches, but a rival and equally probable theory is that they were the heavenly representatives of the churches and that they are being held responsible for what takes place on earth. This would be entirely in line with the general outline of Apocalyptic speeches.

ii. The second part of the book opens with chapter iv and goes down to the end of chapter vi. It begins by showing the vision of heaven, with the twenty-four elders and the four "living creatures" whose characteristics were afterwards taken as the symbols of the four Evangelists. The seer then perceives that there is a book with seven seals, which no one can open until at last the Lamb, who is in some way identified with the lion of Judah, is declared able to break the seals. The seals are then broken, and with each successive seal more and more disasters come upon the earth until after the fourth seal. The first disaster is Conquest, the second is War, the third Famine and the fourth Death, followed by Hell. Each of these is represented by a man riding a horse. The fifth seal represented the souls of the martyrs waiting under the altar for their deliverance; the sixth seal is the story of the sealing of the tribes and a great multitude chosen from among the Gentiles; the seventh [5] (chapter viii.1) introduces a new series of disasters, each heralded by an angel who blows a trumpet.

[4] Tertullian, *De praescrip. Haer.*, 36, and Eusebius *Hist. Eccl.* iii.18 and 20.

[5] Rev. viii.1 ff.

The first trumpet brings fire on earth;[6] the second destruction at sea;[7] the third a falling star,[8] named Wormwood, which poisons all the water on earth; the fourth a number of falling stars and an eagle crying "Woe, woe, woe";[9] the fifth a plague of smoke and locusts which represent the first Woe.[10] The second Woe[11] is a plague of horses with lions' and serpents' tails, headed by four angels who have been previously bound on the bank of the river Euphrates. These introduce an angel with feet like pillars of fire, who is bringing a book which the writer of the Apocalypse is commanded to hear. Then come the measuring of the Temple and two witnesses who are killed. Finally, the seventh trumpet apparently brings the third Woe,[12] but also the triumph of the Kingdom of Christ and the praise offered by the elders.

Much ingenuity has been expended on the attempt to find some meaning in this series of visions. It is very doubtful whether any of it has been successful; they are more likely to represent the general impression of the writer that great tribulation was coming on the earth, which he describes by a number of images taken mostly from other Apocalypses.

iii. The third part of the book begins with chapter xii. It is introduced by the story of a woman who gives birth to a child, which is attacked by the Dragon who is the Devil, but is rescued by being taken up to heaven. Then follows the story of war in heaven and the defeat of the Devil, who goes down to earth and attacks the woman. To help the Dragon there comes a mysterious beast out of the sea,[13] but in chapter xiv we are given a picture of the Lamb and those who are sealed to his worship. It is generally recognised that the child who is born of a woman is the Christ and that the Lamb also rep-

[6] Rev. viii.7.
[7] Rev. viii.8 ff.
[8] Rev. viii.10 ff.
[9] Rev. viii.13.
[10] Rev. ix.1-11.
[11] Rev. ix.13-xi.13.
[12] Rev. xi.15 ff.
[13] Rev. xiii.1 ff.

resents the risen Lord of the Christians, but the identity of the Beast is obscure. Whether it symbolises the power of Rome, or some supernatural power, has been and is likely to be much controverted.

In chapter xiv three angels appear, one of them announcing the Gospel; the second the Fall of Babylon, which obviously means Rome; and the third denouncing those who worship the Beast and blessing the Christian dead especially, apparently, martyrs.[14] There follows the description of the angels who conduct the harvest of the world and the treading of the wine press of the wrath of God.[15] These are succeeded by seven more angels who have the seven plagues which complete the wrath of God. The last plague which comes with the pouring out of the seventh vial of wrath is the Fall of Babylon.[16] This paves the way for another picture, which is a new representation of the Fall of Babylon, the rejoicing over its Fall, and the coming of the End (introduced by the Word of God riding on a white horse), the casting out of the Beast and the False Prophet into the lake of fire, and the Millennium and first Resurrection. After the Millennium,[17] which is the reign of Christ for a thousand years, accompanied by the martyrs who are raised from the dead in order to share in it with him, Satan is loosed for a time, but a great battle [18] leads to his defeat and the end of This Age. The conclusion of the whole is the vision of the Final Judgement by one who sits on the great white throne and of the New World from which Evil and suffering have been abolished.

The date of this curious book is a matter of doubt. Traditionally, it was written in the time of Domitian or of Trajan,[19] but some modern writers are inclined to think that it is much earlier. To us it would seem that no arguments on this ques-

[14] Rev. xiv.13 ff.
[15] Rev. xiv.14-20.
[16] Rev. xvi.17.
[17] Rev. xx.4 ff.
[18] Rev. xx.7 ff.
[19] So Eusebius, who thinks that John survived to the time of Trajan.

tion are anything but precarious. They are discussed in English in R. H. Charles' *Commentary on the Apocalypse* and an excellent exposition of the interpretation of the book can be found in Hastings' *Bible Dictionary* and also in the *Encyclopedia Biblica.*

The value of the book as a contribution to theology, especially Western theology, cannot be overestimated. In our day, both the imagery and the ideas which the imagery represents are largely obsolete, but no one can understand the attitude of mediaeval Christians, especially in the West, unless they realise how important this book was to the ordinary Christian. There have always been a few, such as Origen in the third century and his spiritual descendants through the centuries, who have recoiled from the generally blood-stained nature of the prophecies in this book. But the ordinary Christian took it perfectly literally and seriously for centuries and usually thought that it was all a prophecy of what was still to come.

For the scholar today the question is, largely, at what point the delineation of the past ceases and that of the future begins. Are, for instance, the first twelve chapters to be regarded as a picture of the past; the birth of the child and his taking up into heaven as a representation of the story of Jesus; and the rest of the book as portraying the immediate future? That is, at least, not impossible.

The importance of the book for the history of art should also be noted. It is curious that there are very few manuscripts in Greek with illustrations of the Apocalypse,[20] but almost all Eastern churches, if they have any decoration at all, are largely embellished by terrifying scenes representing its more spectacular episodes. Greek artists and Italian artists in the Renaissance were especially fond of representing the horrible aspect of the Beast and of the Dragon. In the West, the great commentary of Beatus [21] on the Apocalypse was not infrequently decorated by illustrations, many of which have been published,

[20] See H. R. Willoughby, *The Elizabeth Day McCormick Apocalypse,* J B L 1933, pp. 89 ff.

[21] See H. A. Sanders *Beati in Apocalypsim, libri xii,* American Academy in Rome, 1930.

and in the Middle Ages the genius of Dürer in Nuremberg [22] and, a little later, of the French artist Duvet, contributed a series of remarkable illustrations of the Apocalypse, especially of the earlier part of it. Later on, a more symbolic interpretation was adopted by Blake, and many other imaginative artists have tried to illustrate a book which is in some respects the exact opposite of the immaterial reality of the philosophers, for the world of the Apocalypse is imaginable, but quite inconceivable.

[22] See especially the beautiful reproductions by Schram, unfortunately extremely expensive, and the cheaper collection known as *Klassiker der Kunst: Dürer.*

PART TWO

THE BACKGROUND OF THE NEW TESTAMENT

CHAPTER XVIII

The Jewish Historical and Political Background

TO understand the New Testament properly, it is well to remember that it is not, like the Old Testament, the story of a people living in a corner of the western edge of the Semitic world, but of a group—not a people—which started from the eastern edge of the Greco-Roman world and spread all over the west. In the Old Testament the background is the world of Babylon or Persia, but in the New Testament it is the Roman Empire. The process of Hellenisation, to say nothing of Romanisation, was by no means complete in the first century, but many Jews were already looking towards the west and not towards the east.

Seven hundred years earlier Syria, Palestine and Trans-Jordan (Peraea) had been inhabited by a number of Semitic tribes,—Aramites, Phoenicians, Moabites, Ammonites, Edomites, Ishmaelites, Ephraimites and Judahites,—with a non-Semitic race, the Philistines, holding the coast from Carmel to Egypt. These all lived on terms of the most neighbourly enmity, which was broken up when the Assyrians and Babylonians conquered the country. A little later, the Persians took over the whole district, which was divided into Persian satrapies. From this time on, the Jews, who had returned from exile, occupied Jerusalem and a mixed race, the "people of the land," [1] with whom the Jews refused to have friendly relations, occupied the rest. Their world was still Semitic-speaking and Semitic-thinking, for, though the Persians were Iranians and not Semites, the commercial language of their

[1] The *Am ha Arez.* For this phrase in the acquired sense of a non-observant Jew, see Strack-Billerbeck, II, pp. 494 ff. and G. F. Moore in *Beginnings,* I, Appendix E, pp. 439 ff.

empire was always that which they had inherited from Babylonia.[2]

Within the span of a single life Alexander's conquests changed the whole situation. The Greeks came pouring across Asia Minor, through Syria into Egypt in one direction, and as far as the boundaries of India in the other. Though the Aramaic which the Babylonian empire had spoken did not die out it had, from that moment, a serious rival in Greek,—so that Greek thought, Greek customs, Greek law, and above all the Greek language gradually supplanted the inheritance of Babylon.

But the successors of Alexander were not able to work together. They incessantly quarreled, and the result, among other things, was a rivalry between the house of Seleucus in the north and that of the Ptolemies in Egypt.[3] Palestine fell first under the rule of the Ptolemies, who left the Jews largely alone, and afterwards under that of the House of Seleucus which did not.

The Ptolemaic kings encouraged the growth of the Jewish community in Egypt. In Alexandria it was allowed to have its own laws, its own magistrates and its own quarter of the city. It learnt to use Greek, wrote books in Greek, and produced a translation of the Old Testament into Greek (the Septuagint) which differed from our present Hebrew both in text and in contents.[4] Moreover, it became Hellenised in thought, though it will always be a problem how far this Hellenisation spread.

So long as the Ptolemies held Palestine the Jews in Jerusa-

[2] This was Aramaic. The Jews still retained Hebrew for religious purposes, but only for them.

[3] See *Cambridge Ancient History*, Vols. VI and VII and the full bibliography given in them.

[4] See H. B. Swete's *Introduction to the Old Testament*, Cambridge, 1900; the various books and articles of P. de Lagarde and A. Rahlfs, A. E. Brooke and N. Maclean's *The Old Testament in Greek*, Cambridge, 1906, and the article on the Septuagint by E. Nestle in Hastings. There is a growing literature on Ptolemaic history, to which the *Cambridge Ancient History* provides an adequate introduction, but a student of Judaism in this period should read especially the *Letter of Aristeas* and *III Maccabees*.

lem were reasonably happy; the kings of the house of Seleucus,[5] on the other hand, as the heirs of Alexander in Syria, endeavoured to go as far as possible in introducing Greek customs and the Greek language throughout the East. They imposed Greek civilisation on Jerusalem, without waiting for the Jews to ask for it, and for a time had some success. But Antiochus Epiphanes endeavoured to force the pace too rapidly, and was handicapped by war and sedition. The result was that he lost his temper at Jewish ingratitude and the Jews lost theirs at Greek oppression; persecution and rebellion mutually encouraged each other.

So long as Antiochus lived, he was able to hold down the Jews by force, but his immediate successors were incompetent and a successful rebellion under the Maccabees first detached Judaea and Galilee and ultimately resulted in the gradual break-up of the whole territory of the Seleucids, to the accompaniment of disorder and civil war. The Maccabees not only succeeded in reconquering for the Jews the Jewish portions of Palestine, including Jerusalem, but destroyed or conquered most of the purely Greek cities such as Samaria, Caesarea (Stratonis Turris) and the Decapolis, and tyrannised over the non-Jewish inhabitants of Palestine.

The inability of the Ptolemies and the house of Seleucus either to control the mixed populations of the East, to conquer one another or to co-operate with one another, opened the way for the Roman Empire to inherit their property.[6] The will of Attalus and the genius of Pompey, Caesar, Antony and Augustus combined to make the Roman Empire the sole legatee of Alexander's conquest.

The Maccabees soon saw their chance of fishing in the troubled waters, solicited alliance with Rome,[7] and took part in the quarrels of the various Roman parties, endeavouring to divine and help the probable winner. When Pompey entered

[5] See E. Bevan, *The House of Seleucus;* the articles on the various members of the dynasty in Pauly-Wissowa and E. Schurer, *G.J.V.*

[6] See Mommsen's *History of Rome,* or, as a shorter statement, *Beginnings,* Vol. I, 9 ff.

[7] See Josephus, *Antiq.* xii.10.6.

Palestine in 63 B.C. he recognised the Maccabaean kingdom, but freed the Greek cities of Palestine from its rule.

Then followed a strange episode. A man named Antipater, half-Jew half-Arab, made himself the intelligently unscrupulous agent of the Romans and indispensable to the last of the Maccabees. His son, Herod,[8] inherited his ability and convinced Augustus that, although he had supported Antony, he would be a faithful and valuable ally to any one who was successful. A man of infinite talent and unwearied energy, untrammeled by scruples, he was entrusted by Rome with the government of all Palestine. He did not continue the policy of the Maccabees, but adopted that of the Romans, and under his rule Greeks and Jews were equally protected in their own domains.

The animosity not unnaturally felt towards Herod by Josephus and later on by Christian writers has caused many to overlook the great qualities which he showed as a governor. With far-sighted vision, though not without brutality, he suppressed banditry and rebellion and bestowed equal benefits on the Jews in Jerusalem and on the Greeks elsewhere, realising that the business of a ruler of Palestine was to be a Jew in Jerusalem and a Greek in Samaria or Caesarea. He restored Jerusalem to something approaching the glory which it had in the time of the Persians. He greatly enlarged the Temple, adding to it among other things a tower for the garrison, overlooking the whole area, and on the other side of the city built a palace for himself and his soldiers at the spot which is now police headquarters in Jerusalem. He rebuilt Stratonis Turris on the coast and Samaria in the hill country, calling the former Caesarea and the latter Sebaste, in honour of Augustus. In Sebaste he erected a temple to the Emperor and apparently encouraged the worship of Kore.

[8] See Appendix A (p. 253) for the family tree of the Herods. For a different view of Herod see Klausner, *Jesus of Nazareth*, Book II. We cannot ourselves see the evidence in favour of a Palestine which was ever completely Jewish; Herod and the Romans doubtless undid much of the Maccabean work, but there was always a large non-Jewish population which the Maccabees oppressed and Herod governed with reasonable justice.

That this policy secured for him tolerance rather than friendship from both Greeks and Jews was inevitable, but few rulers were ever more successful than he in keeping Palestine in a condition of relative peace, without injuring the reasonable rights of either of the hostile races.

To what extent Herod was in any sense subject to the Roman governor of Syria is open to question.[9] So long as he was successful (and he was throughout his life) he was probably not interfered with, but it may be guessed rather than proved that the Legatus of Syria was his immediate guide, even if not his official superior. In any case, the Legatus of Syria lived a long way off. Syria was an immense province and at the time of Herod, the Romans were more concerned with the northern part of it and with Cilicia, which was attached to it as part of the same province, than they could be with Palestine, which was nominally independent.

With the death of Herod the Great, a new period began. The Romans were forced to choose between permitting internecine strife between Herod's children, of whom he had allowed a few to survive, or of changing the constitution of Palestine. They naturally chose the latter alternative. They abolished the title of King and established one son, Archelaus, as the Tetrarch of Judaea and Samaria, and another, Antipas (the Herod of the greater part of the Gospel story) as Tetrarch in Galilee and Peraea (Trans-Jordan). Archelaus was a failure and in his place a subordinate Roman official with the title of Procurator was sent to take charge of Judaea and Samaria. There were a succession of these officials and at the time of Christ Pontius Pilate was in power.[10]

The Procurator was in fact the High Commissioner of the period and had the same problems to deal with. He had at his disposal a body of troops including legionaries and auxiliaries. These were the Palestinian police of the period and probably

[9] The relation of the Procurator to the governor of Syria is open to discussion, see especially Mommsen, *Rom. Gesch.* ed. 10, Vol. V, p. 509.

[10] It is unfortunate that no Procurator left his memoirs for posterity. An admirable attempt to supply this deficiency has been made by W. P. Crozier in his *Letters of Pontius Pilate*.

there was a centurion (the equivalent of a sergeant) in control of each of the small districts. The Procurator appointed the High Priest,[11] in fact if not wholly in theory, and managed the taxes by means of men who 'farmed' them, so that there was a multitude of collectors, the 'Publicans' of the Gospels. The taxes were partly 'tribute' to Rome, partly 'octroi' for local use.[12]

Thus it came to pass that in the time of Jesus both the Procurator of Judaea, Pontius Pilate, and the Tetrarch of Galilee, Herod Antipas, controlled districts inhabited partly by Jews, partly by non-Jews (who were then called Greeks and now Arabs).[13] Rome expected its delegates to govern in such a way that there should be as few disturbances as possible, but the Jews were at least partially conciliated by being allowed a very large degree of freedom to manage their own affairs. They were curiously divided and their organisation in Jerusalem differed from that in other places.

In Jerusalem, the Temple was the centre of Jewish life. It was nominally under the control of the High Priest, but in practice the High Priest was the temporary representative of a group of great families [14] who quarrelled among themselves,

[11] The legitimate Aaronic line had disappeared at the time of the captivity when the High Priest went to Leontopolis where a Jewish temple existed for many years. The High Priest in Jerusalem in the Roman period was appointed by being given the official robes. These were in the tower Antonia and were given to the selected person by the Keeper of the Robes, who was sometimes the Procurator and later the representative of the Herod family,—Agrippa I, Herod of Chalcis and finally Agrippa II.

[12] The point was that there was a whole army of collectors who were given districts from which to collect a fixed amount, with the privilege of keeping all they could get above this amount. Each man subdivided his district and sold the privilege of collection. Thus had any "publican" taken literally John the Baptist's admonition, (not to collect more than was assigned to him) he would have starved.

[13] They were not Greeks then, nor are they Arabs now, but the name followed the language, not the race, and Greek was then what Arabic is now.

[14] The Boethusians, the family of Ananos and the family of Phabi were perhaps the chief. They are spoken of with enmity in the Talmud, e.g. Pesahim 57 a: "They are high priests and their sons are 'sagans' and their servants beat the people with sticks."

but cooperated against all others. These families are often referred to as "the High Priests" and were undoubtedly the richest and most powerful of the Jews. But they were unpopular. They made the Temple a source of wealth by exploiting the rule that sacrifices should be only of perfect animals, which were to be bought from them, and that alms should be paid in Jewish money, which they provided in exchange for Roman coins, charging of course a commission on the exchange. They also levied a tax on all Jews for the upkeep of the Temple which probably included at least some of their own houses. They were inclined to "Hellenise," accept Greco-Roman customs, and be friendly with the Romans. This was, in chief part at least, their ruin. As has always been the case in the East, the people submitted to extortion but rebelled against civilisation.

In addition to his position in the Temple, the High Priest, whose office was no longer held for life, but only during efficient service, was at the head of the Sanhedrin, a Greek word (*synedrion*) [15] meaning 'council'. It was composed, theoretically at least, of seventy members chosen from among the priests, scribes and elders. We know less about it than might be desired, because our information is derived from the Mishna, which was compiled two or three generations after the destruction of Jerusalem, and is primarily a legislative rather than an historical document; it gives, at least in some points, a picture of an ideal Sanhedrin, not of one which ever existed.

In other places where Jews were dominant there may have been minor Sanhedria, but the real centres of local government and of Jewish life generally were the synagogues, the origin of which is not quite clear.[16] They were not only churches, but also law courts, and were controlled by the

[15] A full statement of the tradition about the Sanhedrin may be found in the article on that subject by Bacher in Hastings' *Dictionary of the Bible*. The possibility that Herod appointed a secondary assembly in Jerusalem, with the same title, is found in Otto's article in Pauly-Wissowa. See also Strack-Billerbeck and George Foot Moore's *Judaism*.

[16] For the history, organisation, officials and religious services of the Synagogues there is nothing comparable to Strack-Billerbeck, IV, pp. 115-414. Cf. also G. F. Moore, *Judaism*, I, pp. 281-307.

Rabbis, who were learned in the Law of Israel. In Jerusalem, they were less obviously powerful, and much less wealthy than the priests, for though there were many synagogues in Jerusalem, each with its own rulers, they were overshadowed by the Temple and the Sanhedrin. Outside of Jerusalem, they were really the governing bodies of the Jews, and when the Temple and the Priesthood disappeared in the ruin of Jerusalem, the synagogues continued their work with but little change. Judaism discovered that the Temple and the Priesthood had only an emotional value, and that the Law was an adequate substitute for the sacrifice in the Temple.[17]

Apart from the functional difference between the Priests and the Rabbis (Scribes), the Jews, according to Josephus, recognised in the first century three chief political or theological parties, the Sadducees, the Pharisees, and the "fourth Philosophy." The Gospels mention one other, the Herodians (Mark iii.6 and xii.13). Apart from these references, we know nothing about the last.

The Sadducees,[18] whose name may or may not mean 'the followers of Zadok,' were believers in the Law, but not more than the Law. They rejected later developments of Judaism, such as a belief in a resurrection or in angels (cf. Mark xii.18 and Acts xxiii.8).

Most of the priests belonged to this party, which perished with the destruction of the Temple. The generally hostile references in the Talmud suggest that the Sadducees were often Hellenisers, accepting much Greek thought, but it should be remembered that statements about the Sadducees from this source are peculiarly untrustworthy because in the Middle Ages the Censor forbade all hostile reference to Christians and in order to cover their meaning, the Jewish scribes often referred to "the Sadducees" statements which had been originally

[17] Cf. the beautiful story that when leaving Jerusalem Jokanan ben Zakkai said that henceforth the Jews had nothing save the Almighty and his Law—but that would suffice.

[18] See the many references to Sadducees in Strack-Billerbeck, especially in IV, pp. 335-352, and G. F. Moore, *Judaism,* especially I, 68, but see also his index.

intended to apply to the Christians. It is, therefore, not always certain whether any one allusion to the Sadducees really applies to them.

The Pharisees were probably the most influential party outside Jerusalem. Their exact origin is not known, but they first appear in the time of the Maccabees and seem to be in some way connected with those who were known as the Chasidim or 'holy ones.'[19]

The word 'Pharisee' is probably connected etymologically with the verb that means to separate, but in what sense it is not clear. The purpose of the Pharisees was to insist upon a life in accordance with the Law, and they devoted much time to interpreting the difficulties in its practice. Their decisions were preserved either by memory or in writing and were formulated in the second century as the Mishna (literally 'repetition') or 'Explanation of the Law.' This again was expounded by still later Rabbis and became the basis of the Talmud, preserved in two forms (the Jerusalem and the Babylonian) which are our main source of information for orthodox Judaism. None of these rules were regarded as additions to the Law, but as explanations intended to render it easier for an ordinary man to avoid transgression.[20]

Those who regarded the Law as positive and found pleasure in living according to it, naturally welcomed the teaching of the Pharisees; and some of these, such as Johanan ben Zacchai, seem to have been men of great spiritual beauty.[21] For those who regarded the Law as chiefly negative,—a series of prohibitions,—the Pharisaic amplifications must have been intolerable. It should, however, be remembered in using the Talmud that orthodox Judaism as we have known it since the fourth century is not necessarily identical in all respects with the Judaism which was current in Galilee, or even in Jerusalem, in the first century.

[19] See Strack-Billerbeck IV, 334-352.

[20] See *Beginnings*, Vol. I, pp. 436 ff.

[21] See C. G. Montefiore's beautiful essay on the Spirit of Judaism in *Beginnings*, Vol. I.

It is usually held to be probable that the *Psalms of Solomon* would be more correctly entitled the *Psalms of the Pharisees*.[22] This curious document is remarkable for two things: *a.* it is the most explicit statement (Ps. Sol. xviii) extant of the "Messianic" expectation of a Davidic prince in the first century before Christ, *b.* it constantly distinguishes between the "righteous" and the "sinners," meaning Pharisees and non-Pharisees. This affords an interesting comment on the "sinners" of the gospels.

The 'fourth Philosophy' is a term found in Josephus. He obviously used 'philosophia' in the sense of 'party' (an interesting comment on the deterioration of the word) and by 'fourth Philosophy' he meant the supporters of Judas of Galilee, in the time of the census of Quirinius A.D. 6, and their successors. Agreeing with the Pharisees in general they shared the Apocalyptic hope for a "good time" for the Jews [23] and tried to hasten its coming. They thought it wicked to acknowledge any ruler except God, and advocated strong action to eject the usurping Romans.

From the point of view of Roman officials, the most dangerous phenomenon in Palestine was the existence of this class of patriots. They became prominent in the days immediately preceding and during the Jewish wars, and the name of "Zealot" was given to one part of them,–the followers of John of Gischala. The members of the Patriotic party clashed with the priestly party, especially in regard to Rome. The High Priests were, of course, not wholly favourable to the rule of Rome or of Herod, but, so long as they were allowed to manage the Temple in their own way and accumulate money, they were not actively hostile to the government and cooperated with it in order to keep the people in order. For that reason, in the days immediately preceding the war, the systematic and steady assassination of the Priests was one of the main features of the policy of the Patriotic party.

22 See Ryle and James, *Psalms of the Pharisees,* and G. B. Gray in R. H. Charles, *Apocrypha and Pseudepigrapha of the Old Testament,* Vol. II, pp. 625 ff.

23 See also p. 204.

The party of the 'Herodians' is not mentioned except in the gospels.[24] The termination of the word (*-ianos*) certainly means "partisan of," but we have only guesses to tell us anything more about the Herodians. Probably they were those who preferred the House of Herod to the Procurator of the Emperor, and ultimately succeeded in securing Herod Agrippa I as king of Judaea. But there is no evidence.

[24] Mark iii.6, xii.13, Matt. xxii.16.

CHAPTER XIX

THE INTELLECTUAL LIFE OF JUDAISM IN PALESTINE

THE sources for our knowledge of this subject are the synoptic gospels, Josephus, the Talmud and the Apocalyptic writings. Each of these is valuable and the final picture of the intellectual life of Judaism must contain elements drawn from them all, but their emphasis is different and the first step is a summary of the value and prejudices of each separately:

i. The synoptic gospels share with Josephus the advantage of date. They were written not long after and not much before A.D. 70. The Jerusalem of the days when the Temple was still standing and the High Priests were in power was known to the authors, either directly or indirectly, but they were definitely hostile to orthodox Jews, especially the Pharisees, and human nature being what it is, undoubtedly magnified the faults and were blind to the virtues of their opponents.

ii. Josephus [1] is the exact opposite of the men who wrote the gospels. He was a Jew trying to present Judaism in a favourable light. Hence his great book, *The Antiquities of the Jews,* must be read with some caution. On points of fact his description does not differ greatly from that in the gospels, but his criticism does. Like the gospels, he recognises the two parties of Sadducees and Pharisees, but he clearly prefers the latter. He has no love for the Priests and is hostile to the Herods

[1] The best edition is Niese's and the Loeb Classical Library provides an excellent translation and valuable notes. See also H. St. J. Thackeray, *Josephus, the Man and the Historian,* R. Laqueur, *Der jüdische historiker Flavius Josephus.* Josephus probably also wrote an Aramaic version, and the Slavonic version, which differs greatly from the Greek, has been thought to preserve traces of the Aramaic or to have been made from it. This seems to us very improbable, but the Slavonic Josephus is a curious problem.

(except Agrippa II) and to the Procurators. Just as Luke, in writing Acts, was interested in Christian propaganda, so Josephus wrote propaganda for the Rabbis who, after the fall of Jerusalem in 70, had become the Jewish national leaders. The almost complete omission of eschatological or Messianic elements, so prominent in the Gospels, is a striking feature of his work. Clearly Josephus did not himself believe these things and was not anxious to let the Romans know that many of his countrymen did. In this respect, he was probably a fair representative of the educated Jews of his own time.

iii. *Talmud* means 'instruction' and the mass of literature known by this term was collected in two recensions,—the Babylonian and the Palestinian. It is not all contemporary but consists of discussions which lasted for some two centuries and arose in the following manner [2]:

In the synagogues of the first and second centuries the Law was expounded in one of two alternative ways—by comment on a portion of Scripture read each day, in the order which is still followed, and by comment on subjects, arranged in a system ascribed to Akiba. This formal exposition of both types was written down and has survived in the treatises on Exodus (the *Mekilta*), Leviticus (the *Siphra*) and Numbers-Deuteronomy (the *Siphre*) which follow the first method, and in the *Mishna* and *Tosephta* which follow the second. In addition to the official *Mishna,* composed by Judah "the Patriarch" about A.D. 200, there were a number of similar works which are known to us only by quotations in the Talmud, which refers to them as *Baraita,* or traditions extraneous to the official *Mishna.*[3]

[2] The following paragraphs are a necessary compression of a difficult and tangled subject. It should be studied further in G. F. Moore, *Judaism,* Vol. 1, pp. 125-216, in the article by S. Schechter in the supplementary volume of Hastings' *Dictionary of the Bible,* pp. 57 ff., and in H. L. Strack, *Einleitung in den Talmud,* 1894. There is an English translation of the Talmud by Epstein and of the Mishna by Danby, and the French works of M. Schwab, and the German ones of L. Goldschmidt, A. Wünsche, and H. L. Strack are of great value to those, who, like ourselves, find the reading of the Talmud in the original to be beyond their powers.

[3] The earlier Rabbis quoted in the Talmud are called *Tannaim* (makers of tradition) the later ones *Amoraim* (lecturers). The legal matter is

After the compilation of the *Mishna,* however, Jewish scholars continued to discuss both it and other traditions and these later discussions, together with the *Mishna,* form the *Talmud,* of which the Palestinian recension came to an end in the fifth century and the Babylonian fifty to seventy years later. But discussion did not cease even with the Talmuds and further compilations were made between the fifth century and the Middle Ages. These are the *Midrashim* and are mainly homiletic. Roughly speaking, they represent the preachers in the synagogue, while the *Talmud* is the work of the great schools of the learned.

From this short sketch of Rabbinical sources, it will be seen that they are relatively useless for the discovery of historical facts, which would be valuable for Christian investigators, or for a description of the first century. The Rabbis seem to have been singularly uninterested in events; even the revolt of Bar-Cochba in the time of Hadrian is unmentioned.

iv. The Apocalyptic literature represents a theory of the past and a forecast of the future. It arose during the Greek period, chiefly in order to explain the non-fulfilment of prophecy. Just as the difficulties of the Law produced the *Mishna,* so the difficulties in the Prophets produced the Apocalyptic literature.

This consists, in the main, of *Daniel,* the *Assumption of Moses,* the Ethiopic *Enoch,* the Slavonic *Enoch,* the *Apocalypse of Ezra* (*II Esdras* iv-xiv in the King James' Version and also frequently quoted as *IV Ezra*), the Syriac *Apocalypse of Baruch,* the Greek *Life of Adam,* the Latin *Life of Adam and Eve.* To these may be added the *Psalms of Solomon* (often quoted as the *Psalms of the Pharisees*), *Jubilees,* the *Testament of the Twelve Patriarchs* and the *Sibylline Oracles.*[4]

Halaka (rules to go by), the anecdotal *Hagada* (teaching). Finally, it should be noted that *Gemara* is a synonym for "Talmud," used in relatively modern Jewish books in deference to Christian censors, who were suspicious of the very word Talmud (see also p. 194).

[4] For a convenient collection of these books see R. H. Charles, *Apocrypha and Pseudepigrapha of the Old Testament;* the best text of the Sibylline Oracles is that by Geffcken in the Berlin edition of *Die griechischen christlichen Schriftsteller d. ersten drei Jahrhunderte,* cf. E. Bevan,

All of these sources imply or even emphasise the main points of Jewish thought. The basis of their whole intellectual edifice was the triple belief that there is only one God, who should be worshipped; he is the creator of all things; he has given a Law which reveals his will and must therefore be obeyed implicitly.

It should be noted that Greeks must have had mixed feelings with regard to the proposition that there is only one God. Many would have admitted without hesitation that there was only one 'first cause,' if there were one at all, though many would have questioned whether the 'first cause' was a 'being.' But they would have greatly doubted whether there were not other supernatural beings who could be called gods. The possible existence of such beings was met in Jewish thought by postulating an infinite number of angels, whose powers and functions were much the same as those of gods in Greek thought, and there is not much essential difference between a Greek theology with Zeus at the top and minor deities as his assistants, and Jewish theology with Jehovah at the top and angels as his assistants.

The question of creation was, and is, more difficult. Apparently, Judaism of all schools was wedded to creationism. Greek thought was not; to it it was just as easy, or just as difficult, to believe in a universe which never had a beginning, as in one which had. Many Greeks believed in gods, but not that any one of the gods was the cause of the universe.

The third point—the Law—was the strength and weakness of Palestinian Judaism. Human nature usually seeks for an infallible guide, especially in conduct. It is, at least, a great economy of thought. The Greeks welcomed the idea of a revealed code of conduct. But the details of the code displeased them. In the Dispersion the Jews were beginning to accommodate the Law for Greek use by means of allegory, and Christianity

---

Sibyls and Seers, Geffcken, *Komposition und Entstehungszeit der Oracula Sibyllina* in *T.U.*, N.F. VIII, 1, and the discussion in Schürer, *G.J.V.*, Vol. III. For a brief introduction to Apocalyptic literature, F. C. Burkitt's *Jewish and Christian Apocalypses* is unrivalled. For IV Ezra, see G. H. Box, *The Apocalypse of Ezra* and B. Violet, *Die Ezra-apocalypse* in the Berlin Academy's edition of *Die griechischen christlichen Schriftsteller.*

completed this process; but in Palestine no compromise was made. It is doubtless vain to think what might have been, but there is more than one element of truth in the epigram that the Palestinian Scribes saved their souls and lost the Greek world. However, no clear-cut issue was dominant in the Palestinian world. The sources show us a maelstrom, rather than a calm sea.

So far as we can judge, then, from four main sources, the intellectual situation was somewhat as follows. In Jerusalem a secretly 'modernistic' or 'Hellenised' aristocratic class made the Temple their centre. We know painfully little about them, but it is at least possible that they were going the same way as the Roman aristocracy.[5] 'Observance,' not theology, was their view of religion. Over against them was the party of Pharisees, who were unconsciously paving the way for the creation of 'normative' [6] Judaism and the Talmud. Just as the Sadducean Priests are vaguely parallel to the Roman aristocracy, so the Pharisees are vaguely parallel to the Stoics; both developed a code of ethics, though of course the Pharisees were much more theistic than the Stoics, and their ethics dealt more with minute details of conduct.

For the history of Judaism, the Pharisees supply far the most important elements in the Jewish thought of the first century, but they are not really very important for the history of Christianity, which from the beginning broke away from the Pharisaic tradition. There remained a few Jewish Christians in Palestine, but they were driven out of the synagogues and have left no trace in the literature of the New Testament. Jesus was anti-Pharisaic, and for his successors Hellenistic, not Palestinian Judaism provides the background of thought.

Far more important for the growth of Christianity is the contribution of the Apocalyptic school of thought, though it played very little part in the formation of normative Judaism

[5] See pp. 213 f.

[6] We use this word because it has become familiar, but it distorts the facts; "Talmudic Judaism" would be far better. "Normative" seems to imply "dominant" and one can see the falsity of it if one tries to imagine what Annas and Caiaphas would have said on the subject.

and was in the main rejected by it. Opinion has oscillated between two extremes. There are those who think that the survival of normative Judaism shows that the Apocalyptic school was always an eccentricity. They are opposed, with an infinite variety of emphasis, by those who think that the survival of Christianity proves that the Apocalyptic school was extremely influential. To us it seems that there has been a tendency to forget that thought was very free in Jewish circles. Probably neither the Sadducean Caiaphas nor the Pharisaic Gamaliel were much interested in the Apocalyptic school of literature, but the amount of it which has survived shows that it had many adherents, and IV Ezra is a proof that among them were men of education and intellect. Thus, for an introduction to the New Testament it is essential to outline the general principles of Apocalyptic thought. It may be summed up in the following propositions:

i. Space is divided into two sections, heaven and earth. Heaven is inhabited by God, the angels and the representatives of the kingdoms on earth, whose actions are closely and perhaps causally connected with events on earth.

ii. Part of the heavenly population had "gone wrong" and become wicked angels, demons and unclean spirits, who cause sin, suffering and evil on earth and have corrupted mankind.

iii. Just as space is divided into heaven and earth, so time is divided into 'this age' and 'the age to come.'

The *Present Age* is the period in which men are living. Evil has corrupted society but God intends speedily to intervene and put an end to This Age, not merely closing a period of time, but ending society as it is. Evil will be eliminated and evil beings, such as fallen angels, wicked men and demons will be thrown into the *Outer Darkness* where there is weeping and gnashing of teeth,—otherwise described as *Gehenna* "where their worm dieth not and their fire is not quenched."

On the other hand all good men will pass into the *Life of the Age to Come,* the "olam haba" of Judaism. This is often spoken of in the gospels as the "Life of the Age" (ζωὴ αἰώνιὸς). In its original sense there is no doubt that this should be translated as the "Life of the Age to Come," but in Greek it is capable of meaning "Life everlasting" or, with a slightly different philosophical implication, "Life eternal." It seems possible that it has this later sense in the Gospel of John, but certain that it has not in the synoptic gospels. A good deal of confusion is therefore caused by translating it in the same way both in the synoptic gospels and in the Gospel of John. It is the same phrase, but with a different meaning. The underlying idea in the original was not that of a different world or of unending time, but a new period in which men will live in this present world, or, as we should say, on this present earth, but under new conditions from which all evil has been eliminated. Between the *Present Age* and the *Age to Come* will intervene not only the *End* (i.e. the end of the *Present Age*), but also the *Resurrection* and *Judgement.*

iv. There was sometimes a belief that before the *End* (i.e. the division between the two Ages), there would be a period of great prosperity and power for the Jews. In some circles, such as the Pharisaic one represented by the Psalms of Solomon, it was believed that the ruler of the Jews in those days would be a prince of the House of David; in others, represented by the Testament of the Twelve Patriarchs, it was thought that he would be a priest of the tribe of Levi. The duration of this period of prosperity was apparently not always defined in the same way. In IV Ezra it was 400 years,[7] in the Revelation of John [8] a thousand years (the Millennium). Some held that it would be preceded by a preliminary resurrection, so that righteous Jews who had died earlier should not lose their share in the prosperity which they had deserved but not enjoyed. This belief is the development of the hope, so prominent in Isaiah, Zechariah etc. of the coming of a great 'anointed' king, of the permanent prosperity of Israel and of its domination over the Gentiles. It was not originally eschatological, but became so when the figure of the Man from Heaven and of the Davidic prince coalesced. It may be doubted whether this coalescing was ever complete in Judaism until the Middle Ages, but it was thoroughly accepted in very

[7] IV Ezra vii.28. [8] Rev. xx.1 ff.

early Christianity, in which Jesus is both the Judge at the End and also the Son of David, who reigns with his saints throughout the Millennium.

One cause of this coalescing is the gradual deterioration of the meaning attached to the word 'Messiah.' Messiah means 'anointed,' and anointing was the means whereby a man was indicated as especially appointed by God for some purpose. Thus the phrase 'the Lord's Anointed' was used of kings and of high priests. Later it was used, in the Testament of the Twelve Patriarchs, quite especially of the Davidic prince who would come before the End; and also, in the book of Enoch as well as in the synoptic gospels, as the title of the Man who was coming from heaven on the clouds; and in the Mishna 'Anointed' is a designation of the High Priest.

That, of course, does not mean that in the first century the Davidic prince or the High Priest who were on earth and the Man who was coming from heaven on the clouds were regarded as one and the same person,--they merely had the same title. But when on the one hand 'Messiah' came to be used by Jews almost exclusively of the Davidic prince, and in Christian circles Jesus was regarded as the fulfilment both of the prophecy of the Davidic Messiah and also of the prophecy of the Man who was coming on the clouds, it is obvious that the word began to lose its meaning. Thus it was possible and usual to speak of *the Messiah* and to attribute to this person all the characteristics of anyone called Messiah in the older literature.

v. In Acts it is said that the Pharisees believed in a Resurrection and that the Sadducees did not. This is confirmed at least partially by Josephus.[9] It is often forgotten that Judaism did not make this a test of membership in the Synagogue of Israel. If a man did not believe in a future life, and the writer of Ecclesiastes surely did not, it did not much matter. The Judge at the End would not ask what his opinion had been, but what had been his conduct.

By 'resurrection' a majority of Jews probably meant a resuscitation of the body which had been buried, and the Sadducees

[9] Acts xxiii.6 ff.; Jos. *B.J.* ii.8.14.

were opposed to this opinion. An intermediate group represented by the Wisdom of Solomon seems to us to suggest a close approximation to the Pauline theory of a transmutation of flesh into Spirit rather than a clear-cut doctrine either of resurrection or immortality.

vi. *The Judgement* is described more fully than elsewhere in the synoptic gospels in the parable of the Sheep and the Goats,[10] which is really not a parable at all but a picture. In it are shown the Son of Man as the Judge (obviously Jesus in the mind of the Evangelist) and three groups of human beings; on the right hand the Righteous Heathen, on the left hand the Wicked Heathen, and, standing by the side of the Judge, his Brethren. The Heathen are tested by their behaviour to the Brethren, who in the gospel are certainly intended to be the Christians but probably represent an originally Jewish conception in which the Brethren are the Jews.

The divine Judgement at the End includes both the living and the risen dead. On its decision the wicked will be sent into Outer Darkness, where they will suffer eternal torture, while the righteous will pass into the Life of the World to Come.

The *Outer Darkness* is also the place appointed for the Devil, his angels and the demons. A wide-spread doctrine of the period, assumed though not stated in the gospels, held that the Devil was a fallen angel, the chief of those who had been appointed "Watchers" over mankind and had proved unfaithful. The demons were the ghosts of wicked men, especially of the giants who had been the off-spring of wicked angels and of women whom they had seduced in the days before the Flood. These giants had all been drowned, but their ghosts lived on, taking possession of men and women whenever possible, and producing sin and disease.[11]

vii. It was thought by Enoch, by the Christians and by IV

[10] Matt. xxv.31 ff.

[11] For this demonology Enoch and Jubilees are the fullest sources. See also H. Gressmann, *Israelitische-jüdische Eschatologie,* Volz, *Jüdische Eschatologie,* but especially Strack-Billerbeck, IV, pp. 501-535 and 764-1212.

Ezra that the Judgement will be presided over by God's representative, a Man who was reserved by God and will come from heaven on the clouds.[12]

This Man is the centre of a difficult problem, very important for the New Testament student. In Dan. vii.13, Daniel sees a vision of a human being in heaven, contrasted with the beasts (a winged lion, a bear, a leopard and a "different beast") of the earlier part of his vision. A formula was used in Aramaic to express a human being which, literally translated, is a 'son of man,' though an idiomatic translation would simply render it 'a man' or, perhaps better still 'a human being.' The Septuagint, as so often, adopted the literal rather than the idiomatic rendering and thus the rather impossible phrase 'son of man' passed into translation-Greek and translation-English.[13]

The human being whom Daniel sees in heaven is explained in the following section as representing the "kingdom of the saints of the Most High," just as the lion represented Babylon and so on. The "kingdom of the saints of the Most High" doubtless means the Jews. For the student of the Old Testament and its thoughts it is a very important question whether the writer meant this as a mere symbol or as part of his belief that in heaven, besides God and his angels, there were the supernatural representatives of the nations. It is at least possible that these representatives were regarded as real and as belonging to the category of angels, for later on in the book of Daniel a different vision shows Michael as the representative of Israel.

Of course, if one were certain that the book was all by one author, which is very doubtful, one might argue that Michael is the same as the "human being" of the earlier part. But this is a question of Old Testament criticism and does not really belong to our subject.

12 The usual doctrine was that the Judgement would be presided over by God. Only in Enoch and IV Ezra the Messiah from heaven is the representative of God.

13 On "Son of Man" see H. Lietzmann, *Der Menschensohn,* 1896; Fiebig, *Der Menschensohn,* 1901; Dalman, *Worte Jesu;* J. Wellhausen, *Skizzen und Vorarbeiten,* VI, 200 ff.; W. C. Allen's *Matthew* (*I.C.C.*), pp. lxxi ff., and *Beginnings,* Vol. I, pp. 368-384.

Much more important is the use which was made in Enoch of the phrase 'son of man,' apparently in dependence from the vision in Daniel. Like Daniel, Enoch sees a human being in heaven and asks the angel who is acting as his guide, who is this "human being" or "son of man"? The angel tells him that it is the Elect one, referred to also as 'Messiah,' who was appointed before the creation of the world, and that he will remain in heaven until the End when he will act as Judge. This is, of course, by no means the same as the meaning of the passage in Daniel, but seems to be a corruption of it. Such a perversion of meaning is not unusual in Apocalyptic literature, the authors of which seem to have been unusually gifted in abusing rather than using the writings of their predecessors.

The same use of 'son of man' seems to be found in the synoptic gospels, where he is, at least in some passages, undoubtedly the Judge who will come on the clouds of heaven. It is, however, very strange that there are no other instances of this usage, so far as we are aware, in Jewish Apocalyptic literature. It is as though the line of descent went from Daniel to Enoch and from Enoch to the gospels, with no other extant representatives of it. IV Ezra has the belief in the Man who is reserved for the End, but in the obscure textual tradition of the book there is no trace of 'son of man' in Greek. In other words, IV Ezra, like Paul, translated idiomatically not literally, as did Enoch and the Evangelists.

This Apocalyptic literature represents a type of thought which Josephus disliked and the Rabbis minimised, though it would be untrue to say that they rejected it completely. The part which the Rabbis accepted was the coming of the Davidic prince, who is still prayed for in the Eighteen Benedictions in the synagogue. The main difference between Jewish and Christian belief was that the Christians thought that Jesus was the Davidic prince, as well as the Man from heaven and regarded a belief in this identification as essential, while the Jews did not agree. It must always be remembered that the Jews were much less "creedal" than Christians. To be a good Jew it is necessary to believe in and love God and to keep his Law; on all other theological matters opinion is free.

CHAPTER XX

The Background in the Greek-Speaking World

WITH the second part of the Acts of the Apostles, the story of early Christianity passes from Palestine, a little country only partly populated by men of Jewish race and religion, to the Roman Empire, with its many nations and religions.[1]

It was, in the main, a Greek world, not a Roman, except for purposes of government. Rome, the city, not the Empire, was still predominantly Latin; the upper classes, at least, were not Greek, still less Oriental. But for the rest of the Empire, the language was Greek and the thought was Greek; yet not the Greek of Athens, but of that curiously 'Hellenistic' world which started from Macedonia.

If one took a map and painted it in various shades of blue to indicate the extent to which Greek culture had spread, the deepest color would probably be in the cities of Asia Minor or of Egypt, not in Europe at all. But these Asiatic or Egyptian cities, though they were predominantly Greek superstructures, retained Oriental bases. The submerged nations, Phrygians, Syrians, Galatians and Egyptians, remained recognisable by custom and worship, but they were mostly bilingual and had been so impregnated by Greek thought and so overrun by Greek traders, that they had become superficially more Greek than anything else. The weak spot in this cosmopolitan civilisation was that the combination of races produced not a synthesis but a smudge. The Greeks found difficulty in penetrating the East in government, rather than in persuasion or thought: the Romans in persuasion or thought, not in government.

[1] Besides Mommsen, see J. B. Bury's *History of the Roman Empire* and the chapter on Rome in Rostovtzeff's *Social and Economic History of the Roman Empire*.

The main feature of the Roman government was its difference from the earlier world empires of Babylon and Assyria, and, though not to the same extent, of Persia. The Babylonians and Assyrians had tried to adopt the policy of the melting-pot and to enforce a homogeneous system. They had desired to have an empire in which all the inhabitants were "100% Babylonian" in despite of language, race, origin and history. To accomplish their purpose, they had made use of enforced migration; Jews had been planted in Mesopotamia and Mesopotamians in Palestine. The experiment had not been very successful; the melting-pot had melted nothing. It had spoiled Jews for being good Jews, and had made undoubtedly bad Palestinians out of possibly good Mesopotamians.

The Persian kings dropped the experiment; they allowed a considerable amount of local autonomy, and were probably more successful than is realised by any one who looks only through glasses supplied by Herodotus and the Greek tragedians, but in the end their system of government collapsed. First the Greeks and then the Romans took over the empire.

The Romans, consciously or unconsciously, developed and improved the Persian system. They recognised the autonomy, at least in small matters, of every part of the enormous realm which they had inherited, or won, from the peoples of the East. No one was forced to adopt Roman customs or Roman ideas, except in so far as they were necessary for the peace and order of the whole. The various countries retained to a large extent their own forms of government and their own forms of speech. Rome had seen, though she had scarcely formulated, the vision of "a common superior of nations."

The government of the Empire was nominally divided between the Emperor and the Senate.[2] As often happens in history, the position of the Emperor was very different in theory from what it was in practice. The imperial power was nominally held only for a short but undefined period, and the Emperor was therefore "acclaimed" at frequent but irregular intervals. He also held, as a kind of connecting link with

[2] See Mommsen's *Roman Provinces,* Tenney Frank's *History of Rome* and *Beginnings,* I, pp. 171 ff.

the past, the tribunician power, to which he was annually appointed. As Emperor he was in control of all the more recent provinces, which are therefore called 'Imperial.' The other provinces were governed by representatives of the Senate, which appointed a governor of consular rank. These are the Senatorial provinces. In practice, of course, the Emperor's choice was largely instrumental in the Senate's nomination.

The governor of a Senatorial province was called the *Proconsul* in Latin or ἀνθύπατος in Greek; the governor of an Imperial province was called *Propraetor* in Latin or ἀντιστράτηγος in Greek. He might also be called the *Legatus,* or in Greek ἡγέμων.

Each governor of an Imperial province had troops assigned to him, legionaries and auxiliaries. These filled the function of police as well as soldiers. The commandant of a legion was a *tribunus,* or in Greek a χιλιάρχος, literally a "captain over a thousand"; his subordinates, who would today be something between subalterns and non-commissioned officers, were the centurions, or "officers over a hundred men." The Greek for 'centurion' was sometimes κεντυρίων and sometimes ἑκατοντάρχης.

The governor was, of course, the chief magistrate in a province and ruled partly by Roman law, partly by local custom; but it should be remembered that the Romans made much use of *coercitio*—compulsion [3]—which was administrative police action, governed chiefly by the policeman's or the magistrate's idea of what was desirable.

In the various cities of the Empire there were naturally subordinate magistrates, with varying titles regulated largely by local usage. Their general title in the New Testament is ἄρχοντες, but in Philippi they appear to have been also called στρατηγοί, which probably represents *duoviri* rather than praetors. In Thessalonica (Acts xvii.6) they are called πολιτάρχαι,—a characteristically Macedonian name. The officers of these magistrates, at least in some cities, were called *lictors* or in Greek 'ραβδοῦχοι, though they were lictors only in a limited sense,—they carried the fasces but not the axes.

[3] See Mommsen's *Strafrecht.*

The general practice of Roman administration was to leave all minor cases, not affecting life or fiscal questions, to magistrates whose verdicts were based on local law and custom. It is not quite clear whether Roman citizens were in all respects free from the jurisdiction of native courts, but certainly a Roman citizen could always insist on a hearing before a Roman official.

The strength of the Roman Empire was that, dealing with a very complex and heterogeneous situation, it did not try to be either simple or homogeneous. Each city, with the country surrounding it, was governed by a compromise between the ideas which Roman governors brought with them and the customs which they found obtaining in their provinces. Moreover, there was a noticeable difference between colonies,[4] free cities and cities which were neither colonies nor free. In each case, the practice of government was considered on its merits.

The Jews especially, not only in Palestine but also in at least some of the great cities of the Empire, were in a peculiar position. They were regarded as a separate nation, and were allowed to inflict punishment, including scourging and possibly death, on their compatriots. This was especially true in Alexandria,[5] where the Jews had their own *ethnarch* (also called *alabarch),* their own laws and even their own quarter of the city. The extent to which this Jewish nation in Alexandria was Hellenised is one of the most obscure problems in the history of Judaism and also one of the most important for the understanding of the evolution of early Christianity.

It is obvious, for instance, that this raised the question "When is a Jew not a Jew and therefore excluded from the privileges of his race?" Was the answer "When he is a Christian"? The point is that if Christians were Jews, and they at least claimed to be "the ancient people of God" and "the true Israel," they could claim the privileges of the synagogue, but would then also be subject to its discipline. If, on the other

[4] See Kornemann's article in Pauly-Wissowa, **IV**, s.v. *Coloniae;* Marquardt, *Staatsverwaltung,* I (2d ed.) pp. 86 ff., 118 ff.; W. T. Arnold, *Roman Provincial Administration,* pp. 219 ff.

[5] See E. R. Goodenough, *The Jurisprudence of Jewish Courts in Egypt.*

hand, they were free from the synagogue, they were subject to the Roman Empire, which frowned on foreign cults if they could not claim to belong to a recognised nation. Very soon this attitude of Rome led to, or contributed to, the definite condemnation of Christians as such.

The evolution of this process is clearly marked in the New Testament. In the synoptic gospels, Jesus is a Jew; in the Epistles Paul boasts that he is a Jew, and in Acts he is always represented as going to the synagogue first,—the attitude of the writer of Acts is, in effect, that Christians are the true Israel, that their troubles are due to bad Jews, and that reputable magistrates never condemned them. Hostility to the Jews is clear on every page, so that Acts is partly a polemic, partly an apologia. Before long, however, the Romans not unnaturally accepted the opinion of the Jews, that Christians had no claim to Jewish privileges; Christians were told *non licet esse vos,* and to be a Christian became a crime. I Peter and the Apocalypse are as clearly later than this situation as the synoptic gospels and Acts are earlier than it. Unfortunately there is no evidence to enable us to say exactly when the change took place.

Turning to the question of thought, the dividing lines between theology, philosophy and ethics were somewhat confused. In the upper classes, the traditional theology was dead; but religious observance, as distinct from theology, was preserved by a real affection for the *mos maiorum,* as well as by political expediency and social convention, which perceived the advantage of preserving old customs and ancient institutions.[6] A good Roman used to attend the religious services in the temples, but only because he was a good Roman, not because he believed in any theological system connected with

[6] More satisfactorily than in any technical book, this attitude is pictured in Walter Pater's *Marius the Epicurean,* a novel which all students of early Christianity ought to read. Among technical works G. Wissowa's *Religion und cultus der Römer* and W. Warde Fowler's *Religious Experience of the Roman People* are the most important. The bibliography in the *Cambridge Ancient History* can be consulted for books on special points.

those temples,—for the philosophers, especially the Stoics and Epicureans, had pulverised the belief in the gods by argument and ridicule, which were repeated by Christian apologists in the second century.

What had taken the place of the old theology in the lives of educated Romans? The answer can partly be found by reading such books as Lucretius' *De rerum natura,* Cicero's *De natura deorum,* his Tusculan orations or his treatise *De divinatione,* and also some of the treatises of Plutarch such as *De Iside et Osiride.*[7] From these it appears that there was a tendency, varying considerably in intensity, to allegorise myths and to reinterpret the old phraseology in such a way as to make it a medium for imparting philosophic thought. The problems of philosophy and the differences between philosophic sects were smoothed over by using an idiom markedly suitable to obscure the distinctions of thought by the ambiguities of language. Something of the sort was obviously needed if the temples were not to collapse entirely.

To replace the naive creationism of more primitive times, three main theories were substituted,[8] though with many variations:

i. The 'theory of the elements' chiefly held by Stoics. This originally postulated the eternal existence of four elements: Earth, Water, Air, Fire; ultimately Spirit (which may have been thought of as a mixture of Air and Fire) was added as a fifth element and considered the governing force of the world.

ii. The 'theory of atoms,' chiefly held by Epicureans. This postulated the eternal existence of atoms, the *primordia* which

[7] The two best editions of Lucretius are those of H. A. J. Munro and of C. Bailey; of the *De natura deorum* that of J. B. Mayor; a good commentary on Plutarch's *De Iside et Osiride* is still to be written but there is a good translation in the *Loeb Classical Library.*

[8] Probably the quickest way to gain some insight into this question is to begin to read in E. Zeller's *History of Philosophy,* but E. Bevan's *Stoics and Sceptics,* C. Bailey's *The Greek Atomists and Epicurus,* and Dill's *Roman Society from Nero to Marcus Aurelius* should be added. C. Bailey has given an excellent account of the *Advent of Philosophy* in the *Cambridge Ancient History,* Vol. VIII, pp. 454-459, but nothing replaces P. Wendland's *Die Hellenistisch-römische Kultur,* in Lietzmann's *Handbuch.*

could not be 'cut up.' These atoms, unlimited by time, existed in 'the void' which was unlimited by space. The atoms were always falling towards a bottom which was not there, so that they never stopped. As they fell, they collided, coagulated for a longer or a shorter time into larger or smaller entities, then separated again. These coagulations are never permanent, but the atoms themselves are eternal and, given unending time, all possible combinations or coagulations are certain to return.

iii. The theory of 'immaterial reality' derived from Plato. This regards Mind and Thought as more real than Matter and possibly as the cause of it. From it come 'Values' or 'Universals' (to adopt a later terminology), which the Stoics and Epicureans regarded as the transient opinions of ephemeral beings.

Thus for Stoics and Epicureans, reality was material, but for Platonists immaterial. The existence of gods was not always or necessarily denied, but their importance was minimised. Moreover, the word 'God' was preserved as convenient to denote the governing principle of the Universe, so that by Platonists it might be used to denote Mind, the immaterial reality which created and governed the universe, while for Stoics who thought that material Spirit was the governing force it was easy to equate God and Spirit.

Speaking generally, Stoicism was the most prevalent philosophy among educated Romans in the first century. To them, matter was eternal, though its form constantly changed. Men were one form of matter, gods were possibly another; but neither men nor gods had created matter, and both were subject to Fate. Fate was not a person, but a principle which was in the nature of things, inexorable and inevitable. Yet it was not necessarily hostile, and 'Providentia' was often used to express the benignant side of Fate.

Had men no power of choice? The educated Roman did not know any more than the modern psychologist; but, like ourselves, he recognised that ethics are based on the assumption that choice is possible. Stoic ethics were an elaborate and admirable system, which was not unlike that of the synagogue, so that in the ethical parts of the Pauline Epistles it is often impossible to say whether Paul was influenced by Jewish teaching or by Stoic thought,[9] which he might have absorbed in Tarsus.

Naturally, this practically non-theistic philosophy, which cheerfully accepts Fate and tries to live in cooperation with it, not in futile attempts to escape, was as a rule dominant only among influential persons of high education and position; for just as Thackeray noted the relative ease of virtue combined with "ten thousand a year," so Fate is more cheerfully accepted by those to whom it has given lavishly.

This philosophy, in which ethics were becoming more important than metaphysics, was increasingly the basis of the view of the Universe held by educated men. But obviously this was not their religion, as distinct from their theology,—still less was it the religion of the Empire as a whole.

The situation is obscured by the extent to which *religio* (the reverse of "negligence") meant the proper performance of rites, not the acceptance of opinions.[10] Augustus laid great stress on this proper performance, and did all he could to rebuild temples and to revivify interest in them. But, though attending services of which the original meaning has been abandoned may be called *religio* in Latin, it is scarcely what 'religion' means in modern language, which tries to distinguish the spiritual attitude which is 'religion' from 'theology' which expresses that attitude, and still more from the general *Weltanschauung* which is bound up with the theology.

This makes it hard to define or describe either the religion,—in the modern sense,—or the theology of the educated Roman. His real religion was probably a sense that the individual was somehow concerned with the progress of the

[9] The general similarity of Paul's ethics (not his theology) to that of the Stoics, led to the mediaeval belief that Seneca was a Christian and to the fictitious correspondence of Paul and Seneca. See also R. Bultmann, *Stoisch-cynisch Diatribe und Paulus*. For Tarsus, see Böhlig, *Geisteskultur von Tarsus*.

[10] But this is not the meaning of the word in Lucretius, where it is consistently used as meaning, or at least including, the false opinions which cause so much misery to mankind.

whole, that he was both part of the general scheme of things and also an agent in producing its result. His theology, therefore, would vary as he took a different view, partly rational, partly imaginative, of what the scheme of things really is. Is there behind it a Being or a number of Beings who have greater powers than men? Or is there nothing behind it except Fate, beneficent as it may be, but unchangeable? Or is there a possible combination of the idea of God, whose Will can be modified and whose actions change, and the inscrutable, unchangeable nature of Fate,—so that men can speak of a certain Providence which may be almost completely personified and to whom prayer can be lifted?

Then as now educated men naturally felt the difficulty of forming a clear statement in theological terminology of that which was itself not clear or more than partially perceptible to the human mind. It was doubtless, however, this belief in the validity of the scheme of things and in the part which man has to play in its progress which induced many educated Romans to accept the institutions of inherited religion,—to support the temples, not as a statement of theology but as an institution of society.

This same problem of the scheme of things took a different form when educated Romans were outside of Italy, in countries with which they had no inherited affinity. Were they to accept the temples of the local gods in the same way that they had accepted those of their own country? To some extent that was doubtless their practice, and a more or less conscious (and also more or less artificial) equation was made between the gods and the temples of Rome and those of the provinces. But the genius of Augustus and his friends not only revivified the moribund temples in Rome, but provided a new focus for the real religion of the Romans in the provinces. They had all felt the wonder and miracle of the Empire which they administered. The true Roman felt that he was serving a cause better, nobler, and more enduring than himself. Augustus was probably a hard, cold man, but the *Res gestae Divi Augusti*[11]

[11] The most convenient edition is Hardy's *Monumentum Ancyranum*, though Mommsen's edition of the *Res Gestae* is still invaluable; W. M.

seem to have, in a prosaic way, something of the true religious spirit which breathes in the Aeneid.

For this religious devotion to Rome Augustus provided a focus in the new temples,[12] which he built for his ancestors and especially for Divus Julius, from which rapidly developed what became the most fundamental element in Roman religion in the first and following centuries, the cult of the Emperors. Its origin is somewhat obscure, but certainly it began in the provinces, not in Italy, and therefore is probably similar to the cult sketched in the foregoing paragraph. The Roman officials needed something to express their belief in the creative and permanent value of the Emperor in the general scheme of things. A belief in the actual divinity of the reigning monarch was thus always very close to the surface; but whether it was Herod, as has been suggested, or someone else who started it, undoubtedly the practice soon grew of introducing the Emperor into the temples. Thus, the cult of the Emperor meant in practice the recognition by the nations of Rome as their common superior; it was a binding element in a curious amalgam of different races, and behind the cult of the Emperor was the philosophical belief that he was the centre of that complex of factors which make up the position of government in the general scheme of things in the world, to serve which is a real and not ignoble religion.

In less fortunate circles, which were not Latin, or even Greek, by origin, a curious situation arose. The words and ceremonies of the old national religions[13] such as those of Egypt or Phrygia remained, but their meaning and probably their details were changed. Ceasing to be national, they became private religions; for, instead of purporting to support

---

Ramsay's *Monumentum Antiochenum* in *Clio,* 1927; further references in the *Cambridge Ancient History,* Vol. X, p. 896.

[12] See Warde Fowler's *Religious Experience of the Roman People.*

[13] See F. Cumont, *Religions orientales dans l'Empire Romain.* This book has been translated, but for those who read French, the original has the merit of charm as well as learning. Moreover the English represents the 2nd edition, which Cumont has greatly revised in the later French editions.

the existence and well-being of national life, they offered salvation to individuals. This 'private salvation' was effected in various ways, but in each case the general outline was as follows:

There was a belief in a supernatural being who had found the way,—generally with pain and grief and suffering,—to achieve salvation, in the sense of acquiring happiness and immortality. If it be understood that the word 'god' is used in the Greek and not the Jewish sense, he had become a god. He had left behind the secret of how he did it and the ceremonies of the religion were mainly intended to enable others to repeat his experience. This was the secret, or 'Mystery,' and the supernatural being at the head of it was usually referred to as its 'Lord.' All nationality has disappeared in these cults. The worship of Isis no longer belonged exclusively, or even chiefly, to Egyptians; nor did that of the Great Mother belong only to Phrygians.

These cults were not competitive with each other in any exclusive sense. Doubtless the priests were anxious to obtain converts to their own way of doing things, but they did not deny that other cults had a right to exist. Furthermore, to some extent, many of these cults were interpreted in the light of philosophy, so that the combination of philosophy and ceremony made them attractive to the ignorant and palatable to the instructed.

It is very hard to say whether these religions ought to be described as being 'Hellenised,' or the religion of the Empire as being 'Orientalised.' Doubtless the truth lies somewhere between the two extremes. If it had been merely a contest between the undisputed religions of the East and Greek philosophy in its strictest form, no compromise between the two would ever have been reached. But two elements seem to have served as what chemists call a catalyst.

In the first place, there was the combination of the two cognate systems of Orphism and Dionysianism.[14] Whether these were originally Oriental religions, representing a previ-

[14] See Rohde's *Psyche,* Th. Reinach's *Orpheus,* and Miss Jane Harrison's *Prolegomena* and *Themis.*

ous wave of invasion into Greek thinking, or were originally Thracian cults, does not very much matter for the present purpose. Certainly Orphism and Dionysianism had entered into the spirit of many Greeks and were sufficiently allied to some of the Oriental religions to effect a union between them and other elements of Greek thought.

Equally important and operating on a higher level was neo-Pythagoreanism. The teaching of Pythagoras, of which less is known than we should like, was more emotional, more fitted to comfort those who were seeking release from trouble, than the stricter metaphysics of Aristotle or the Stoics. It proved itself, even in the days of Plato himself, well adapted for union with Platonism; and, on the other hand, presenting as it did a doctrine of future life and the relation between that life and conduct in this life, it was a very convenient medium of reconciling Greek metaphysics and Greek ethics with Orphism, Dionysianism, the Mysteries of Eleusis, and ultimately with Oriental cults.

In the first century B.C. Posidonius [15] was probably largely instrumental in producing a curiously eclectic new philosophy, in which the basis of metaphysics was Pythagorean and Platonic, but many of the details were borrowed from Stoicism, —the fundamental materialism of which Posidonius probably did not accept. This philosopher played a considerable part immediately before and after Christ. He is admirably adapted to serve as a subject for interesting discussion, as none of his writings are extant and little is known about him, except for scattered references in other writers. A few years ago, he was treated in some quarters as the ultimate solution of all problems dealing with the history of philosophy, though it has since been recognised that this was exaggerated. But whether it was due to Posidonius or to someone else, the fact is almost certain that it was this compromising metaphysics which was dominant in the first century.

Especially interesting is the attitude of these religions to Fate and to Astrology, though, unfortunately, it is not clear

[15] See K. Reinhardt, *Posidonios* and S. Hennemann, *Posidonios' Metaphysische Schrift.*

when this was first adopted. Apparently it was almost universally believed that the stars were the instruments and the signals of Fate (Manilius [16] is the classical example), so that their arrangement at the day of any one's birth decided the course of all his life. The only cure for birth under an evil star was to be born again, and this rebirth was effected by the sacraments of the cults of private salvation, by which it was possible to "contract out of fate." In the second century, this was certainly a wide-spread belief and was also applied to Christian Baptism. It is less certain how far it existed in the first century.

Probably all these Oriental cults carried on some degree of philanthropic activity among those who belonged to them. But there seems to have been an essential difference on this point between them and Christianity. The cults insisted on excluding "publicans and sinners"; Celsus pointed this out and attacked the Church for its foolishness in admitting all the broken-down failures of society, to whom the other cults closed their doors firmly. It is noteworthy that only the Church survived.

Finally, it is extremely likely that these cults, like the Synagogue and the Church, also gave instruction in ethics, but the proof of this point is much less strong than might be desired. The truth is that we know sadly little about their organisation or activities.

It would be natural to suppose that the religion of the Jews, living outside Palestine, would have changed in the same way as the other denationalised cults. Formerly it was thought that this was not the case, and that Judaism was an exception. But probably this is a mistake; further study of Hellenistic Judaism [17] has shown that it also was going the same way as the other Oriental religions in the first century. The recognition of this fact is due to two factors. Archaeological investigation

[16] A. E. Housman's edition is the best, and the preface added to the gaiety as well as to the learning, if not to the good feeling, of scholars.

[17] E. R. Goodenough seems to us to have made this clear, but the matter is still hotly disputed. See especially his *By Light, Light.*

has shown that Greek was far more prevalent in Jewish circles than had been supposed, and the accommodation of Jewish theology to Greek philosophy and to sacramentalism, in the circle dominated by Philo, has been emphasised.

The evidence is, unfortunately, somewhat obscure, partly because after the first century there was a reaction in Judaism against all Hellenism, which produced what is rather unfortunately called 'normative' Judaism. The Hellenistic Jews either voluntarily abandoned Judaism, or were driven out of the synagogues. For their point of view we have two main sources, the Wisdom literature and Philo.

i. The earlier books of the Wisdom literature, such as Proverbs and Ecclesiastes, were written in Hebrew and used in Jerusalem as Scripture. They probably represent the point of view of the Sadducees. The Wisdom of Solomon, however, was written in Greek. It was considered as Scripture by Alexandrian Jews and accepted as such by the early Christians, but rejected by the orthodox Rabbis, though it was probably well known to educated Jews in Jerusalem. It possibly represents the views of Josephus, influenced Paul in many passages, and Matthew's account of the crucifixion has clearly been "written up" with the help of Wisdom ii. On the one hand it may be contrasted with Daniel's belief in a resurrection, the typical background of Apocalyptic literature and probably the belief of the Pharisees, and, on the other, with Ecclesiastes' negation of all future life, the usual opinion of the Sadducees. It had great influence on the Greek Christianity of the second century; but there is little evidence that it had any influence on Jesus.

The basic idea is that 'Wisdom' is the point of connection between God and man, the surrogate in some way of the Spirit of the Lord, or the 'Hand of the Lord' of earlier literature. Thus it paved the way for a theory of inspiration such as is found, or at least adumbrated, in Paul. It attributed to Divine action not merely spasmodic and intermittent effects, such as are contemplated in earlier documents dealing with inspiration, but also permanent qualities, with which men can be endowed if they choose rightly.

ii. In Alexandria we have Philo,[18] a Jew who had been educated in Greek learning and was recognised by men of all nations as a profound philosopher. He was one of the leaders of the nation of Jews in Egypt and was their representative on a deputation to the Emperor Gaius. The Christian Church preserved many of his writings, from which we can reconstruct the theology of at least one highly educated Hellenistic Jew. Roughly speaking, he accepted in the main the philosophy of those Greeks who had produced a mixture of Pythagoreanism and Platonism, adding many details from Stoicism, but rejecting its fundamentals. To convert the Jewish Law into a means of teaching this philosophy, Philo employed Allegory much as it was used by others to deal with Isis and Osiris. God was identified with Light, and religion was the process of enlightenment to which the Law, the Prophets, the example of the Patriarchs and the ordinances of religion all served as means.

Philo admits that there were other Jews who went even further than himself. He adhered to the details of the Law, but others did not. That is to say, whereas he accepted both the historical and the allegorical meaning of the Law, others accepted only the allegorical. It has been held that Philo is a unique specimen, rather than a highly educated example of what, in more or less degree, was to be found in all the synagogues throughout the Empire. But that he is not unique can be seen in his reference to those who went further than himself, and the tendency of the past has been to underestimate the amount of Hellenisation of Judaism in the Empire.

A point of great importance, which is certain to be the centre of future controversy, is the extent to which the introduction of 'Sacrament' or 'mystery' in the other religions found a parallel in this Hellenistic Judaism. Certainly, some parts of Philo can be cited as showing that he regarded salvation as

[18] The standard text is Cohn and Wendland's. There is an excellent account of Philo's writings in E. Schürer, *G.J.V.*, Vol. III. The translation in the Bohn series is sometimes but not always a help. It will be replaced by the *Loeb* edition, when that is complete. See also C. Bigg, *Christian Platonists of Alexandria,* J. Drummond, *Philo Judaeus* and Brehier, *Idées de Philon d'Alexandria.*

possible to those who united themselves in some mystic way with the great leaders of the Jewish race, by fulfilling the Law which they had inculcated. Philo's language seems to take some steps toward making sacramental the observance of Jewish Law; but to what extent this went, or what importance should be attached to it, is one of the most difficult problems in Hellenistic Judaism, though it is obviously crucial for a true understanding of the background of the early days of the Christian Church.

The further this Hellenisation of Judaism may be supposed to have gone, the easier became the position of those honorary members [19] of the synagogue who are perhaps referred to in Acts as "God-fearers" and are often called 'half-proselytes' in modern books. Whether 'God-fearers' was really the technical name of a recognised part of the synagogue is doubtful, but it is certain that there was a fringe of heathen who constantly attended the synagogue and at least seemed to be on the way to becoming proselytes.

These honorary members of the synagogue must have consisted of heathen who were attracted by the monotheism of the Jewish religion and by its stern ethics, so similar to that of the best of the Stoics. If we may suppose that the synagogue had been largely impregnated with Greek philosophy, its attractiveness becomes still plainer. Presumably what prevented men from becoming full-fledged proselytes was their objection to circumcision and to the ceremonial food laws of the Jews. It is obvious that these would be decisive hindrances to many Gentiles, and that, when Paul came into the synagogue and preached a new form of Judaism, he would have met with an enthusiastic reception from Gentiles who found that he had given up the very points which they regarded as obstacles. Moreover, when the Rabbis saw those whom they regarded as future proselytes turning aside after a heresy, their irritation was as natural as severe.

It is, of course, clear that the denationalised religions, none of them claiming an exclusive hold on complete truth, could

[19] See *Beginnings*, Vol. V, pp. 74-96.

not remain in a state of isolation. Converts who had probably visited the meetings of more than one cult would inevitably introduce new ideas from one to the other. The same would also be true of the God-fearers in the synagogue. Thus it is not surprising to find a growing mass of evidence that there were syncretistic religions combining features taken from several sources, which under the influence of the monotheistic leanings of philosophy tended to identify the one supreme God with one or the other of the gods of their various cults.[20] To those chiefly attracted to Judaism this would be the God of the Jews; to Syrians it might be Attis; and the tendency was to describe this supreme God as 'the Highest God' or 'the Lord of all,' or some similar title. We have, unfortunately, too little accurate knowledge of the early years of these syncretistic religions.

The causes which produced these results can be imagined with probable correctness, but the evidence is lamentably scarce. Partly at least they are due to the spread of that Greek thinking which led to the abandonment of the cruder elements of anthropomorphic, and especially of theriomorphic, theology. A hybrid was produced between theology and science which used scientific words such as 'mind,' 'reason,' 'power,' 'desire,' 'wisdom,' etc., but personified them. Probably there was a wide range of difference between those who completely personified the scientific phraseology, so that it became a new mythology, and those who emphasised the original meaning of the words, so that it became a scientific theology, devoid of anthropomorphism.

It is also possible that some phrases and some stories which had played a part in Oriental myths, Iranian, Babylonian, or Egyptian, were adapted for service in this new theology,—but they were used by it, rather than were its origin. Finally, there was a rapidly developing "astral" theology which adopted the Greek (especially Stoic) doctrine of Fate and of the Planets (including Sun and Moon) as the instruments of Fate.[21]

Thus, these new religions were partly concerned with the

[20] See Cumont's article in Pauly-Wissowa on *Hypsistos.*

[21] See F. Cumont's *Astrology and Religion.*

propitiation of the astral powers, and partly with the effort to find a way to be born again under a more satisfactory star than human nativity had supplied. It is not unlikely that this is alluded to in Col. ii.8, for the word translated 'rudiments' in the Authorized Version is that commonly employed for 'planets' in the theological or philosophical Greek of the later periods.

This syncretism was probably more influenced by philosophy or science than were the denationalised religions in the narrower sense. Very little is known of its beginnings, least of all its exact date, or probably ever will be known,—though it may be guessed that its earliest days were kaleidoscopic. The evidence, such as it is, suggests that the most popular basis was a mixture of Oriental mythologies, including Judaism. This is illustrated in magical papyri, in the Hermetic literature,[22] and in the curious document called a "Mithras-liturgie" by its first editor. Later on Christians either adopted or influenced this syncretistic movement and the result was the various sects which, rather improperly, are grouped together as 'Gnosticism' or 'Knowledgeism,' to coin a translation. Naturally, perhaps, the use of 'scientific' terminology was more marked in the later syncretistic cults than in the earlier ones.

Discovery, in the form of inscriptions and papyri, will doubtless throw somewhat more light on the subject, but it would be optimistic to expect much.

[22] See W. Scott, *Hermetica* (4 vols., 1924-5, ff.). The book of Reitzenstein, called *Poimandres,* is fascinating but capricious. There is as yet no satisfactory text, but it has been rumoured for the last ten years that Prof. A. D. Nock has an edition in preparation.

CHAPTER XXI

The Relation of the New Testament to Its Background

THE purpose of the present chapter is to discuss the main problems concerned with the relation of the New Testament to the background described in the previous chapters.

The first problem is the relation of Jesus and his immediate disciples to the Judaism of Palestine. Christianity rejected some elements in this Judaism and emphasised others. Then the scene shifts to the Roman Empire, and again the Church was influenced in its formulation by some of the elements of thought in the denationalised sacramental religions, effecting a synthesis between these elements and its original Jewish foundation. Finally, it effected a further synthesis with the philosophic ideas of the period, adding them to the Judaism of its earliest period and the sacramentalism which it had adopted.

When the details derived from the various sources enumerated in the last three chapters are combined, a general picture can be formed of the social, political and intellectual world against which the story of Jesus and his disciples in Palestine must be placed, and certain points should be noted especially.

In the first place, there was much discussion and controversy about the Law, and the New Testament represents a strong reaction against the Pharisaic exposition. From the social point of view, no one was regarded as a good Jew, living in a creditable manner, unless he observed the Law, and ostracism was employed in order to enforce this view. But the Law was already very difficult to follow. The result was that the Sadducees in Jerusalem, the rich Priests, took a stricter view of what was necessary than did anyone else. Their wealth enabled them to lead a life which was in accordance with the letter of the Law. They could offer the correct sacrifices at the correct moment; and, having plenty of servants, it was possible for them to do no work contrary to the Law, and to avoid all ceremonial defilement. How far they always observed the Law in so far as it directed that servants should obey it as well as masters may be open to doubt. Unfortunately, we have little evidence. The Talmud often represents what ought to have been rather than what actually was.

On the other hand, the Pharisees, often living outside Jerusalem under conditions where sacrifices, being impossible, were not nearly so important an item of the Law as were the regulations of conduct, saw that an explanation had to be given of many precepts which in themselves were either ambiguous or impossible. They therefore explained the Law,—and thus modified it,—so as to make it practicable for a larger circle.

Nevertheless, there must have been many who found it impossible to live up to the Pharisaic interpretation of the Law and were therefore outside respectable Jewish society. Such persons are described in the Gospels as "publicans and sinners." It was to them that the message of Jesus obviously appealed with the greatest force. The Scribes had produced a standard of life which, however carefully worked out in detail, was really lower in essentials than what the Law had contemplated. But Jesus' message was that the purpose of the Law was more important than its letter, and that the grave defect of Jewish life was that the purpose was over-shadowed by the consideration of the letter. He, therefore, insisted that true righteousness must exceed that of the Scribes and Pharisees.

On the other hand, he fully recognised the impossibility of living up to the Law, especially when it was interpreted in this way, and emphasised God's willingness to accept the penitent. In this respect he did not go further than the best rabbis of his time, but the fact that he refused to join in the usual ostracism of "sinners and publicans" and extended to them the hope of entry into the life of the world to come if they did but repent, in combination with his emphasis on the purpose of the Law and the heightening of standards which this implied, created great hostility among the professional exponents of the Law and corresponding loyalty from the ostracised multitude, which they condemned but he accepted.

Doubtless it was this controversy about the Law which led to the expulsion of Jesus from the Synagogue, but one may suppose that his teaching that men should love their enemies, which he certainly did not mean to apply only to private grudges, was equally important in producing unpopularity for him among the members of the Patriotic Party and the events of the Jewish war, then still in the future, show how powerful that party must have been outside Jerusalem.

Moreover, the existence of the Patriotic Party is extremely important for the understanding of the gospels. Obviously Jesus was opposed to it and doubtless many other Jews shared his opinion on the subject. This opposition party probably had some name. Is it too much to guess that its members took to themselves the Old Testament term of 'Anawim' ('the Poor')? If so, it is possible that the word translated 'the meek' or 'the poor' in the New Testament may represent this opposition party which believed that the right policy of the Jews was to keep quiet and submit to any government which was over them, until it pleased God to intervene. Much of the New Testament, especially the Sermon on the Mount, is illuminated by a brilliant light if it be read with this suggestion in mind. It would then appear that part of the teaching of Jesus was a strong polemic against the Zealots, as they were afterwards called, and in favour of the Poor and the Meek.

This much is tolerably certain: doubtless Zealots and Anawim ceased to be important when the Church left Palestine, but the question of the Law did not cease to be discussed. It remained a subject of controversy between Jews and Christians, though in the gospels there is very little evidence of the details of this controversy. It is, of course, possible to read the influence of later controversy into every verse and to explain away all traces of the work of Jesus himself, but this makes nonsense of the gospels. Soberly considered, the wonder is that there are so few traces of "community influence" in the records.

There is, however, a noticeable difference between Matthew and Luke in their treatment of the Law and in each case we would seem to have the influence of later controversy developing the original position of Jesus. In Matthew, there seems to be a tendency to put forward the teaching of Jesus as a supplement to the Law; in Luke as a substitute. Matthew would seem to be the nearer to the teaching of Jesus, but these Gospels, or, more accurately, the differences between them reflect two points of view in the early Church.[1]

Finally, it should be noted that there is a real difference between the gospels, whether Matthew or Luke, and the Epistles of Paul. The Pauline position is that righteousness comes from a new creation, depending on faith and grace. It is not regarded as wholly in the power of man to obtain righteousness, least of all can he do so by obedience to the Law, or, indeed, to any law. Paul's objection is not to the Law, still less to any part of the Law, but to anything of a legal nature if it be regarded as a means of obtaining righteousness. On the other hand, he fully recognises that the righteous man will, in point of fact, live up to the Law in many points and even go beyond it; but he will do so because such conduct is the expression of his nature, not because he is living up to an external code.[2]

The synoptic gospels and the Pauline Epistles represent Jesus as the man who will come at the End of the World as God's appointed Judge.[3] Only the most indefensible use of the critical knife could eliminate all the passages which plainly have this meaning. It is also clear that in the Gospel of Mark and the other synoptics, Jesus is represented as himself recognising that this was his position. The problem which has constantly disturbed New Testament scholars is whether this is really the attitude which he himself adopted. Unless the gospels are very far from the facts, he obviously expected the

[1] See above pp. 42 and 47.

[2] See W. Morgan, *The Religion and Theology of Paul*, 1907, and Lake's *Paul, his Heritage and Legacy*.

[3] See pp. 207 f.

coming of the Man from Heaven, but whether he thought that he himself was that Man has often been disputed, not without reasonable arguments on both sides.

It is also interesting to notice that the Apocalypse represents an exact survival of the Jewish belief, found in IV Ezra, of a preliminary kingdom of a Davidic Messiah, whose rule would have a definite termination at the end of a fixed period. The same idea apparently recurs in I Corinthians xv, where Paul looks forward to a Resurrection, not of all men, but of Christians, who will be with Christ until he hands over the kingdom to God. But Paul does not have anything to say about the length of this kingdom, except that it is limited.

The synoptic gospels, on the other hand, seem to have no trace of this belief. The teaching of Jesus as represented in them is that the End is coming quite soon and what will follow it is quite obviously not the Kingdom of the Davidic Messiah, but the Reign of God realised in the Life of the World to Come. This is clear because the Judgement in the synoptic gospels always precedes the Resurrection and the Reign of God and there is no trace of any previous reign; in the other documents the Resurrection always comes after and not before the kingdom of the Davidic prince.

The emphasis which Jesus laid on the eschatological expectation of the End and Judgement must have been popular, at least in some circles, for it was an important element in the thought of his time.

The key-word which dominates this whole conception is the *Kingdom of God*[4]; the concept is common in the later books of the Old Testament, but the phrase, though it is frequently found in the Rabbinical writings, is as unknown to the Old Testament as it is common in the New. This meant primarily the Sovereignty of God as the supreme ruler of the universe. But its secondary meaning included the circumstances which would make complete and perfect the universal recognition of this Sovereignty of God, and the time at which it would be

[4] See J. Klausner, *Die Messianischen Vorstellungen des jüdischen Volkes im Zeitalter der Tannaiten;* Strack-Billerbeck, IV, 799 ff.; G. F. Moore, *Judaism,* I, 228 ff., 432 ff., II, 323 ff.; and *Beginnings,* Vol. I, pp. 269 ff.

in force. Thus, in one context the Kingdom of God might mean the recognition of the Sovereignty of God in his personal life by the individual, and in another context it might mean the time when the whole world would be living under the direct rule of God and recognising his rule in a manner never yet achieved. The question may be raised, whether *Kingdom of God*,—the phrase, not the concept—like *Gospel*, and perhaps *Apostle* was not a Christian contribution to the vocabulary of Greco-Jewish religion.

As was said on pp. 206 f., in some circles, mainly represented by Enoch and the gospels, it was held that the Judgement would be entrusted by God to the *Man*, who had been appointed from the beginning of the world and was reserved in Heaven until the *End*, when he would be sent on the clouds.

It was pointed out on p. 207 that the Aramaic term used in referring to this figure merely means 'a certain man' or 'a human being,' but might be translated literally, not idiomatically, by 'a son of man.' In the Greek version of the Book of Enoch [5] the Elect one is referred to as "that son of man" and thus this phrase, as unnatural in Greek as in English, came to be treated in Christian circles as the title of the Man in Heaven. Doubtless this is its meaning in many passages in the gospels: e.g. Mark viii.38, xiii.26, Matthew xvi.27, xix.28, and xxiv.30. It would, however, be a grave error for the student of the New Testament to think that there are no problems left in connexion with the use of 'Son of Man.' The following may be suggested:

i. Does 'Son of Man' ever represent simply 'man,' not of course in the intention of the writer, but in that of Jesus? This question has been put especially with regard to Mark ii. 10 and 28 where many interpreters think that 'Son of Man' can well have been intended by Jesus to mean 'a human being.'

[5] See Flemming and Radermacher, *Das Buch Henoch*, in the Berlin *Griechischen-christlichen Schriftsteller;* C. Bonner, *A Fragment of the Greek Text of Enoch*, in *Studies and Documents*, viii.; and R. H. Charles, *The Book of Enoch*. The latter book should be used with caution, as it often provides a translation of conjectures rather than of the text.

ii. Did Jesus ever follow the precedent of Ezekiel and refer to himself in Hebrew, in a non-eschatological sense, as 'Son of Man' (Ben-Adam)?

iii. Did Jesus in his own intention, mean to identify himself with or to distinguish himself from the "Son of Man" in Mark viii.38 or xiv.62? Certainly the Church soon made the identification and modified the original Jewish belief in order to facilitate it. In the Apocalyptic scheme in Enoch "the Son of Man" was by definition reserved in heaven until the last day, but the belief of the Church was that the 'Son of Man' was to come twice, first to suffer, then to judge.

It should be said that all interpreters agree on one point,— in Galilee Jesus did not announce himself to the people as Messiah or as Son of Man. To the Galileans he was the herald of the Kingdom, the preacher of repentance, a great exorcist and a great healer. It is interesting that in the Lucan writings the Message of Jesus in the gospel is always 'the Kingdom,' and in Acts that of the Apostles is always Jesus.[6]

Three lines of interpretation of the position adopted by Jesus in regard to the Son of Man have had, and are likely to have, varying degrees of popularity:

The first is that Jesus did not think of himself as the Son of Man or as Messiah until after he left Galilee, but did so then. This view is perhaps best expressed by J. Wellhausen; it was held also by G. F. Moore.

The second is that Jesus probably did not identify himself as any special Messiah, but was conscious of a divine commission,— a Messiahship,[7]—of which the exact nature and purpose was not yet fully revealed; but the crowd, and possibly some of his disciples, thought that he was the Davidic Messiah, a figure in which Mark xii.35-37 suggests that Jesus himself did not believe. The Apostles, on the other hand, believed that he was the "Son of Man" who would come on the clouds of heaven at the End, and thought that Jesus himself believed

[6] See especially W. Wrede's *Das Messiasgeheimnis.*

[7] See especially Schweitzer's *Quest of the Historic Jesus* for a history of criticism, and for the theory suggested see Lake, *Paul, His Heritage and Legacy.*

this, but had been unwilling to say so openly until God should make it known by raising him from the dead.

The third view is that the whole eschatological element in the gospels is an accretion made by Jewish Christians, and no part of the original teaching of Jesus.

A somewhat mediating view presented by T. W. Manson must be mentioned. In his very interesting book, *The Teaching of Jesus*, he argued that 'Son of Man' is derived from the prophetic doctrine of 'the Remnant ideal,' and that Jesus was the Son of Man by embodying that ideal. This is an interesting speculation, but it does not seem to us to be adequately based on the Gospels.

Of these theories, none are impossible, but the second seems to us most probable, though it cannot be proved. The third is at present the least generally accepted, but it may be revived, since some of the developments of *Formgeschichte* may be expected to fit into it very well.

But Christianity in the first century was related not only to a Jewish background, but also to that provided by the Greco-Oriental world of the Roman Empire. This is a very obscure subject because we have so little evidence.

A series of problems may be presented:

i. What was the legal position of the Church in the Empire? Acts was certainly written to show that there was no unfavourable decision given against it by competent magistrates. But Tacitus partially, and Pliny definitely, show that before long it was a capital offence to be a Christian. This attitude is reflected in I Peter and the Apocalypse.

ii. What was the relation of the Church to the 'mystery,' or denationalised religions? The chief difficulty in the treatment of this question is that we know more about Christianity than about any other sacramental religion.

The main facts to remember are best seen by beginning with the middle of the second century. Christianity was then a completely sacramental religion.[8] In all essentials of doc-

[8] See, for example, the writings of Ignatius and Justin.

trine it was the Catholic Church. Christian writers recognised its similarity to the other cults, but explained this as due to deliberate imitation by demons, who wished to pass off the heathen worship as being what Christianity really is,—a supernatural means of salvation. Thus the similarity then subsisting between Christianity and the cults is incontrovertible. A certain general set of ideas as to Fate, Life, Death, Regeneration and Sacraments was current and as common to all cults as the ideas of causality or evolution are to the modern world. It influenced both heathen cults and Christianity, but the suggestion that either imitated the other is absurd.

Thus there is no doubt about the character of the Church in the second century, but most modern writers are equally convinced that the teaching of Jesus, as given in the synoptic gospels, was not sacramental, but in many ways far more akin to Judaism, and especially to the Jewish Apocalyptic party, than to the heathen cults. His teaching as to God, the Judgement and the World to Come is Jewish; his ethical teaching is the development of the teaching of the prophets, and shows no trace of Hellenistic or Oriental influence.

This, however, is not true of the Gospel of John, which is thoroughly sacramental. It is, therefore, possible to argue that the Gospel of John really gives the historical truth, and shows that Christianity was the same in all essentials in the days of Jesus as in the second century. In this case it is the synoptic gospels which have diverged from the main stream and their origin is the really difficult problem.

To most Protestant scholars this view seems unacceptable and they maintain the priority and superior accuracy of the synoptics. For them the main problem should be to explain the origin of the sacramental element in the Pauline Epistles and in John. Unfortunately, many books, especially those inspired by Harnack,[9] have scarcely seen that this problem exists,—just as many Catholic writers have scarcely seen that the

9 Especially in his *Das Wesen des Christentums,* translated as *What is Christianity,* in which Harnack's hopes for the future seem to have coloured his representation of the past.

existence, not the analysis, of the synoptics is the main problem for those who accept Johannine Christianity as original and to be traced back to Jesus.

Few living scholars now deny that sacramental Christianity existed in the Pauline churches, though many doubt whether it was derived from Paul himself. It is widely,—and in our opinion, correctly,—held that sacramental Christianity was the result of the Church's rapid penetration of the Hellenistic world in which sacraments were normal and expected by converts, who produced the sacramental worship found in the second century by giving their own interpretation to three salient points, Baptism, the Eucharist and the term 'Lord.'

Baptism[10] may originally have been part of a Jewish ceremony of initiation for proselytes, retained and Christianised when circumcision was given up. It was, however, soon connected with the gift of the Spirit, was readily adopted by Greek converts and treated by them as a sacrament of regeneration.

The Lord's Supper[11] may have been merely a commemorative meal, reminding Christians of the death of Jesus and his impending return in judgement. This too could readily have been interpreted by Greeks as a sacramental meal, and Paul in I Corinthians x certainly did nothing to hinder this view, and, as it seems, probably shared it.

A question of great importance to the early history of Christianity is the changed terminology with regard to Jesus found in the Pauline Epistles and to some extent repeated in Acts. In the earliest forms of the synoptic gospels, Jesus is referred to either as the 'Son of Man,' as the 'Christ,' or as the 'Son of God.' Of these, the last is very vague and it is doubtful in

[10] See W. Brandt, *Jüdische Baptismen,* Strack-Billerbeck, G. F. Moore, *Judaism,* I, 332 ff., W. Heitmüller, *Taufe and Abendmahl bei Paulus,* and the article on Baptism in Hastings *Encyclopedia of Religion and Ethics.*

[11] Out of a mass of literature see especially Goguel, *L'Eucharistie;* G. H. MacGregor, *Eucharistic Origins,* and A. Schweitzer, *Das Abendmahl im Zusammenhang mit dem Leben Jesu und der Geschichte des Urchristentums.*

what sense it was intended. It survived into Acts and Epistles but is not the most prominent title of Jesus in the New Testament, though it soon became so. The word 'Christ' is undoubtedly a translation of the Hebrew title 'Messiah,' but in the Pauline Epistles and in some places in Acts it is used as though it were a proper name and 'Jesus the Christ' becomes "Jesus Christ." This is a curious illustration of the extent to which the words of the Septuagint were not really intelligible in Greek-speaking synagogues. 'Messiah' would mean much to Jews: 'Christ' would mean nothing to Greeks.

In the Epistles, and largely in Acts, another word has taken the place of almost all other titles. This is 'Lord.'[12] In considering it, two points must be distinguished. In the first place, what was the origin of the word? In the second, what was its implication in the ears of Greek hearers?

It was probably the Greek rendering of the Aramaic word *mar,* which is preserved, strangely and fortunately enough, in the phrase 'Maran atha,' in I Corinthians xvi.22. This shows that the Aramaic of this word was for a time actually used in Greek-speaking synagogues.

Mar implies in Aramaic that the person so addressed is of considerable importance. It was used for kings and other persons of distinction, but does not imply divinity and is not the usual appellation of God. It is still used in Syriac, which is, after all, only modern Aramaic, in the title of a bishop. The implication of the word in Greek circles where it was translated by the Greek word for Lord (Kyrios) is very important, for 'Kyrios' was customarily used by the members of the Greek sacramental cults as the title of their supernatural head. It therefore implies a cult-relationship between the divine being in question and the worshipper. Thus, for instance, Osiris was a god and generally recognised as such by all heathen, but he was 'Lord' only to those who were initiated into his cult. When, therefore, Jesus was referred to as 'Lord,' it would immediately imply to Greek minds a claim that he was the

[12] Bousset's *Kyrios Christos* is the outstanding book; a summary is given in *Beginnings,* I, pp. 408 ff.

head of a sacramental cult, whose initiates, to whom he was 'Lord,' were the Christians.

A 'Lord' had a supernatural nature which may or may not be described as divinity in proportion as Greek or Jewish forms of thought are being observed. To the Jew 'God' means the Creator, an omnipotent being beside whom there is no other. To the Greek 'God' is a generic title of a whole class of supernatural beings who are neither creators of the world, nor omnipotent, nor omniscient. They resemble much more closely the angels of Hebrew theology than the God; and Justin Martyr not unnaturally described them as demons. In this sense, the lords of the various cults were all gods and it would be natural enough for the Greeks to interpret thus the statement that Jesus was the Lord.

Of course, the problem would soon arise of how this was to be reconciled with the belief inherited from Judaism that there is but one God; especially since the same word, Lord, is used in Greek to render 'Jehovah.' Much of the controversy of early Christian theology goes back to this fact; but that it was not felt to be insuperable can be seen from the statement of Paul that, whereas to the Gentile world there were many gods and many lords, to the Christians there is but one God, the Father, and one Lord, Jesus Christ. One of the puzzles in the exegesis of the Epistles is the exact distinction between those words in the mind of Paul, but it seems, at least, not improbable that the word Lord became popular in Gentile Christian circles, because there was no adequate rendering for the Aramaic word 'Messiah.' 'Christ,' its verbal equivalent, became a proper name and the word 'Lord' took its place and was interpreted in the light of its connotation in Greek religions. It should never be forgotten that the Christian idea of God is neither Jewish nor Gentile, but Christian, and that it is not a compromise, so much as an attempt at a synthesis of two different ways of regarding the deity.

Thus, a comparison of the relation of the synoptic gospels to the background provided by Palestinian Judaism, with the relation of the earlier Epistles of Paul and Acts to the background provided by the Hellenistic world, suggests that the Apostolic Church effected an important synthesis. It came to terms with the Hellenistic need for the general setting of the denationalised religions of salvation and became sacramental.

A further synthesis with another element in the Hellenistic background remained necessary. Just as the Church had become sacramental, so it became syncretistic, though in a more limited sense than did Gnosticism. The Pythagorean-Platonic theory of life and reality, partly a metaphysical speculation, partly a mystical experience, was adopted. This is illustrated by the later Epistles of Paul and the Johannine writings. Jesus was the eschatological Messiah to the first Jewish Christians; he was the Lord of a sacramental cult to the Hellenistic Christians of I Corinthians, and probably to Paul himself; in addition to these, he became the Logos,—the divine reality which is at once the object of human choice and quest and the inspiration and power which enables choice and quest, distinct from the invisible and incomprehensible God, yet never separate from him.

To us it seems that, except for the actual use of the word Logos, a more advanced synthesis of this character appears in Hebrews and Colossians than in John, but John seems to portray a deeper and more intense mysticism. To carry this point further would transgress the limits of this book, but two observations may be permitted:

Were these syntheses made consecutively or simultaneously? The older view, which is—roughly speaking—that of the Catholic Church, maintains that they were made simultaneously and by Jesus himself. They are all original and primitive parts of his teaching, but various groups of Christians emphasised various parts in varying manners. The only synthesis, properly so-called, of the various elements in the teaching of Jesus and the Apostles was that made by the Catholic Church. The more recent view, which is—again roughly speaking—that of liberal Protestantism, maintains that the syntheses sketched above were real changes, and were effected consecutively. The two later syntheses represent points of view which were unknown to Jesus.

In the main we agree with the more recent view, but the last word has not been said. The result of archaeology is to show that Palestine was more Hellenistic than had been supposed. The question of whether Jesus himself was not a product of Hellenistic as well as of Apocalyptic Judaism has not yet been solved. If it was possible for Simon Magus to call himself the "Great Power" of God, why could not Jesus have called himself the "Logos" of God? Both phrases are good Philonic Greek and though we personally think that Jesus did not so call himself, this is because we think that the evidence points that way, not because of antecedent improbability.

In the second place, it is vitally important to realise that both in the sacramental theory of salvation and in the Johannine theory of the Logos it is desirable to distinguish experience and expression. We seek a reality, higher than and distinct from ourselves. We believe that we find it. That is experience: whether it be real or illusion is a matter for enquiry. We then proceed, if we can, to express that experience in terms of our own view of the universe: whether that expression be logical is also a matter for enquiry. But these two enquiries are not identical, and the student of historical theology has an especial need to keep them distinct, for they have so frequently been confused. The experience does not necessarily validate the expression; the mystical experience of John does not prove that a Logos-theory is objectively true. Still more important is it to remember that belief in the expression does not confer the experience. No understanding, however perfect, of Johannine theology will necessarily confer the experience which the Logos Evangelist agonised to explain.

APPENDICES

APPENDIX A

The Chronology of the New Testament

THE GOSPELS

The Birth of Jesus. According to Matthew, Jesus was born in the reign of Herod the Great. Herod died in B.C. 4, so that would be the latest possible date for the birth of Jesus. But, according to Luke ii.1ff, Jesus was born at the time of a census made by Quirinius, the governor of Syria, and began his ministry in or after the fifteenth year of Tiberius (A.D. 29). Luke also states that Jesus was then "about thirty years old." If the last statement is correct, he was born in or about 2 B.C.

But he further says in i.5 that John the Baptist and, by implication, Jesus were born in the days of Herod the King, which might possibly mean in the days of Archelaus, but much more probably means in the time of Herod the Great.

This combination of statements in Luke leads to great and probably insoluble difficulties. According to Josephus, the census of Quirinius was made in A.D. 6 after Archelaus had been deposed from the rule of Judaea, and there is no evidence in Josephus or elsewhere that any earlier census was held. Thus there is a difference of about ten years not only between Matthew and Luke, but also between Luke's own statements.

It is widely held that this can be explained by assuming that Quirinius was twice governor of Syria, and that there was a census of Judaea in his first period of office as well as in his second. But the evidence for this is not strong. In support of the earlier governorship of Quirinius an inscription (*C.I.L.* xiv, 3613, and Dessau, 918) from Tivoli can be alleged. This records the career of a man who was governor of Syria and Phoenicia. His name is missing, but the reconstruction of San Clemente (in *De Vulgaris aerae emendatione,* Rome, 1793, pp. 414 ff.) who restored the name of Quirinius was accepted by Mommsen and is often regarded as certain by commentators, who forget that it is, after all, only a guess as to the missing word. In historical circles, however, it has been seriously questioned, for instance by Lily Ross Taylor (*American Journal of Philology,* LIV. 2) and Groag (*Jahreshefte,* Beiblatt, xxii,

1924, pp. 445 ff.). Miss Taylor suggests M. Titus and Groag M. Plautius Silvanus as alternatives to Quirinius. In favour of the theory that Quirinius held a census twice, see W. M. Ramsay, *Was Christ Born in Bethlehem?* The real difficulty is that even if Quirinius was twice governor of Syria, and even if Augustus did order a census of the whole world,–for which there is no evidence except the statement in Luke,–it seems doubtful if Quirinius was in Palestine (which was outside his province) before the death of Herod; more doubtful that he could have extended such a census into the kingdom of Herod; and most doubtful of all that such a census could have failed to have raised revolt, just as it did in A.D. 6, or to have been noticed by Josephus.

Thus, on the evidence as it stands, it is only possible to say that there are signs of two traditions as to the date of the birth of Jesus, one that he was born in the reign of Herod the Great, i.e. before 4 B.C., and the other that he was born in the time of the census made by Quirinius in A.D. 6. No one can say which tradition is right, and the attempts to reconcile them are not quite successful. If it were necessary to choose, obviously the date in the reign of Herod, which is found in both Matthew and Luke, and agrees with the statement that Jesus began his ministry when he was thirty years old, has the better evidence.

The Beginning of John the Baptist's Ministry. The date for this is given in Luke iii.1 as the fifteenth year of Tiberius. This is A.D. 29, unless the years of Tiberius be reckoned from the time when he was associated with Augustus in the rule of the provinces and of the armies, but such a method of reckoning the years of Tiberius is not found elsewhere and in any case he was not Emperor until the death of Augustus. There is, however, some difficulty in connection with John's criticism of Herodias and Antipas. Their marriage was probably not much later than A.D. 23, as Herodias was in a position to help Agrippa by her influence with Antipas not long after the death of Drusus. Yet the Gospel-narrative seems to imply that the marriage was recent when John protested. But it must be admitted that all this is speculative (see *Beginnings* Vol. I, p. 17).

The other data given by Luke in iii.1-2 present many difficulties, and throw no further light on the question.

He says that Lysanias was then tetrarch of Abilene. This is open to the criticism that there is no evidence that there ever was such a person at that time. It is possible that Luke has confused the facts and is thinking of Lysanias who was King of Chalcis in 6 B.C. If he knew the writings of Josephus, as has often been suggested, this is possible, as Josephus, in explaining how Agrippa II obtained Abila in A.D. 53, says that this "had been" the tetrarchy of Lysanias. It is conceivable that the district of Abila was often called the "tetrarchy of Lysanias" but scarcely possible that there was a Lysanias ruling it in the reign of Tiberius. The whole question of Luke's use of Josephus is dealt with in Krenkel's *Josephus und Lukas,* 1894, F. C. Burkitt's *Gospel History and its Transmission,* pp. 105 ff. and *Beginnings,* Vol. II, pp. 355 ff.

Luke also says that Annas and Caiaphas were high priests. There never were two high priests at the same time, and there is no evidence to support the common assumption that Annas was regarded as the high priest *de iure* and Caiaphas *de facto.* Luke seems to have had unusual ideas about the succession of High Priests, which is tolerably well established in Josephus. In Acts iv.6, Annas is described as the High Priest, and Caiaphas is merely one of his companions. The possibility that Luke really mentioned Annas as the High Priest and that Caiaphas is an interpolation in the text of Lk. iii.2 is discussed in *Beginnings,* Vol. IV, pp. 41 ff.

The Beginning of the Ministry of Jesus. According to all three Synoptic Gospels, the public preaching of Jesus began after the end of the Baptist's ministry; but according to John before it. It is nowhere stated how long the Baptist preached, so that there is a gap in the evidence, and we cannot say when Jesus began his work in Galilee. As will be seen, according to the most probable scheme of chronology, John's work cannot have lasted long, unless Luke's fifteenth year of Tiberius is quite wrong.

The Duration of the Ministry. There is no clear evidence for fixing this period. Taking the Marcan narrative first, two points are to be noted. The episode of the disciples plucking the corn as it stood in the fields must have been in May or early June. Moreover, there is no green grass in Palestine, so far as our experience goes, after the middle of May. Therefore, the feeding of the Five Thousand on the "green grass" was most probably in the following spring, and the crucifixion can hardly have been before the Passover of the year after that. Thus, if the crucifixion was in A.D. 30, the feeding of the Five Thousand was in A.D. 29, and the eating of the corn in the fields was in A.D. 28.

Admittedly, this chronology rests on scanty data, but it is all that we have. There is a difference of opinion among experts as to whether Mark gives a disconnected series of episodes. Our own opinion is that he intended to give the story in chronological order; if he did not, all argument is useless.

It will be seen later, that if we accept the chronology of Galatians i.15 ff. as correct, A.D. 30 is almost the latest possible date for the crucifixion, but if we accept the forgoing deductions from Mark, the ministry of Jesus began not later than A.D. 28. This does not quite fit the statement of Luke that John the Baptist began to preach in A.D. 29, the fifteenth year of Tiberius. Three suggestions are possible to meet this difficulty:

i. The fifteenth year of Tiberius is not reckoned from his accession, but from the time when he was coordinated with Augustus in his provinces. This seems to us very unlikely, but it has its supporters.

ii. Mark's arrangement is not chronological. The "green grass" of Mark vi.39 may refer to an earlier time than the standing corn of Mark ii.23. If so, the ministry of Jesus may have lasted only one year, A.D. 29-30.

iii. Luke may have made a mistake in saying the "fifteenth year" of Tiberius.

The Johannine evidence as to the length of the ministry and the date of the crucifixion is much fuller than the Marcan. The chronological notices in John as to the length of the ministry before the final Passover are:

i. "And the Passover of the Jews was near and Jesus went up to Jerusalem" (ii.13): "And he was in Jerusalem at the Passover" (ii.23).

ii. "After these things was a feast (or the feast) of the Jews and Jesus went up to Jerusalem" (v.1).

iii. "And the Passover, the feast of the Jews, was near" (vi.4).

iv. "And the Tabernacles, the feast of the Jews, was near" (vii.2).

v. "And it was then the Dedication in Jerusalem" (x.22).

Thus three Passovers, including that of the Passion, are mentioned. If the final (the third) Passover was in A.D. 30, the second was in 29, and the first was in 28. This agrees remarkably well with the Marcan chronology. It has, however, been suggested, especially by Westcott and Hort, that the text of John vi.4 is doubtful, for Irenaeus (who thought that the ministry lasted ten years) counts v.1 as a Passover, but ignores vi.4, and Origen, Cyril and the Alogi may have omitted the word "Passover" in vi.4. It should, however, be observed that the argument is largely inferential, and that there is no textual evidence for the omission. The case for omitting "Passover" in vi.4 is best given in Westcott and Hort's *New Testament in Greek,* Vol. II, p. 77, but the opposite case is convincingly stated by Turner in Hastings' *Dictionary of the Bible,* on "Chronology," Vol. I, p. 407 ff.

The Crucifixion. The difficulties involved in fixing this date increase the more they are considered. The fixed point is that the crucifixion was on a Friday. Mark and Matthew also state that the Last Supper was the Paschal meal on Nisan 14 (Mark xiv.12-16; Matt. xxvi.17-19), but John implies that it was the day before the Passover, Nisan 13, and Luke is perhaps ambiguous.

Mark's meaning is clear, but he and Luke (not Matthew) complicate the point by saying that "on the first day of unleavened bread when they killed the Passover" Jesus sent his disciples to prepare for the Last Supper. Strictly, the first day of unleavened bread was the fifteenth day of Nisan, and the Lamb was killed on the fourteenth, but it would seem that in popular use (especially among Greek-speaking Jews) the terms Passover (i.e. the meal at which the Lamb was eaten) and the "week of unleavened bread" which followed were confused. The best discussion of this point is in Strack-Billerbeck. Thus, if Mark be accepted, Jesus was tried and crucified on the fifteenth of Nisan and this day was a Friday. The question might then seem a simple problem in astronomy. The fifteenth of Nisan was the full moon after the equinox. In what years was the full moon on a Friday? Astronomers can easily answer that question, but we do not know how the Jews in Jerusalem in the time of Christ would have answered it, and unluckily that is the only important question. According to the Talmud, the new moon of Nisan 1 was fixed by observation, so that, if the sky was cloudy on the evening when the new moon ought to have been seen, Nisan 1 was postponed (and consequently Nisan 14). Many scholars, nevertheless, think that in point of fact, a calendar was actually used, and the "observation" forced into agreement with it. This is not improbable, but there is no evidence for it. A similar difficulty is that we do not know to what date the Jews assigned the equinox. In the fourth century A.D. March 21st was accepted, Anatolius of Laodicaea (*c.* A.D. 277) put it on March 19th (cf. Eusebius, *H.E.* vii.32) and Hippolytus half a century earlier put it on March 16th.

Obviously these complications prevent certainty, but if observation was followed and if the sky was clear in A.D. 30, Nisan 15 probably was on Friday, April 18th.

In John, as in Mark, the crucifixion is placed on a Friday, but on Nisan 14. The general considerations given above, of course, apply equally to this point, but A.D. 29 fits better than A.D. 30.

Few pursuits are more unprofitable than the attempt to fix the date of the crucifixion along these lines. From the nature of the case, we can never find out accurately in which years the fifteenth of Nisan was on a Friday. If the Johannine story be accepted, A.D. 29 is the most probable date, but if Mark be followed A.D. 30 is preferable.

The matter is made harder by the fact that a reasonable argument can be adduced to explain either date as due to the influence of later ecclesiastical practice and opinion. The date of Nisan 15 for the crucifixion makes the Last Supper a Passover, and thus the Eucharist is the legitimate successor of the Passover; the date of Nisan 14 makes the crucifixion itself the Paschal sacrifice and the death of Jesus becomes the substitute for, or the fulfilment of the Passover. Both ideas were common in the early Church; either may have affected the narrative. But who can say which?

ACTS AND EPISTLES

For the chronology of these books there are three relatively certain fixed points, from and to which everything must be reckoned:—the death of Herod and the Famine, the Proconsulship of Gallio, and the Procuratorship of Festus.

The Death of Herod and the Famine. Herod almost certainly died in A.D. 44. The evidence is given in Josephus, *Antiq.* xviii.6.10, xix.8.2, and is discussed by E. Schwartz, *Zur Chronologie des Paulus, in Gött. Nachrichten,* 1907, and *Beginnings,* Vol. V, pp. 446 ff. The famine probably came in A.D. 45. The evidence for this date is given in *Antiq.* xix.9.2, which puts it in the time of Fadus or perhaps of Tiberius Alexander or both. Fadus was procurator in A.D. 45 and Tiberius Alexander in 46 (see *Beginnings,* Vol. V, p. 453). This fixes within narrow limits the visit of Paul and Barnabas mentioned in Acts xi.30 and xii.25. If the arguments given on pp. 79 ff. be accepted, this was also the occasion of the visit described in Gal. ii.1-10 and probably also in Acts xv. But Paul says in Gal. ii.1 that this was fourteen years after the conversion, so that if the "Famine relief visit" be placed in 45 or 46, the conversion was not later than A.D. 32 and Paul's first visit to Jerusalem was in A.D. 34 or 35. Paul's words in Gal. ii.1 might be interpreted to mean that his second visit to Jerusalem was fourteen years after his first visit, not his conversion, but this renders the chronology much more difficult.

The first missionary journey must have begun in 45 or 46 and a process of dead reckoning will give approximate dates for the events in it.

Gallio. An inscription of Delphi of which at least four fragments are extant (Delphi 2178, 2271, 3883, 4001 and perhaps also 500, 2311 and 728, published in Nikitsky, *Epigraphical Studies at Delphi*, D. Plooij, *De Chronologie van het leven van Paulus*, and *Beginnings*, Vol. V, pp. 460 ff.) shows that Gallio was proconsul of Achaea in the year A.D. 52. We do not, it is true, know how long he was in office. The normal length of a proconsulate was only one year, but two years was not unprecedented, and Gallio may, therefore, have been proconsul as early as 50 or as late as 54. Thus ± A.D. 52 dates Paul's appearance before Gallio. But again, we do not know whether this was at the beginning, middle or end of Paul's stay of eighteen months (Acts xviii.11). Paul's arrival in Corinth, then, cannot be dated certainly, but if, as would be normal, Gallio was in office only one year, and Paul came before his court at the beginning of this period (the usual interpretation of Acts xviii.12) Paul reached Corinth in 49 or 50.

Festus. The confused and partly contradictory data in Josephus and Tacitus make it probable that Festus succeeded Felix as procurator of Judaea in A.D. 55. The chief difficulty is in Acts xxiv.27, "And when two years were completed Felix was succeeded by Porcius Festus." It is impossible to say whether this means "when Felix had been in office for two years" or "when Paul had been in prison for two years." We believe the former view is the more probable. If so, Paul must have reached Rome in A.D. 56 or 57. If he was in prison in Caesarea for two years, he must have reached Jerusalem on his last visit in A.D. 54 or 55. This leaves about the right space for his three years in Ephesus (see Josephus, *Ant.*, xx.8 and Tacitus, *Ann.* xii.54).

The chronology of the Epistles, apart from Acts, is relatively certain in the case of Thessalonians, Corinthians and Romans, all of which were written during Paul's stay in Corinth and Ephesus, i.e. between 49 and 54. The date of Galatians (see p. 125) is very doubtful, and that of the other Epistles is worse.

It is obvious that though a relatively probable chronology of Acts and of some Epistles can be fixed on the basis of these dates, there is a margin of doubt covering perhaps two years. But it assumes as certain Paul's statement that his conversion was fourteen years before his second visit to Jerusalem. There is no doubt that "fourteen" is the reading of all the manuscripts, but after all it depends on the accuracy of one *iota* in the original text of the Corpus Paulinum, for in Greek numerals the difference between four and fourteen is only one stroke of the pen (Δ or I Δ). What happened in those fourteen years will always be an enigma, and if it were possible to read "four" for "fourteen," the whole chronology of the New Testament would be easier.

The results reached in the preceding paragraphs can be formulated thus:

The Birth of Jesus	Before 4 B.C.
The Baptism	A.D. 28
The Crucifixion	A.D. 30
Paul's Conversion	A.D. 32
The Death of Herod Agrippa	A.D. 44
The Famine	A.D. 45
The Apostolic Council	A.D. 46
Paul in Corinth	A.D. 49
Paul in Jerusalem	A.D. 55
Festus	A.D. 55 or 56
Paul in Rome	A.D. 55, 56 or 57

The best sources for more detailed discussion are C. H. Turner's article on Chronology in Hastings *Dictionary of the Bible,* A. von Harnack, *Chronologie der altchristliche Literatur,* Vol. I, pp. 236 ff., and for Acts, Jackson and Lake, *Beginnings,* Vol. V, pp. 445-474, and D. Plooij, *De Chronologie van het leven van Paulus.*

Subsidiary aids to chronological studies will be found in the following lists, to which details can be added from the *Prosopographia Imperii Romani,* but this invaluable book is now rather old, and the new edition which is in process of appearing will certainly revise many statements in it. At the moment of writing this has only reached the letter C.

The High Priests of Jerusalem

The Priesthood had long ceased to be a lifelong office, and in the first century, the High Priests changed rapidly. Our evidence is derived from Josephus, *Antiq.* xviii and xix. There are various minor problems (e.g. that of Ishmael in the time of Claudius, cf. *Beginnings* V, p. 455), but the following list is approximately correct.

The High Priests from A.D. *6 to* A.D. *66*

Annas or Ananos, A.D. 6-14	appointed by Quirinius
Ishmael, son of Phabi Eleazar, son of Ananos Simon, son of Kamithos Joseph also called Caiaphas	appointed by Gratus between A.D. 14 and 25
Jonathan, son of Ananos Theophilos, son of Ananos	appointed by Vitellius after A.D. 37
Simon Kantheras Matthias Elionaeos	appointed by Agrippa I A.D. 38-44
Joseph Camei Ananios Nebedaeos	appointed by Herod of Chalcis A.D. 45-48
Jonathan Ishmael, son of Phabi Joseph Cabi	appointed by Agrippa II 48-66
Ananos Jesus Damneos Jesus, son of Gamaliel Matthias, son of Theophilos	appointed by Agrippa II 48-66

The Roman Emperors from Augustus to Marcus Aurelius

[The dates given are those of the Emperors' deaths.]

Augustus, A.D. 14
Tiberius, A.D. 37
Gaius (Caligula), A.D. 41
Claudius, A.D. 54
Nero, A.D. 68
Galba, A.D. 69 (January)
Otho, A.D. 69 (April 17th)
Vitellius, A.D. 69 (December 20th)
Vespasian, A.D. 79
Titus, A.D. 81
Domitian, A.D. 96
Nerva, A.D. 98
Trajan, A.D. 117
Hadrian, A.D. 138
Antoninus Pius, A.D. 161
Marcus Aurelius, A.D. 180

The Kings and Procurators of Judaea from A.D. *6 to* A.D. *60*
(Accession dates)

Herod the Great, King	37 B.C.
Archelaus, Ethnarch	4 B.C.
Coponius, Procurator	A.D. 6
M. Ambibulus, Procurator	A.D. 9
Annius Rufus, "	A.D. 12
Valerius Gratus, "	A.D. 15
Pontius Pilate, "	A.D. 26
Marcellus, "	A.D. 37
Herennius Capito, "	A.D. 38
Agrippa I, King	A.D. 41
C. Cuspius Fadus, Procurator	A.D. 45
Tiberius Alexander, "	A.D. 46
Ventidius Cumanus, "	A.D. 48
Antonius Felix, "	A.D. 52
Porcius Festus, "	A.D. 55
Lucceius Albinus, "	A.D. 57
Gessius Florus, "	A.D. 60?

It is impossible to discuss here the orthography of these names or the dates. In the main we have followed the *Prosopographia Imperii Romani,* which may be open to emendation.

The Legates of Syria from 6 B.C. *to* A.D. *66*

P. Quinctilius Varus	6 B.C.–4 B.C.
P. Sulpicius Quirinius??	3 B.C.–2 B.C.
C. Caesar	1 B.C.–4? A.D.
L. Volusius Saturninus	A.D. 4–A.D. 5
P. Sulpicius Quirinius	A.D. 6–A.D. 7
Q. Caecilius Metellus Creticus Silanus	A.D. 12–A.D. 17
Cn. Calpurnius Piso	A.D. 17–A.D. 19
Cn. Sentius Saturninus	A.D. 19–A.D. 21
L. Aelius Lamia	Before A.D. 32
L. Pomponius Flaccus	A.D. 32–A.D. 35
L. Vitellius	A.D. 35–A.D. 39
P. Petronius	A.D. 39–A.D. 42
C. Vibius Marsus	A.D. 42–A.D. 44
C. Cassius Longinus	A.D. 45–A.D. 49/50
P. Anteius	A.D. 55
C. Ummidius Durmius Quadratus	A.D. 56–A.D. 58
Cn. Domitius Corbulo	A.D. 60–A.D. 63
C. Cestius Gallus	A.D. 63–A.D. 66

The Herodian Family

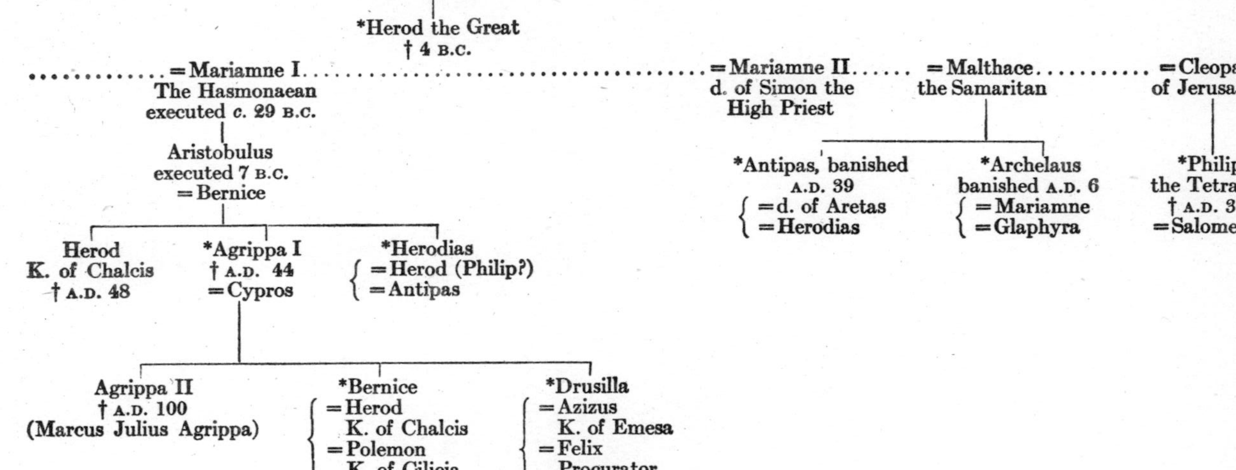

This "tree" shows the relationship of all the Herods mentioned in the New Testament. There were also many other members of the Herod family who are omitted here for the sake of clarity, as they have no connection with the story of the Gospels. A fuller discussion is given in *Beginnings*, Vol. V, pp. 487 ff. with a complete "tree" taken from the Loeb Classical Library, Josephus, Vol. II. We have here queried the identification of the first husband of Herodias as Herod Philip, as that is very doubtful; it is more probable that he was an otherwise unknown "Herod."

APPENDIX B

The Topography of the New Testament

PALESTINE AND SYRIA

Palestine is a strip of land, much longer than it is wide, running north and south along the eastern end of the Mediterranean. The narrow coastal plain and the lower slopes of the hills that bound it are fertile until to the south, near Gaza, the Sinai desert intrudes its scattered outposts—sand dunes which under the constant pressure of the wind "walk" across the country-side.

Through the centre of the country run the mountains, the slopes terraced elaborately to preserve what little soil may cling to them, the numerous valleys reasonably fertile. Eastward the mountains drop abruptly into the valley of the Jordan and Dead Sea, the opposing mountains of Moab (modern Transjordania) rising again almost as abruptly. A narrow oasis runs along on each side of the river, spreading wherever springs or irrigation permit, but the hills are barren.

Many thousands of years ago one of the greatest upheavals in geologic time overtook the Near East. The surface of the earth cracked, in an almost north-south line, from a point near the Caucasus to one deep in Africa. This is known as the "Great Rift" and a part of it forms the Sea of Galilee, the Jordan Valley and the Dead Sea, fixing the permanent and very peculiar conditions of life in Palestine. The surface of the Sea of Galilee is about six hundred feet below sea-level, that of the Dead Sea about twelve hundred.

The great spur of Mt. Carmel juts from the mountains of Palestine into the Mediterranean, bounding the coastal plain on the north, and beyond it a broad fertile valley cuts through the mountains from east to west. This is Esdraelon and the valley of Jezreel,—really two valleys sloping west to the Mediterranean and east to the Jordan from a low watershed.

North of Esdraelon come the hills again,—first the hills of Galilee, then those of Syria, running up to the snow-capped heights of the Lebanon. Through this region the coastal plain is much narrower and frequently disappears altogether as the hills come right down to the sea, forming more and better harbours than are found south of Carmel.

To the east of the Lebanon is the range of the Anti-Lebanon, and between the two the broad and very fertile valley of Coele-Syria (Hollow Syria), separated from the Sea of Galilee on the south by the heights of Mt. Hermon and watered by two rivers. These rise at almost the same spot, not far north of Baalbek (Heliopolis), the Leontes (the Litane) flowing south and breaking through the mountains at one end of the Lebanon, the Orontes flowing north around the other end of the Lebanon and entering the sea at Alexandretta.

East of the Anti-Lebanon is the great Syrian desert with the large and amazingly fertile oasis of Damascus lying in it to the east of Hermon. Southward from Damascus came the predominantly Greek cities of the Decapolis, the limits of whose territories are not too well defined, with the narrow district of Peraea facing Judaea from the opposite side of the Jordan.

The territory of Palestine was divided into three large sections: Judaea in the south, Samaria and Galilee. The last of these, and particularly the shores of the Sea of Galilee and the hills west of it, is the country of Jesus.

All the sites mentioned in the Gospels have been identified, at least to the satisfaction of the modern dragoman. The difficulty is that not all the identifications are valid. There are three grounds on which they can be made: literary, archaeological and the survival of the ancient names.

i. *Literary evidence.* This is, first of all, the New Testament; then Josephus and other historians or geographers of the first century; various Fathers of the Church,—Justin Martyr, Origen, Eusebius, Jerome, etc.; pious pilgrims like the famous one from Bordeaux in the fourth century. Unfortunately the Gospels and the historians frequently fail to characterise places except by name and are therefore useless without other evidence. Certainly in Jerusalem and probably throughout Palestine there was a dislocation of tradition after the fall of Jerusalem, but in the third century Origen renewed an interest in sacred sites. Doubtless he inquired of them from local Christians, who can hardly be supposed to have denied themselves the pleasure of response, even when some of the details had grown hazy in the intervening centuries, especially in a country where admission of ignorance is considered bad manners. The pious energy of the Empress Helena pushed certainty another step forward and from her time on the greater part of the identifications were firmly established and repeated from generation to generation of pilgrims.

ii. *Archaeological evidence.* Excavations of a site may increase the probability of an identification by uncovering walls and buildings which correspond to the literary tradition of the place. Very occasionally, it may make it quite certain, by producing an inscription mentioning the site by name, but,—especially in Palestine,—this is rare.

iii. *Survival of names.* Frequently the present colloquial name of a town can be recognised as a corruption of the name supposed to have pertained to it in New Testament times. The difficulty is, however, that mentioned above. Many of the identifications go back to the third or fourth century,—not to the first. Thus the modern names may also derive from that period. Sixteen hundred years is quite long enough to establish an idea firmly in the background of the peasant mentality of any country.

Thus it will be seen that the establishment of the identity of New Testament sites is a matter of delicate balance of judgement and perfectly adequately equipped critics may quite well disagree in their conclusions.

Aenon near to Salim: (Jn. iii.23). The Salim near Nablus (Neapolis) up in the hills, can hardly be intended and no other village of this name is known. Tradition, however, has placed the Salim of John (with its accompanying Aenon) at various points along the Jordan valley, where there are springs.

Arimathaea: (Mt. xxvii.57, Mk. xv.43, Lk. xxiii.51, Jn. xix.38). A town of this name is mentioned also by Josephus and in Maccabees. Eusebius identifies it with Elkanah, a town which he locates not far from Lydda. This is not contradicted by the slight indications in the Gospels.

Bethany: (Mt. xxi.17, xxvi.6, Mk. xi.1, 11, 12, xiv. 3, Lk. xix.29, xxiv.50, Jn. i.28, xi.1, 18, xii.1). Known in antiquity only from the Gospels and identified from about the fourth century on with the village of El-Azariyeh,—in the name of which is seen a corruption of "Lazarus." This village is on the road to Jericho on the east side of the Mount of Olives and fits what little data are given in the Synoptic Gospels.

The Bethany of Jn. i.28, however, cannot be intended as the same place. No "Bethany across Jordan" is known and it is possible that John confused the name, but the textual evidence is clear that this is the term originally used in his Gospel. The difficulty was early perceived and Origen, though admitting that the manuscript evidence supports "Bethany," preferred to emend the name to "Bethabara"—in which he was followed by later manuscripts.

Bethlehem: (Mt. ii.1, 5, 6, 8, 16, Lk. ii.2, 15, Jn. vii.42). The city of Jesus' birth is traditionally placed a few miles south-east of Jerusalem. This site was apparently known to Justin Martyr, about 150 A.D. and a very beautiful Constantinian basilica marks the supposed stable.

Of recent years, some critics have questioned whether Jesus was not born in another Bethlehem, about six miles west of Nazareth. Since, however, the Gospels specify "Bethlehem of Judaea" this seems to us unlikely.

Bethphage: (Mt. xxi.1, Mk. xi.1, Lk. xix.29). This village is not mentioned elsewhere and cannot be located accurately. The evidence must first be considered from the point of view of the textual critic. Apparently the original text of Mark told how, as Jesus and his disciples were approaching Jerusalem and Bethany, he was tired and sent his disciples "into the village over against you" (unnamed) to fetch a colt. Matthew, on the other hand, says "when they drew nigh to Jerusalem and were come to Bethphage, to the Mount of Olives," Jesus sent disciples to the village "over against you" to fetch an ass. Luke combines the two, as do later texts of Matthew and Mark, and mentions both Bethany and Bethphage. The interpretation of these facts would be that Bethany was near Jerusalem, high on the Mount of Olives, as it must have been if Jesus went out to it each night, and that Bethphage was at the foot of the last steep climb, where Jesus would have felt he needed a beast to carry him up, and was the village to which he sent for a donkey. Thus the Markan tradition would preserve the name of Jesus' destination, the village in which he planned to lodge, and the Matthean tradition the name of the village in which he could get help. If this be so, Bethphage must have been located on the east slope of the Mount of Olives, at the bottom of the last steep pitch, and much lower than the site now shown—for which there is no literary or archaeological evidence.

Bethsaida: (Mt. xi.21, Mk. vi.45, viii.22, Lk. ix.10, x.13, Jn. i.44, xii.21). The site of this town is not certain, although the favourite identification is with et-Tell, to the north of the Sea of Galilee and not far east of the Jordan. Others place it at Mas'adiyeh, on the Sea, east of the mouth of the Jordan. Josephus says (*Ant.* xviii.2.1): "He (Philip) also advanced the village Bethsaida, situate at the lake of Gennesareth, unto the dignity of a city, . . . and called it by the name *Julia,* the same name with Caesar's daughter," and (*B.J.* ii.9.1) "Philip . . . built . . . also the city Julias, in the lower Gaulonitis. Herod also built the city Tiberias in Galilee, and in Peraea (beyond Jordan another that was also called Julias." The Julias built by Philip would suit either of the traditional sites, as could the description in the *Antiquities,* though perhaps it is more suitable for Mas-aliyeh.

Some scholars, while admitting the probable locality of Josephus' Bethsaida, have felt it necessary to assume a second town of the same name, in order to fit in certain New Testament references. This, however, does not seem to be the case.

For example, in Mk. vii.45 Jesus, who is apparently on the west side of the Sea of Galilee, tells his disciples to "go to the other side . . . unto Bethsaida." The argument is that any of the proposed sites for Bethsaida and for the feeding of the Five Thousand are near the northern end of the lake,—not the "other side" of it, in relation to each other. There are two objections to this argument: In the first place, they are on opposite sides of the north end of the lake, where the Jordan enters it; in the second, the phrase does not necessarily imply a passage across the width of the lake. Josephus uses it of a journey from Tiberias to Tarichaeae.

In Jn. xii.21 Andrew, Peter and Philip are referred to as "of Bethsaida of Galilee." Again, a second Bethsaida is not necessary. Josephus refers to other places, further to the east, as "of Galilee"; probably by 66 A.D., and perhaps earlier, the east coast of the lake was included in the jurisdiction of Galilee; finally Bethsaida was so close to the Jordan that it may well have been thought of as "of Galilee" even when not formally included.

Capernaum: (Mt. iv.13, viii.5, xi.23, xvii.24, Mk. i.21, ii.1, ix.33, Lk. iv.23, 31, vii.1, x.15, Jn. ii.12, iv.46, vi.17, 24, 59). The exact site of Capernaum is uncertain but it was probably on or near the north-western shore of the Sea of Galilee. It is first mentioned in the gospels and in Josephus, and no spot now records it by name, unless it be assumed that Tell-Hum represents Tell-Nahum. Two sites, only two to three miles apart, divide the favour of modern critics: Tell-Hum and Khan-Minyeh, "the village of heretics." Jerome and Theodosius seem to indicate the former; Josephus' description fits the latter, as do the descriptions of medieval pilgrims. The evidence in the New Testament is not decisive,—stating merely that this town was on the sea of Galilee and had a synagogue and customs-house. The excavation of an elaborate synagogue at Tell-Hum a few years ago was acclaimed by some critics as decisive, but there is no evidence that there was not also a synagogue at Khan-Minyeh, and the building excavated is not old enough to have been the one seen by Jesus. Either site might have had a customs-house and a guard under a centurion—probably an indication that it was on the main road between Tiberias and Damascus, which went around the northern end of the lake. Probably opinion has been influenced by a feeling that Tell-Hum is a corruption of Tell Nahum, but why should the strong syllable have been lost rather than the weak?

Caesarea Philippi: (Mt. xvi.13, Mk. viii.27). A city built by Philip the tetrarch at the source of the Jordan, just under Hermon, on or near the site of the ancient Paulas. Apparently Jesus went, not to the city itself, but to the villages of the district surrounding it.

Cana: (Jn. ii.1, 11, iv. 46, xxi.2). This town is known only from the fourth Gospel, where the only additional information given is that it is in Galilee and somewhat higher than Capernaum. Two modern villages, perhaps because of their Arabic names, traditionally and at the present time, divide the support of those who wish to establish an identification. They are Kefr Kenna, some three to four miles north-east of Nazareth and Khirbet Kana (Kana el Gelil) about eight miles north of the same city. But Cana remains one of the more doubtful gospel sites.

Canaanite: (Mt. x.4, Mk. iii.18). This is probably not a local name at all, but a transliteration of the Aramaic word "zealous." In the parallel passage in Luke, the phrase is not "Simon the Canaanite," but "Simon the Zealot" (see pp. 196 f.).

Chorazin: (Mt. xi.21, Lk. x.13). From the context this town seems to be in the same general region as Bethsaida and Capernaum. Possibly it is to be located in a valley about a mile inland from Tell-Hum, where some ruins are found, including a large synagogue with Corinthian columns, which bear the name Kerazeh.

Cyrenian: (Mt. xxvii.32, Mk. xv.21, Lk. xxiii.26). Cyrene is the capital of a district of the north coast of Africa, between the territories of Egypt and Carthage. The name is preserved in the Italian north African colony of Cyrenaica. The ancient Cyrene had a very large Jewish population.

Dalmanutha: (Mk. viii.10). Probably this name, which is not known elsewhere, is a mistake. The Matthean parallel is Mageda(n) or Magdala(n) and this is the reading in Mark in many important ancient manuscripts. It is probably the correct reading in Mark as well as in Matthew. In any case, if there was a village called Dalmanutha it cannot be located, except as presumably somewhere on the shore of the Sea of Galilee.

The Decapolis: (Mt. iv.25, Mk. v.20, vii.31). A league of at first ten and later more cities, inhabited chiefly by Greeks. Their territory was not continuous, but extended north and south from Damascus to Philadelphia and, while lying chiefly to the east of the Jordan and the Sea of Galilee, included Scythopolis to the west. The original ten seem to have been: Scythopolis, Pella, Gadara, Hippos, Dion, Gerasa, Philadelphia, Raphana, Kanatha and Damascus. This is the list given by Pliny (*H.N.* 5.16 (18)). Thus the "coasts of the Decapolis," mentioned by Matthew, is a large and loosely defined area mostly east of the Jordan and the Sea of Galilee, but extending to the south-west and separating Judaea from Galilee.

Emmaus: (Lk. xxiv.13). There are two places called Emmaus mentioned by Josephus. One of them is the well-known city also called Nicopolis. Eusebius and others thought that this was the Emmaus of Luke xxiv.13, but this is impossible as it is fully twenty miles from Jerusalem. The influence of this tradition can be seen in the variant reading in Luke which makes Emmaus one hundred and sixty, instead of sixty, stadia from Jerusalem. Obviously this is an impossible distance for the walk of the disciples. The other Emmaus is referred to in Josephus, *B.J.* vii.6.6, as the place in which Vespasian settled eight hundred veterans. He says that it was thirty stadia (not quite four miles) from Jerusalem, but in the worse manuscripts of Josephus (followed in Whiston's translation) this is changed to sixty stadia to harmonise with Luke. Most modern critics identify this with the present Kolonieh (Colonia) which is about the right distance from Jerusalem as Josephus gives it. Perhaps Luke was giving the distance of the walk from Jerusalem and back.

Ephraim: (Jn. xi.54). The difficulties raised by this allusion have been discussed from every view-point. One suggestion is that "Ephraim" is a scribal error for "Jericho"—which brings the Johannine story into accord with the Synoptic. Others are that the city "Ephraim" is to be identified with the "Baal-Hazor" of II Sam. xiii.23 or the "Ephron" of II Chron. xiii.19. These identifications, even if either be correct, only put the difficulty one stage back—since the sites of Baal-Hazor and Ephron cannot be said to be fixed.

The Country of the Gadarenes (Gerasenes, Gergasenes): (Mt. viii.28, Mk. v.1, Lk. viii.26, 37). The text of these passages is obscure and complex. Probably *Gerasenes* is the original text of Mark and Luke; *Gadarenes* of Matthew; *Gerga-*

senes is an emendation of Origen, who perhaps intended the village called Khersa on the east coast of the Sea of Galilee; but all three variants are found in some manuscripts of each Gospel. The facts about the three places are as follows:

i. Gerasa is the well-known Greek city (Jerash). It can hardly be the scene of the story of the demoniac and the swine if they really ran down into the sea, but possibly "sea" is an error in tradition, and they ran down into the deep "wady" near Gerasa.

ii. Gadara is an equally well-known city only six miles from the sea; it may be a Matthean emendation, and if so is valuable evidence that "Matthew" knew Palestine, and saw the difficulty of Gerasa.

iii. Gergasa is an Origenian emendation; it helps to identify the character of manuscripts which preserve it, and it is a question whether the village Khersa is the source of Origen's guess, or perpetuates it.

Khersa, whether a corruption of Gergesa or of Gerasa (in the latter case, a small and otherwise unknown village of the same name as the great city) is not an unconvincing site. It is about opposite Tiberias and fulfills all the requirements of the story.

Galilee: The boundaries of Galilee varied from time to time, but it is described by Josephus (*B.J.* iii.3.1-2) as follows: "Now Phenicia and Syria encompass about the Galilees, which are two, and called the Upper Galilee and the Lower. They are bounded toward the sun-setting with the borders of the territory belonging to Ptolemais and by Carmel; which mountain had formerly belonged to the Galileans, but now belonged to the Tyrians, to which mountain adjoins Gaba, which is called 'the city of horsemen' because those horsemen that were dismissed by Herod the king dwelt therein; they are bounded on the south with Samaria and Scythopolis, as far as the river Jordan; on the east with Hippene and Gadaris, and also with Gaulonitis and the borders of the kingdom of Agrippa; its northern parts are bounded by Tyre and the country of the Tyrians. As for that Galilee which is called the Lower, it extends in length from Tiberias to Zabulon, and of the maritime places, Ptolemais is its neighbor; its breadth is from the village called Xaloth, which lies in the great plain, as far as Bersabe, from which beginning also is taken the breadth of the Upper Galilee, as far as the village Baca, which divides the land of the Tyrians from it; its length is also from Meloth to Thella, a village near to Jordan.

"These two Galilees, of so great largeness, and encompassed

with so many nations of foreigners, have been always able to make a strong resistance on all occasions of war; for the Galileans are inured to war from their infancy, and have been always very numerous; nor hath the country been ever destitute of men of courage, or wanted a numerous set of them, for their soil is universally rich and fruitful, and full of the plantations of trees of all sorts, insomuch, that it invites the most slothful to take pains in its cultivation by its inhabitants, and no part of it lies idle. Moreover, the cities lie here very thick, and the very many villages there are here are everywhere so full of people, by the richness of their soil, that the very least of them contained above fifteen thousand inhabitants.

"In short, if any one will suppose that Galilee is inferior to Perea in magnitude, he will be obliged to prefer it before it in its strength."

The Sea of Galilee: (Mt. iv.18, xv.29, Mk. i.16, vii.31, Jn. vi.1); also known as the Lake of Gennesaret (Lk. v.1) and the Sea of Tiberias (Jn. vi.1, xxi.1). The use of these various names is a most complicated problem for the textual critic, but has no place here. Set in a cup of hills, six hundred feet below sea-level, it is notorious for its sudden violent storms,—as are mountain lakes elsewhere. It should be noted that any reference in the Gospels to "the sea," without a proper name, should be interpreted as referring to the Sea of Galilee, not the Dead Sea or the Mediterranean (see *Tiberias* and *Gennesaret*).

Gennesaret (*Gennesar*)*:* (Mt. xiv.34, Mk. vi.53, Lk. v.1). A region west of the Sea of Galilee, toward the north, and described by Josephus (*B.J.* iii.10.8) as follows: "The country also that lies over against this lake hath the same name of Gennesareth; its nature is wonderful as well as its beauty; its soil is so fruitful that all sorts of trees can grow upon it, and the inhabitants accordingly plant all sorts of trees there; for the temper of the air is so well mixed that it agrees very well with those several sorts, particularly walnuts, which require the coldest air, flourish there in vast plenty; there are palm trees also, which grow best in hot air; fig trees also and olives grow near them, which yet require an air which is more temperate. One may call this place the ambition of nature, where it forces those plants that are naturally enemies to one another to agree together; it is a happy contention of the seasons, as if every one of them laid claim to this country; for it not only nourishes different sorts of autumnal fruit beyond men's expectation, but preserves them a great while; it supplies men with the principal fruits, with grapes and figs continually, during ten months of the year, and the rest of the fruits as they become ripe together through the whole year: for, besides the good temperature of the air, it is also watered from a most fertile fountain. The people of the country call it Capharnaum; some have thought it to be a vein of the Nile, because it produces the Coracin fish as well as that lake does which is near to Alexandria. The length of the country extends itself along the banks of this lake that bears the same name, for thirty furlongs, and is in breadth twenty. And this is the nature of that place."

Idumaea: (Mk. iii.8). The "Edom" of the Old Testament, a mountainous region with a few fertile valleys, lying to the south of Judaea.

Jericho: (Mt. xx.29, Mk. x.46, Lk. x.30, xviii,35, xix.1, Heb. xi.30). The only large town of the Jordan valley after it leaves the Sea of Galilee. From ancient times to the present day the city has slightly shifted its location, but has been continuously occupied, and the identification is not in doubt.

Jerusalem: (numerous references in the Gospels and Acts: Rom. xv.19, 25, 26, 31, I Cor. xvi.2, Gal. i.17, 18, ii.1, iv.25, 26, Heb. xii.22, Rev. iii.12, xxi.2, 10). The capital of Judaea. It is sometimes forgotten that Jerusalem is on the top of a relatively narrow range of hills, with a steep drop of above 3500 ft. to the Jordan valley on the east, and a somewhat less abrupt descent of nearly 2300 ft. to the coastal plain on the west.

Localities in Jerusalem: See especially Vincent et Abel, *Jerusalem,* the articles in Hastings, G. A. Smith, *Jerusalem,* and *Beginnings,* Vol. V, pp. 474 ff. Ten spots in Jerusalem or just outside it are mentioned in the New Testament.

i. *The Upper room, the tomb of David* and the *house of John Mark* and his mother. Late tradition identifies all these places with the *caenaculum* belonging to the Franciscans in Jerusalem. This is in the modern Sion in the south-west corner of Jerusalem (the ancient Sion was in the south-east, outside the present wall). It is identified with the tomb of David on the basis of Acts ii.29—an obviously absurd exegesis—and is popularly known as En-nebi David. Probably this was the site of the Byzantine Church of the Apostles, and it may represent a third century tradition that here had been the Upper room of Pentecost. The Byzantine church appears to have been founded by Maximus, bishop of Jerusalem between 331 and 349. Before this there may have been an earlier church on the same spot, but the evidence is not quite satisfactory. Epiphanius (*De mensuris et ponderibus,* xiv, Migne, *P.G.* xliii.260 f.) says that when Hadrian visited Jerusalem he found it desolate except for a single synagogue and a church which had been built on the spot where the Apostles had lived in the upper room. Unfortunately, those who use Epiphanius most trust him least. It is ominous that neither Eusebius nor the Pilgrim of Bordeaux says anything about this church, and it is to be feared that the tradition, like the church, is not older than the foundation of Maximus in the fourth century.

ii. *The court-room* of the Sanhedrin. Josephus says it was immediately west of the Temple (Josephus, *B.J.* v.4.2), but the Talmud says it was in the Temple itself. Further details can be found in the *Jewish Encyclopedia,* Vol. xi, p. 72, but they lead nowhere.

iii. *Three prisons* are mentioned. One, that of the Sanhedrin, was possibly beneath the Council chamber, but there is no evidence. The second is that of Herod,—the Praetorium on the west side of the city, close to the present Police Headquarters (possibly Pilate used it when he was in Jerusalem). The third is that of the Roman garrison in the barracks of the tower Antonia overlooking the Temple and connecting with it by a stairway (Acts xxi.40 and Josephus, *B.J.* v.5.8).

iv. *The Temple.* It is impossible here to discuss all the details of the plan of the Temple, but two points are important.

a. There was a door in the east wall of the city leading to the Temple area. This was called the gate of Shushan. There was then a line of three more gates, the first into the court of women, the second from the court of women to the court of men, the third from the court of men into the Holy of Holies. The first of these was called the gate of Nicanor. The important question for the student of the New Testament is, which was the "Beautiful" gate of Acts iii.3? No gate is mentioned by this name in Josephus or in the Talmud, but the gate now called the Golden Gate is an obvious corruption, perhaps not earlier than the Crusades, of a Latin transliteration of the word for beautiful *(orea)* misread as *aurea,* owing to similarity of pronunciation. The present golden gate is perhaps in the place where the Shushan gate once was, but modern scholars, influenced by the stress which is put by Josephus on the splendour of the gate of Nicanor, have thought that this is the gate intended in Acts. Unfortunately, there is an important variation in the text relating the cure of the lame beggar (see *Beginnings,* Vol. IV, note *ad loc.*). According to the Neutral text, the Shushan gate is intended, according to the Western, the Nicanor. This does not help to identify the gate, but it is interesting as indicating knowledge of and interest in the details of the Temple at the time when the text was still being revised. But much more important is the fact that no one would have come through the Shushan gate if he had been living in Jerusalem; it was the entry for persons coming from the Mount of Olives and Bethany.

b. Solomon's Porch. The Temple area probably had a portico along its eastern and southern sides. Apparently the eastern was Solomon's Porch and the southern the Royal Porch. The word "Porch" though traditional in English is unfortunate. The Greek is "Stoa" and means a colonnade (see Josephus, *B.J.* v.5.1 and *Beginnings,* Vol. V, p. 485).

v. *The Grave of Jesus, Calvary and Golgotha.* These places are venerated in Jerusalem at the Holy Sepulchre and the Church of the Anastasis. They have more claim to authenticity than most identifications. The best discussion is that of the Dominican scholars, Fathers Vincent and Abel (to whom we owe many thanks for many things), in their great book on Jerusalem. There is perhaps difficulty in the discovery of the northern wall which would seem to follow a line which would bring the present church within it. The question of the northern wall cannot be settled without more excavation, but the "second wall" seems clearly to lie south of the church, and if the "northern wall" of recent discovery is that of Agrippa, it does not affect the question.

vi. *Bethesda.* It is fairly certain on textual evidence that this place should be spelled *Bethzatha* and it ought to be identical with the district which Josephus calls Bezetha,—the quarter of Jerusalem north of the Temple. But the identification of the pool mentioned in John v.2 is obscure. The Sheep gate was north of the Temple, and it led to Bethzetha but there is no pool there, except one of later date. Conder thought that the pool was the "Virgins' pool" south-east of the Temple and wished to spell the name *Betheshdah* (house of the stream). There is a spring here, and the water does overflow and is "troubled" intermittently. But it is not near the "Sheep gate," though sheep are often watered there (see also under Siloam).

vii. *Siloam.* The evidence of Josephus (*B.J.* v.4.1) confirms the tradition that the pool of Siloam was at the southern end of the Tyropaean valley, which runs through the middle of Jerusalem from north to south. Apparently, the water from the "Pool of the Virgin" (the Ain Sitti Miriam) was dammed up in the Kidron valley east of Jerusalem and used for irrigation. It was afterwards taken through a conduit in the rock and this ultimately led into two reservoirs, of which one was and is called the pool of Siloam, though it now contains more dirt than water (see the article by Sir Charles Wilson in Hastings *Dictionary of the Bible*).

viii. *Cedron:* (John xviii.1). Probably the Kidron valley which divides Olivet from Jerusalem. The fact that Cedron means "Cedars" in Greek seems unimportant.

ix. *Gethsemane.* Apparently this was on the lower part of Olivet, and the traditional site, though doubtless only a guess, is quite plausible.

x. *The Mount of Olives* is the southern part of the ridge to the east of Jerusalem. It is doubtful whether Mount of Olivet (Olivetum = Oliveyard) or Mount of Olives is the right form. It is possibly the former, but the point is scarcely important.

Jordan: (Mt. iii.5, 6, 13, iv.15, 25, xix.1, Mk. 1.5, 9, iii.8, x.1, Lk. iii.3, iv.1, Jn. i.28, iii.26, x.40). The one large river in the region. It is about seventy miles long, originating near Caesarea Philippi, passing through the Sea of Galilee and emptying into the Dead Sea. It was probably along its banks that Jesus travelled on his last journey, from Galilee to Jericho (see Judaea). Although the hills on each side are very barren, there is nothing along its lower reaches which a native of the Eastern Mediterranean would call "desert," until the vicinity of Jericho is reached. It is therefore probable that the preaching of John and the baptism should be located just north of the Dead Sea, although the traditional location is in Galilee.

Judaea: The limits of Judaea varied. It is described by Josephus (*B.J.* iii.3.5) as follows: "In the limits of Samaria and Judaea lies the village Anuath, which is also named Borceos. This is the northern boundary of Judaea. The southern parts of Judaea, if they be measured lengthways, are bounded by a village adjoining to the confines of Arabia; the Jews that dwell there call it Jordan. However, its breadth is extended from the river Jordan to Joppa. The city Jerusalem is situated in the very middle; on which account some have, with sagacity enough, called that city the navel of the country. Nor indeed is Judaea destitute of such delights as come from the sea, since its maritime places extend as far as Ptolemais; it was parted in eleven portions, of which the royal city Jerusalem was the supreme, and presided over all the neighboring country as the head does over the body. As to the other cities that were inferior to it, they presided over their several toparchies; Gophna was the second of those cities, and next to that Acrabatta, after them Thamna, and Lydda and Emmaus and Pella and Idumaea and Engaddi and Herodium and Jericho; and after them came Jamnia and Joppa, as presiding over the neighboring people: and besides these there was the region of Gamala and Gaulonitis and Batanea and Trachonitis, which are also parts of the kingdom of Agrippa. This (last) country begins at mount Libanus and the fountains of Jordan, and reaches breadthways to the lake of Tiberias; and in length is extended from a village called Arpha as far as Julius. Its inhabitants are a mixture of Jews and Syrians."

The majority of New Testament references to Judaea are general, e.g. "a great multitude from Galilee followed him, and from Judaea," etc., or "the brethren which dwelt in Judaea"; but some raise problems.

a. Mk. iii.7-8: It should be noted that in these general references the "Jerusalemites" are frequently distinguished from "those from Judaea," being classed side by side, as if the writers were thinking of the country-folk of Judaea and the city-folk of Jerusalem.

b. Mk. x.1: "And he arose from thence (i.e. Capernaum) and cometh into the coasts of Judaea by the farther side of Jordan." Apparently Capernaum was west of the northern end of the Sea of Galilee and Jesus' route according to this text would be around the east side of the Sea, and down the Jordan valley to some point opposite Judaea. The alternative text "into the coasts of Judaea *and* by the farther side of Jordan" would imply a route along the west side of the Sea and the Jordan to the borders of Judaea, thence down the east side to somewhere opposite Jericho. In either case, the route down the Jordan valley seems obviously indicated.

Mt. iii.1: "the wilderness of Judaea," probably the western side of the Jordan River, north of the Dead Sea. The Jordan, for most of its length, runs through a narrow strip of fertility, though the mountains on either side are barren. As it approaches the Dead Sea, however, the banks become almost as desolate as the surrounding country.

Jn. iv.47, 54: Apparently Galilee and Judaea in the strict meaning of the terms, were at no point contiguous. Either Samaria or the Decapolis had to be traversed. Yet the matter is confused, for Josephus states in one place that Galilee extended down to Mount Carmel and in another that Judaea included the coast as far north as Ptolemais. He also mentions Ginea (modern Jenin) as the boundary of Samaria—thus excluding from it all the Plain of Jezreel and any part of the coast. Moreover, Luke iv.44, Acts ii.9, x.37, xi.1, 29, xxvi.20 seem to reflect a loose usage in which Judaea means Palestine, and Strabo uses it to cover all the country south of the Lebanon.

Magdala or *Magedan:* (Mt. xv.39). This corresponds to "Dalmanutha" in the parallel passage in Mark. No "Magedan" can be located and it is probable that it is a corruption of Magdala. Certainly there was a Galilean town of that name, which is mentioned in the Talmud, and appears in the name Mary *Magdalene.* The Jerusalem and Babylonian Talmuds both mention a Magdala near Tiberias, though they differ slightly in the location.

Nain: (Lk. vii.11). A town where, according to Luke, Jesus raised a dead man. The place is not otherwise known. On the previous day Jesus was in Capernaum. According to Eusebius, and Jerome, Nain was not far from Tabor. This might be associated with a modern village of the same name on the north edge of the plain of Esdraelon. The identification is, however, quite uncertain and even Luke's name for the village is questionable.

Nazareth: See G. F. Moore in *Beginnings,* Vol. I, pp. 426 ff. (Mt. ii.23, iv.13, xxi.11, Mk. i.9, Lk. i.26, ii.4, 39, 51, iv.16, Jn. i.45, 46, Acts x.38). This town, associated in the Gospels with the early life of Jesus, is usually identified with the modern town of the same name (Arab. *al-Nasira*) high in the hills to the north of the plain of Jezreel and looking down upon it. To this identification there is no valid objection, even though it is not supported by any proof.

The modern Nazareth is in Galilee–the one identifying tag supplied by the New Testament–but because the name does not occur in the Old Testament, Josephus or the Talmud, some critics have been inclined to argue that no such place ever existed. Since, however, Nazareth seems to have been a small place and these authorities by no means mention all even of the important cities of Galilee, this seems an unnecessarily complicated hypothesis–especially as it involves the assumption that the authors of the Gospels and Acts misunderstood the adjective "Nazarene" as a local term and invented a "Nazareth" to which it referred. They are then constrained to interpret "Nazarene" as meaning something else, and this has not yet been done satisfactorily.

Until some cogent reason to the contrary is produced, it seems best to assume that "Nazareth" was a town of Galilee, too insignificant to be mentioned except by writers interested in the Jesus who came from there. It was used by them to distinguish him from others who bore this common name. The similarity of the word to the Hebrew for "Branch" (netzer) used in a Messianic sense by Zachariah, was afterwards noted and the connection of Jesus with Nazareth was treated as the fulfilment of prophecy (cf. Mt. ii.23). The identification with the modern Nazareth goes back to the third or fourth century and may be valid.

"Peran"="The other side": (Mt. iv.15, 25, viii.18, 28, xiv.22, xvi.5, xix.1, Mk. iii.8, iv.35, v.1, 21, vi.45, viii.13, x.1, Lk. viii.22, Jn. i.28, iii.26, vi.1, 17, 22, 25, x.40). The term "the people beyond Jordan" is occasionally used to designate the inhabitants of the east bank and probably means those of Peraea in particular. Otherwise the phrase "beyond Jordan" varies from the east bank to the west bank in accordance with the point of view of the narrative, e.g. in Mt. iv.15 and Mk. v.21 it certainly refers to the country west of the river.

The references in John are all connected with John the Baptist and imply that, at least when Jesus came to him, he was baptising on the east bank of the river.

Samaria: (Lk. xvii.11, Jn. iv.4, 5, 7, Acts i.8, viii.1, 5, 9, 14, ix.31, xv.3). The district lying between Judaea and Galilee. Its boundaries varied from time to time, but it was described by Josephus (*B.J.* iii.3.4) as follows: "Now, as to the country of Samaria, it lies between Judaea and Galilee; it begins at a village that is in the great plain called Ginea, and ends at the Acrabbene toparchy, and is of entirely the same nature with Judaea; for both countries are made up of hills and valleys, and are moist enough for agriculture and are very fruitful. They have abundance of trees, and are full of autumnal fruit, both that which grows wild and that which is the effect of cultivation. They are not naturally watered with many rivers, but derive their chief moisture from rain-water, of which they have no want; and for those rivers which they have, all their waters are exceeding sweet: by reason also of the excellent grass they have their cattle yield more milk than do those in other places, and, what is the greatest sign of excellency and abundance, they each of them are very full of people."

"Samaria" was also the name of the capital city of this district from the time of King Omri, its founder, until the time of Herod the Great, who rebuilt a large part of it and renamed it "Sebaste" in honour of Augustus.

The difficulty of many passages lies in this double use of the name, and it is often difficult to determine with certainty whether the city or the district is meant.

"The (or 'a') city of Samaria" in Acts viii is a difficult phrase both textually and historically. The use of the definite article in this way is very rare, if not impossible in Greek. If, however, it is the correct reading, and the manuscript evidence favours it, it would imply that the city referred to was either the capital, or at least the largest or richest town of the district.

By the time when the incidents related in Acts took place, "Samaria" the city had become Sebaste, but it is, of course, possible that colloquially it retained the name under which it had been famous for almost a thousand years. On the other hand, Neapolis (the modern Nablus) was probably the richest town of the district of Samaria and the most active commercially. Either may be the place meant in Acts, or perhaps a quite different town may have been intended,—especially if the correct reading be "*a* city of Samaria," not "*the* city."

Sodom and *Gomorrha:* (Mt. x.15, xi.23, Mk. xi.24, Lk. x.12, xvii.29, Rom. ix.29, II Pet. ii.6, Jude 7, Rev. xi.8). The locality of these cities is still entirely unsettled,—though a position somewhere near the Dead Sea has been traditionally favoured. In any case, they appear in the New Testament only as historic admonition, not as actual places.

Sycher: (Jn. iv.5). This village, otherwise unknown, seems from the context to be close to Jacob's well. This, in turn, is well-known and is less than a mile from Shechem, the ancient city of the Samaritans. From at least the time of Jerome, the possibility that "Sycher" is a mistake for "Shechem" has been entertained by students of the fourth Gospel. This, however, is not certain and it is possible that there was also a "Sycher" within a short distance of Jacob's well.

Syria: (Mt. iv.24, Mk. vii.26, Lk. ii.2). This term is very vague and refers in different writers and at different periods to wider or narrower areas. In its broadest sense, as in Strabo, Pliny and Ptolemy, it included all the territory between the Taurus and the Arabian desert, between the Euphrates and the Mediterranean. More narrowly it was that part of the wider area north of Palestine and east of the sea-coast region of Phoenicia.

Even the boundaries of the Roman province of Syria, which is certainly the meaning of "Syria" in Luke, varied from time to time. It must be remembered that the Romans thought not so much of the boundaries of territories, as of important cities with accompanying, and more or less undefined surrounding areas. At a time when surveying was an unknown art this was inevitable.

The Greek woman of Mk. vii.26 was a native of Phoenicia and Syria. Here the term "Syrian" seems the general indication, "Phoenician" the particular. "Syria" includes the coastal region as well as the interior.

In Mt. iv.24 the sense of "Syrian" is even broader: "And

Jesus went about all Galilee, teaching . . . and preaching . . . and healing . . . And his fame went throughout all Syria: and they brought unto him all sick people . . ."

Mount of Transfiguration: Traditions of the fourth century identify this both with the Mt. of Olives and with Mt. Tabor. The former is most unlikely since Jesus is in Galilee both before and after the event, and there is no indication of the long journey which would have been necessary to reach the vicinity of Jerusalem. Even Mt. Tabor is a considerable distance from the region of Caesarea Philippi, but could easily have been reached if the "six days" mentioned in Mk. ix.2 were spent partly in travel. Modern critics have, on the whole, preferred to think of Mt. Hermon, close above Caesarea Philippi, as the scene of the Transfiguration. There is, however, no evidence for any of these identifications.

Tyre and Sidon: (Mt. xi.21, 22, xv.21, Mk. iii.8, vii.24, 31, Lk. vi.17, x.13, Acts xxi.3, 7, xxvii.3). These two sea-coast towns north of Ptolemais, have preserved a continuous identity down to the present day. In the Gospels they are always mentioned in conjunction, in Acts separately.

Mk. vii.31 is difficult to understand and much ingenuity has been expended upon it. Textual emendation has, of course, taken its part,—perhaps most happily in Wellhausen's suggestion that "through Sidon" should have been translated "to Bethsaida," from an original Aramaic in which the phrases would have been almost indistinguishable. The greatest difficulty with this is that it ignores the following phrase "through the coasts of the Decapolis." No route south or south-eastward from Tyre to Galilee would pass anywhere near the Decapolis. On the other hand, if Jesus started northward from Tyre toward Sidon he would soon have come to the mouth of the river Leontes and turning eastward up this valley could have followed it to the point where it bends sharply north. Here a short but steep climb over a narrow range of hills would bring him into the Jordan valley in the vicinity of Caesarea Philippi and thus down, through what may properly be called "the shores of the Decapolis," to Galilee.

THE MEDITERRANEAN WORLD

If the line of Coele-Syria be followed up as far as it goes to the north, the valley of the river Orontes turns around sharp to the west, and comes out into the Mediterranean almost at the corner of the eastern coast. At this point there was naturally a good harbour, Daphne, until it was silted up, and adjoining it was the great city Antioch, the third in the Roman

Empire, with a variegated population remarkable for its wealth and its wickedness. This city became the second capital of the early Church. Before many years had passed, the migration of persecuted Christians had produced a church there more important than that in Jerusalem, and it became the place from which started the Pauline mission to the rest of the Roman Empire.

The land which the missionaries first had to traverse was divided from them either by the sea or by two rather severe lines of mountains, through which there were but few passes. Not far from Antioch to the north and west are the Syrian gates, which lead the way through Amanus, which is the continuation of the Lebanon to the north. As soon as this pass was traversed, the missionary found himself in Cilicia, of which the most important city was Tarsus, a university town and the home of St. Paul. The other side of Cilicia is the Taurus, a range of great mountains which runs roughly parallel to Amanus and the Lebanon and then bends to the west, so that it runs along the south coast of Asia Minor, and divides it into two very unequal portions. On the south is a narrow coastland, mountainous, rugged and, generally speaking, unadaptable for cultivation, and on the other side of it, to the north, a large plateau, partly fertile, partly barren, considerably elevated above the level of the sea. In this plateau itself, in the middle of Asia Minor, there is another considerable range of mountains, though not nearly so long, called the Sultan Dagh. The middle of this plateau, to the north and west, is very sterile and barren and was not much cultivated in antiquity, so that there was, as it were, an island of barrenness in the middle of a highly populated and fertile district.

The west end of Asia Minor was drained by several large rivers, of which the Indus, the Meander, the Hermus, the Carkos and the Rhyndakos, with their tributaries, are the most important.

This complex of mountains and rivers conditioned both life and travel in Asia Minor. It also went far to fix the limit of the provinces into which it was divided by the Romans. Naturally, the main roads ran east and west rather than north and south. Exactly where they all were is, of course, not completely known, nor will it be until a complete survey is made of Asia Minor, but obviously there had to be a main road from the west coast, beginning at Ephesus towards the south, or at Troas at the north, going across the country north or south of the central desert, as far as the passes across the Taurus, and so into Syria, and across the desert to the Euphrates. Perhaps the chief road of this kind was that which went from Ephesus along the northern foot of the Sultan Dagh, through the passes to the north of the Taurus. But there must have been a subsidiary road to this, which went further to the south, probably branching off from the main road at Iconium, then as now a great junction, then through the Cilician gate and through Tarsus to the Syrian gate, just above the now well-known port of Alexandretta. This road would certainly be the main means of communication between Antioch and Asia Minor and, as will be seen from the map, Tarsus is on and must be on the main road which goes through the Cilician gate; for, just as Antioch is immediately to the south of the Syrian gate, Tarsus is immediately to the south of the Cilician gate. Possibly this was a continuation of the *Via Sebaste*, which was started by the Romans in the time of Augustus and on it would naturally be Lystra and Laranda. A glance at the map (see end-paper) will show that there is a much shorter route from Iconium to the north of the marshes which come exactly east of Lystra. Why was this not the main road, if indeed it was not? Probably because the Romans desired to hold the mountaineers in check and therefore the main road with its colonies, Lystra and Laranda, ran along the base of the mountains, even at the expense of being a little longer.

This country of Asia Minor has been in past history a cockpit of contending nations. In the first century, they were all more or less under the control of Rome, and only some remnants remained of the older ethnological divisions. For many generations the Lydians had occupied the west, the Phrygians the centre, and the Galatians, coming a little after the others, the district in the north-east. Still further to the east were the Cappadocians and south of them the Cilicians. Next to the Cilicians to the west were the Lycaonians, to say nothing of smaller tribes, such as the Isaurians, Pamphylians and Pisidians, all of whom have left their names on the map, even if they have made a somewhat smaller print on the records of history.

The boundaries of the Roman provinces were fixed partly by the date of acquisition and partly by the geography of the country, which in turn largely conditioned the ethnological frontiers of the various nations. The Roman provinces had moved steadily eastward. The first, the legacy of Attalus, became the Province of Asia and included the whole of ancient Lydia, and a great part of Phrygia. To what extent the old languages survived is doubtful; probably they were not entirely extinct, but Greek had taken their place in most of the cities. Possibly the word Asia had been used loosely to describe the Greek-speaking cities, and Phrygia (and Lydia?) was used of the non-Hellenic country. From that spread the fashion of describing the whole province of Asia, and its eastern limits were defined by degrees, not always in the same way.

To the south of "Asia" was the small Province of Lycia, of which the separate name indicates its separate acquisition. Still further to the east was another small, poor and rather sterile country, Pamphylia, which gives its name to a Province. Further to the north was Pisidia, which at the time of the writing of the New Testament, was probably part of the Province of Galatia.

Galatia, a congeries of kingdoms and parts of kingdoms, came to the east of Asia and stretched almost across the country (see further on pp. 125 ff.). To the north-east of Asia and abutting on Galatia was Bithynia, and in the south-east were the remains of Lycaonia, still dignified by the name of the Kingdom of Antiochus, one of the few remaining independent princes whom the Romans kept to assist in the government of the wilder parts of the Empire.

The chief exits from Asia Minor to Europe were the ports of Ephesus and Troas, though of course there were many others of considerable importance. It is hard for the modern mind to remember that in those days it was more difficult to go from Ephesus to Corinth than from Corinth to Ephesus, because the prevalent winds are westerly. For that reason perhaps it was not uncommon to go by land to Troas and then creep along the coast of South Macedonia to Neapolis, the modern Cavalla, just east of Mt. Athos, which was the end of the great Roman road which led across Greece to Dyrrachium, whence there was an easy connection to Brindisi and so to Rome. Greece, like Asia Minor, was divided into provinces, but unlike the Asiatic districts, the provinces of Greece were all senatorial and the country was divided into Thrace, Macedonia and Achaea, each with its subdivisions. Greece, then as now, was badly equipped with roads, chiefly owing to the fact that the country is so difficult. For that reason, in order to go from the north to the south, it was much easier to take a boat which was going down the coast, for which purpose the prevailing winds and the draught off the coast rendered progress moderately easy.

The individual places mentioned in Acts are so well-known, in sharp distinction to those in Palestine, that a map seems sufficient to indicate their locality (see end-paper).

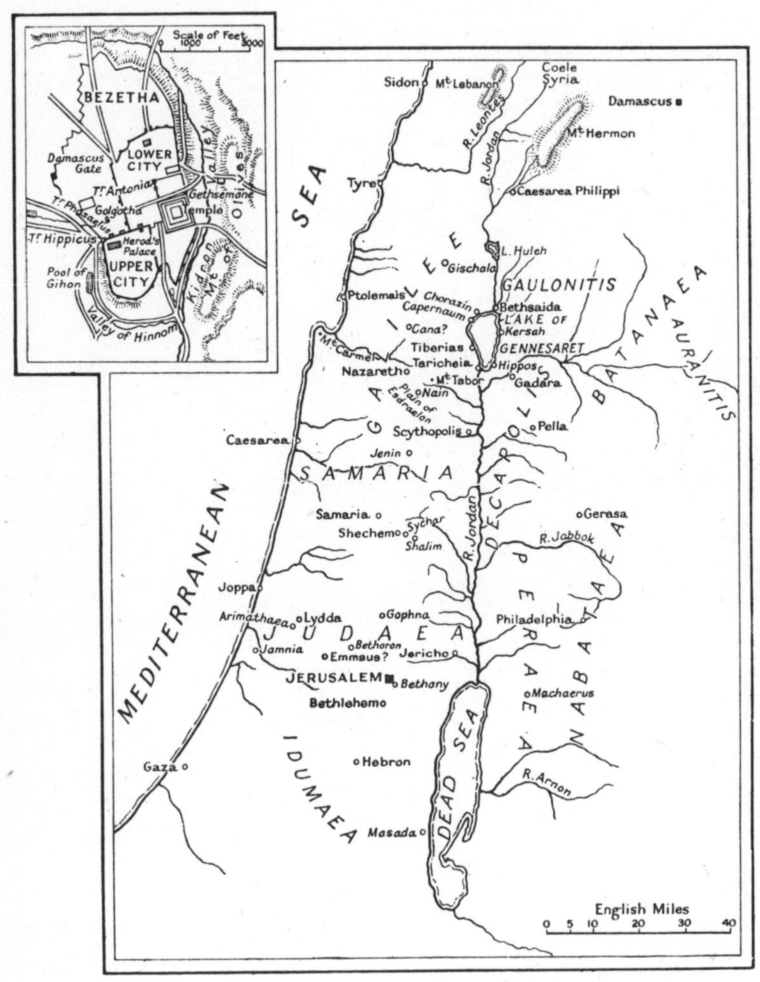

PALESTINE (JERUSALEM INSET)

APPENDIX C

The following quotations supply the main body of "tradition." The list could be greatly increased by adding the evidence of later writers, such as Augustine and Jerome. But these do not seem to contribute anything which may not have been derived from the passages here collected. It should be noted how largely we are dependent on Eusebius and on his fortunate habit of accurate quotation in preference to loose paraphrase.

1. Papias (a) *as reported by Eusebius.*

"Of Papias five treatises are extant which have also the title of 'Interpretation of the Oracles of the Lord.' These are also mentioned by Irenaeus as though his only writing, for he says in one place, 'To these things also Papias, the hearer of John, who was a companion of Polycarp and one of the ancients, bears witness in writing in the fourth of his books, for five books were composed by him.' So says Irenaeus. Yet Papias himself, according to the preface of his treatises, makes plain that he had in no way been a hearer and eyewitness of the sacred Apostles, but teaches that he had received the articles of faith from those who had known them, for he speaks as follows: 'And I shall not hesitate to append to the interpretations all that I ever learnt from the presbyters and remember well, for of their truth I am confident. For unlike most I did not rejoice in them who say much, but in them who teach the truth, nor in them who recount the commandments of others, but in them who repeated those given to the faith by the Lord and derived from truth itself; but if ever anyone came who had followed the presbyters, I inquired into the words of the presbyters, what Andrew or Peter or Philip or Thomas or James or John or Matthew, or any other of the Lord's disciples, had said, and what Aristion and the presbyter John, the Lord's disciple, were saying. For I did not suppose that information from books would help me so much as the word of a living and surviving voice.' It is here worth noting that he twice counts the name of John, and reckons the first John with Peter and James and Matthew and the other Apostles, clearly meaning the Evangelist, but by changing his statement places the second with the others outside the number of the Apostles, putting Aristion before him and clearly calling him a presbyter. This confirms the truth of the story of those who have said that there were two of the same name in Asia, and that there are two tombs at Ephesus both still called John's. This calls for attention: for it is probable that the second (unless anyone prefer the former) saw the revelation which passes under the name of John. The Papias whom we are now treating confesses that he had received the words of the Apostles from their followers, but says that he had actually heard Aristion and the presbyter John. He often quotes them by name and gives their traditions in his writings. Let this suffice to good purpose. But it is worth while to add to the words of Papias already given other sayings of his, in which he tells certain marvels and other details which apparently reached him by tradition. It has already been mentioned that Philip the Apostle lived at Hierapolis with his daughters, but it must now be shown how Papias was with them and received a wonderful story from the daughters of Philip; for he relates the resurrection of a corpse in his time and in another place another miracle connected with Justus surnamed Barsabas, for he drank poison but by the Lord's grace suffered no harm. Of this Justus the Acts relates that the sacred Apostles set him up and prayed him together with Matthias after the ascension of the Lord for the choice of one to fill up their number in place of the traitor Judas, 'and they set forth two, Joseph called Barsabas, who was called Justus, and Matthias; and they prayed and said.' The same writer adduces other accounts, as though they came to him from unwritten tradition, and some strange parables and teachings of the Saviour, and some other more mythical accounts. Among them he says that there will be a millennium after the resurrection of the dead, when the kingdom of Christ will be set up in material form on this earth. I suppose that he got these notions by a perverse reading of the apostolic accounts, not realising that they had spoken mystically and symbolically. For he was a man of very little intelligence as is clear from his books. But he is responsible for the fact that so many Christian writers after him held the same opinions, relying on his antiquity, for instance Irenaeus and whoever else appears to have held the same views.

"In the same writing he also quotes other interpretations of the words of the Lord given by the Aristion mentioned above and traditions of John the presbyter. To them we may dismiss the studious; but we are now obliged to append to the words already quoted from him a tradition about the Mark who wrote the Gospel, which he expounds as follows: 'And the Presbyter used to say this, Mark became Peter's interpreter and wrote accurately all that he remembered, not indeed, in order, of the things said or done by the Lord. For he had not heard the Lord, nor had he followed him, but later on, as I said, followed Peter, who used to give teaching as necessity demanded but not making, as it were, an arrangement of the Lord's oracles, so that Mark did nothing wrong in thus writing down single points as he remembered them. For to one thing he gave attention, to leave out nothing of what he had heard, and to make no false statements in them!' This is related by Papias about Mark, and about Matthew this was said, 'Matthew collected the oracles in the Hebrew language, and each interpreted them as best he could.'

"The same writer used quotations from the first Epistle of John, and likewise from that of Peter, and has expounded another story about a woman who was accused before the Lord of many sins, which the Gospel according to the Hebrews contains."—Eusebius, *Hist. Eccl.,* III. 39.1-17.

(b) *as reported by George Hamartolos (Cod. Coisl. 305).*

. . . "John was considered a martyr. For Papias, the bishop of Hierapolis, being himself a witness to this, states in the second book of the Oracles of the Lord, that he was taken by the Jews, fulfilling plainly with his brother the prophecy of Christ about them."

(c) *as reported by Philip Sidetes.*

"Papias in the second book says that John the theologian and James his brother were slain by the Jews."

2. Clement of Alexandria

"While Peter was preaching openly at Rome in the presence of certain knights of Caesar, and putting forward much evidence to Christ, Mark, the follower of Peter, wrote at their request the Gospel which is called 'according to Mark' out of those things which were said by Peter, in order that they might be able to commit to memory what was told, just as Luke is recognised to have described with his pen the Acts of the Apostles, and to have translated Paul's letter to the Hebrews."—Clement of Alexandria, on I Peter v.13.

3. Irenaeus

"At this time that very disciple whom Jesus loved, John, at once Apostle and Evangelist, still remained alive in Asia, and administered the churches there, for after the death of Domitian, he had returned from his banishment on the island. And that he remained alive until this time may fully be confirmed by two witnesses, and these ought to be trustworthy for they represent the orthodoxy of the church, no less persons than Irenaeus and Clement of Alexandria. The former of these writes in one place in the second of his books, Against the Heresies, as follows: "And all the presbyters who had been associated in Asia with John, the disciple of the Lord, bear witness to his tradition, for he remained with them until the times of Trajan.' And in the third book of the same work, he makes the same statement as follows: 'Now the church at Ephesus was founded by Paul, but John stayed there until the times of Trajan, and it is a true witness of the tradition of the Apostles.' "—Eus. *H.E.* III. 23.1-5.

4. Origen

(*in Eusebius*)

"... as having learned by tradition concerning the four Gospels, which alone are undisputed in the church of God throughout the world, that the Gospel according to Matthew, who was once a publican, but afterwards an apostle of Jesus Christ, was written first. He published it for those who had become converts from Judaism, and composed it in Hebrew; second came that according to Mark, who wrote it as Peter directed him. And in his general epistle, Peter acknowledges him as the son in these words, declaring, 'She that is in Babylon, elect together with you, saluteth you; and so doth Mark my son;' and third came that according to Luke, who had made for converts from the Gentiles the gospel praised by Paul; last of all came that according to John."—Eus. *H.E.* VI. 25.4.

5. Polycrates

(*in Eusebius*)

"In this he mentions both John, Philip the Apostle, and Philip's daughters as follows: 'For the great luminaries sleep in Asia, and they will rise again in the last day of the advent of the Lord, when he shall come with glory from heaven and call back all the saints, such as was Philip, one of the twelve apostles, who sleeps at Hierapolis with his two daughters who grew old as virgins, and his third daughter who lived in the Holy Spirit and rests in Ephesus. And there is also John, who leaned on the Lord's breast, who was a priest wearing the mitre, and martyr and teacher, and he sleeps at Ephesus.' "—Eus. *H.E.* III. 31.2-4.

6. Proclus

(*in Eusebius*)

"After him the four daughters of Philip who were prophetesses were at Hierapolis in Asia. Their grave is there and so is their father's."—Proclus, Eus. *H.E.* III. 31.4.

7. Dionysius of Alexandria

(*in Eusebius*)

"They say that there were two tombs in Ephesus and that each of them was ascribed to John."—Eusebius, *H.E.* VII. 25.16.

8. The Canon of Muratori

This curious fragment is of unknown date and authorship. The bad Latin is generally recognised as a translation from Greek, and a fair case can be shown for thinking that Hippolytus may have been the writer. The fragment is called that of Muratori, because it was published by the Italian scholar Muratori in 1740. It is in Milan, Bibl. Ambros. Cod. 101 and is usually ascribed to the seventh or eighth century.

". . . at which, however, he was present, and so set them down.

"The third book of the Gospel (according to Luke) Luke, that physician whom after the ascension of Christ Paul had taken with him as companion of his journey (?), composed in his own name on the basis of report. However he did not himself see the Lord in the flesh and therefore as he could 'trace the course of events' he set them down. So also he began his story with the birth of John.

"John, one of the disciples, wrote a fourth book of the Gospels *(the text of this line is extremely doubtful)*. At the entreaties of his fellow disciples and his bishops, he said, 'Fast with me for three days from this time, and let us relate to one another what shall be revealed to each of us.' On the same night it was revealed to Andrew, one of the Apostles, that John should write down all things in his own name with the recognition of all . . . and so, though various *principia* are taught, in the separate books of the Gospels, yet they are of no importance for the faith of believers, since by the one supreme (*principali*) Spirit all of them give all the details, concerning the

Nativity, the Passion, the Resurrection, the intercourse of Christ with his disciples, and about his double Advent, first in humility of aspect, which has taken place, the second splendid in royal power, which is still to come. What wonder is it then that John brings forward each detail with so much emphasis even in his Epistles, saying of himself (*or* of his own accord) 'What we have seen with our eyes and heard with our ears and our hands have touched, this we have written.' For thus he professes himself to have been not only a spectator, but also a hearer [and not only a hearer] but also a writer of all the wonderful things of the Lord in order.

"But the Acts of all the Apostles were written in one volume. Luke compiled for 'most excellent Theophilus' what things were done in detail in his presence, as he plainly shows by omitting both the death of Peter and also the departure of Paul from the city, when he departed for Spain. But the Epistles of Paul themselves show to those who are willing to understand what they are, from what place they were written, or for what reason. First of all, he forbids the Corinthians to share in heretical schisms, and the Galatians to practise circumcision, but wrote at greater length to the Romans, showing by a series of quotations (*ordine scripturarum?*) that Christ is the origin of them. But we must deal with certain points concerning them; since the blessed Apostle Paul himself, following the example of his predecessor, John, only wrote to seven churches by name, and in the following order: first to the Corinthians, second to the Ephesians, third to the Philippians, fourth to the Colossians, fifth to the Galatians, sixth to the Thessalonians, seventh to the Romans, for though two letters each were written to the Corinthians and the Thessalonians by way of reproof (*pro correctione*), yet that there is but one Church scattered throughout the whole world, is made plain, for John also in the Apocalypse, though he writes to seven churches, yet speaks to them all. But he wrote one letter to Philemon and one to Titus, and two to Timothy from affection and love. Yet they have been sanctified by the ordinances of ecclesiastical discipline in the honour of the Catholic Church. There is also extant an Epistle to the Laodiceans and another to the Alexandrians which were forged under the name of Paul for the heresy of Marcion. There are many others which cannot be received in the Catholic Church, for gall cannot be mixed with honey. An Epistle of Jude at least, and two ascribed to John, are accepted in the Catholic Church, and the Book of Wisdom was written by his friends in honour of Solomon. Among Apocalypses, we receive only those of John and Peter, though some of our friends do not wish this (*the apocalypse of Peter?*) to be read in the Church. But Hermas wrote the Shepherd quite recently in our own times, in the city of Rome, while his brother Pius was seated on the episcopal throne in Rome. And therefore, it should indeed be read, but it cannot be made public in the Church to the people among the Prophets, the number of whom is complete, nor among the Apostles since it comes at the end of time (*the text and meaning are obscure*).

"But we receive nothing of Arsinoes, or Valentinus or Metiades (*some think that this is a corruption of Tatian*). Also, those who wrote a new book of Psalms for Marcion, together with Basilides and . . . Assianus, the founder of the Cataphrigians" (*the Montanists*) . . . (*it is quite unknown what this sentence means or who is Assianus*).

APPENDIX D

Bibliography

[The Bibliography which appeared in the first edition has been revised and considerably amplified by Professor W. F. Howard, D.D., to whose kindness in undertaking this work and accepting responsibility for it in our absence in the East we are much indebted.

Even now it does not profess to be exhaustive. There are many other books, especially in foreign languages, which might be added. It is, however, submitted as containing most of the relevant material likely to be useful to readers for a further study of the subject.—K. and S.L.]

ENCYCLOPAEDIAS

Die Religion in Geschichte und Gegenwart, 5 vols. 1st ed. 1909-13; 2nd ed., largely re-written, 1927-31.

Encyclopaedia Biblica, 4 vols., 1899-1903.

F. Cabrol and H. Leclercq, *Dictionnaire d'archéologie chrétienne et de liturgie,* 1903.

The Catholic Encyclopaedia, 1909-1914.

Hastings, *Dictionary of the Bible,* 5 vols., 1898-1904.

—— One vol., *Dictionary of the Bible,* 1908.

—— *Dictionary of Christ and the Gospels,* 2 vols., 1906-8.

—— *Dictionary of the Apostolic Church,* 2 vols., 1915-18.

—— *Encyclopaedia of Religion and Ethics,* 13 vols., 1908-26, American edition 1927.

Hauck-Herzog, *Real-encyclopädie für protestantische Theologie und Kirche,* 3rd ed., 1896-1913.

The Jewish Encyclopaedia, 1901-1906.

Pauly-Wissowa, *Real-encyclopädie der classischen Altertumswissenschaft,* vols. i-vii, 1893-1907; neue Bearbeitung von W. Kroll und K. Mittelhaus, 1908-

Smith, *Dictionary of Christian Antiquity,* 1875.

Smith and Wace, *Dictionary of Christian Biography,* 1877.

Vacant and Mangenot, *Dictionnaire de théologie catholique,* 1899.

DICTIONARIES

G. Abbott-Smith, *Manual Greek Lexicon of the New Testament,* 3rd ed., 1937.

Bauer-Preuschen, *Griechisch-Deutsches Wörterbuch zum Neuen Testament,* 1928; 3rd ed., 1937.

G. Kittel, *Theologisches Wörterbuch zum Neuen Testament,* 1932-

J. H. Moulton and G. Milligan, *Vocabulary of the Greek New Testament,* 1914-1929.

F. Preisigke, *Wörterbuch der griechischen Papyrusurkunden,* 1924-1931.

CONCORDANCES

C. H. Bruder, *Concordantia N.T.*, 1888. (This is in some ways preferable, but is difficult to obtain.)

Moulton and Geden, *Concordance to the Greek Testament,* 1897.

Hatch and Redpath, *Concordance to the Septuagint,* 1897.

GRAMMARS

F. M. Abel, *Grammaire du Grec Biblique,* 1927.

F. Blass and A. Debrunner, *Grammatik des neutestamentlichen Griechisch,* 6th ed., 1931.

E. D. Burton, *New Testament Word Studies,* ed. H. R. Willoughby, 1927.

—— *Notes on New Testament Grammar,* rev. ed., 1904.

—— *Syntax of the Moods and Tenses in New Testament Greek,* 1893.

E. Mayser, *Grammatik der griechischen Papyri aus der Ptolemäerzeit,* 1906-1934.

J. H. Moulton, *A Grammar of New Testament Greek,* Vol. I, *Prolegomena,* 3rd ed., 1908. (This ed. revised for German trans. *Die Sprache des Neuen Testaments,* 1911.) Vol. II with W. F. Howard, 1919-29.

L. Radermacher, *Neutestamentliche Grammatik,* in L.H.B., 1.i. 2nd ed. 1925.

H. B. Swete, *Introduction to the Old Testament in Greek.*

H. St. J. Thackeray, *Grammar of the Old Testament in Greek,* 1909 (only first volume published).

SYNOPSES AND HARMONIES

Burton-Goodspeed, *A Harmony of the Synoptic Gospels in Greek,* 1920.

Huck-Lietzmann, *Synopse der drei ersten Evangelier,* 9th edition 1935, also published with the notes in English. (The same arrangement with the text in English instead of Greek was published by R. L. Finney in 1907.) Editions 5 to 8 have a far fuller textual apparatus than the 9th.

GENERAL COMMENTARIES

The Expositor's Greek Testament, 1897 ff.

International Critical Commentary (I.C.C.), 1895 ff. The commentaries in this series are of unequal value.

M.-J. Lagrange, *Etudes Bibliques.* The commentaries on the Gospels are specially strong on the linguistic side.

H. Lietzmann, *Handbuch zum N.T.* (L.H.B.; an introduction and commentary). New editions of the various books appear at irregular intervals.

H. A. W. Meyer, *Kritisch-exegetischer Kommentar zum N.T.* (constantly brought up to date).

The Moffatt New Testament Commentary.

A. S. Peake, *Commentary on the Bible,* 1919. *Supplement,* ed. A. J. Grieve, 1936.

J. Weiss, *Die Schriften des neuen Testaments,* 2 vols., 1905 ff. 3rd ed. in 4 vols., 1917.

J. J. Wetstein, *Novum Testamentum Graecum* 1751 (a still indispensable book, of which a new edition is in preparation).

Th. Zahn, *Kommentar zum N.T.,* 1910 ff.

Das Neue Testament Deutsch (*N.T.D.*), 4 vols., 1932-7.

COMMENTARIES ON INDIVIDUAL BOOKS

The Synoptic Gospels:

E. Klostermann, in L.H.B.

A. Loisy, *Les Evangiles Synoptiques,* 1907.

C. G. Montefiore, *The Synoptic Gospels,* 1909, 2nd ed. 1927.

J. Wellhausen, *Einleitung in die drei ersten Evangelien,* 1905, 2nd ed. 1911.

Matthew:

W. C. Allen, in I.C.C., 1907.

B. W. Bacon, *Studies in Matthew,* 1930.

E. Klostermann, in L.H.B.

A. H. MacNeile, *The Gospel according to St. Matthew,* 1915.

J. Schniewind, in N.T.D., 1937.

J. Wellhausen, *Das Evangelium Matthaei,* 1904.

Mark:

B. W. Bacon, *The Beginnings of the Gospel Story,* 1909.

E. Klostermann, in L.H.B.

A. Menzies, *The Earliest Gospel,* 1910.

A. E. J. Rawlinson, *St. Mark,* 1925.

H. B. Swete, *The Gospel according to St. Mark,* 1902.

J. Wellhausen, *Das Evangelium Marci,* 1903.

J. Schniewind, in N.T.D., 1932.

C. H. Turner, *St. Mark,* 1928 (repr. separately 1931).

Luke:

J. M. Creed, *The Gospel according to St. Luke,* 1930.

B. S. Easton, *The Gospel according to St. Luke,* 1926.

E. Klostermann, in L.H.B.

A. Loisy, *L'Évangile selon Luc,* 1924.

J. Wellhausen, *Das Evangelium Lucae,* 1904.

John:

W. Bauer, in L.H.B.; probably the best modern commentary, but the first and third editions are preferable to the second.
J. H. Bernard, in I.C.C., 2 vols., 1928.
A. E. Brooke, in Peake's Commentary.
A. Loisy, *Le quatrième Evangile,* 1903 (out of print; very useful and stimulating). 2nd ed. 1921 (entirely rewritten. Includes Epistles).
J. Wellhausen, *Das Evangelium Johannis,* 1930.
B. F. Westcott, *The Gospel of John,* 1881 (with Greek text, and Revised Version by A. Westcott, 1908).

Acts:

Jackson and Lake, *Beginnings of Christianity,* Vols. I-V. Vol. IV Commentary, Vol. V Additional Notes, 1933.
A. Loisy, *Les Actes des Apôtres,* 1920.
E. Preuschen, in L.H.B. 1912.
H. Wendt, in Meyer's *Kommentar,* 1913.
Th. Zahn, *Apostelgeschichte,* 1916-1919.

Pauline Epistles:

E. D. Burton, *Epistle to the Galatians,* in I.C.C., 1920.
J. Denney, in *Expositor's Greek Testament* (Romans), 1900.
M. Dibelius, in L.H.B. (all the shorter Epistles).
E. V. Dubschütz, in Meyer's *Kommentar* (Thessalonians), 1909.
C. H. Dodd (Romans), in Moffatt Commentary. 1932.
G. S. Duncan (Galatians), in Moffatt Commentary, 1934.
J. E. Frame, in I.C.C. (Thessalonians), 1913.
H. Lietzmann, in L.H.B. (Romans, Corinthians and Galatians).
J. B. Lightfoot, *St. Paul's Epistle to the Galatians,* 1865, 10th ed. 1890.
G. Milligan (Thessalonians), 1908.
J. Moffatt (1 Corinthians), in Moffatt Commentary, 1938.
A. Plummer (2 Corinthians), in I.C.C., 1915.
W. M. Ramsay, (*A Historical Commentary on Galations,* 1899).
J. A. Robinson (Ephesians), 1903.
J. H. Ropes, *The Singular Problem of the Epistle to the Galatians,* 1929.
Sanday and Headlam, in I.C.C. (Romans), 1895, 5th ed. 1905.
E. F. Scott (Colossians, Ephesians and Philemon), in Moffatt Commentary, 1930.
J. Weiss, in Meyer's *Kommentar,* 9th ed. (1 Corinthians), 1910.
Th. Zahn, *Kommentar zum Neuen Testament* (various editions of different dates for the individual books).

Catholic Epistles:

A. E. Brooke, in I.C.C. (John), 1912.
M. Dibelius, in Meyer's *Kommentar,* 7th ed. (James), 1921.
A. von Harnack, *Uber den III Joh.,* in T.U. xv.3 (John), 1897.
J. B. Mayor (James), 2nd ed. 1897; (2 Peter and Jude), 1907.
J. Moffatt (James, 1 and 2 Peter, Jude), in Moffatt Commentary, 1928.
J. H. Ropes, in I.C.C. (James), 1916.
B. F. Westcott, *The Epistles of John,* 1892.
H. Windisch, in L.H.B. (all). 2nd ed. 1930.

Hebrews:

J. Moffatt, I.C.C., 1924.
A. Nairne, *The Epistle to the Hebrews,* in Camb. Greek Testament, 1917.
B. F. Westcott, *The Epistle to the Hebrews,* 1892.

Apocalypse of John:

W. Bousset, in Meyer's *Kommentar,* 5th ed. 1896, 6th ed. 1906.
R. H. Charles, in I.C.C., 2 vols., 1920.
H. B. Swete, *The Apocalypse of John,* 1907.
E. Lohmeyer, in L.H.B., 1926.

INTRODUCTIONS TO THE NEW TESTAMENT

B. W. Bacon, *An Introduction to the New Testament,* 1900.
Feine-Behm, *Einleitung in das Neue Testament,* 1936.
M. Goguel, *Introduction au Nouveau Testament,* 1923-26.
H. J. Holtzmann, *Lehrbuch der historisch-kritischen Einleitung in das N.T.,* 1892.
—— *Lehrbuch der neutest. Theologie,* 1892.
A. Jülicher and E. Fascher, *Einleitung,* 1931.
A. H. MacNeile, *An Introduction to the Study of the New Testament,* 1927.
J. Moffatt, *An Introduction to the Literature of the New Testament,* 1911, 3rd ed. 1918.
A. S. Peake, *A Critical Introduction to the New Testament,* 1909.
E. F. Scott, *Literature of the New Testament,* 1932.
B. H. Streeter, *The Four Gospels,* 1924, 4th impression, 1930.
G. W. Wade, *New Testament History,* 1922.
Th. Zahn, *Einleitung in das N.T.,* 1924 (transl. from 3rd ed. 1905-07. *Introduction to the New Testament,* 1909).
—— *Forschungen zur Geschicte des N.T.—lichen Kanons und der altkirchl. Literatur,* 1881 ff.

BOOKS ON NEW TESTAMENT QUESTIONS

H. J. Cadbury, *The Style and Literary Method of Luke,* in Harvard Theological Studies, 1920.
B. W. Bacon, *The Fourth Gospel in Research and Debate,* 1910, reprinted 1918.
—— *The Gospel of the Hellenists,* 1933.
R. Bultmann, *Die Erforschung der synoptischen Tradition,* 1925, 2nd ed. 1930.
F. C. Burkitt, *The Gospel History and its Transmission,* 5th impression, 1925.
C. F. Burney, *The Aramaic Origin of the Fourth Gospel,* 1922.
J. Estlin Carpenter, *The First Three Gospels,* 1890, 4th ed. 1906.
—— *The Johannine Writings,* 1927.
M. Dibelius, *Die Formgeschichte des Evangeliums,* 1919, 2nd ed. greatly enlarged 1933 (Transl. *From Tradition to Gospel,* 1934).
E. Fascher, *Die Formgeschichtliche Methode,* 1924.
Sir John Hawkins, *Horae Synopticae,* 2nd ed. completely revised, 1909.
W. F. Howard, *The Fourth Gospel in Recent Criticism and Interpretation,* 1931, 2nd ed. 1935.
C. H. Kraeling, *Anthropos and Son of Man,* 1927.
T. W. Manson, *The Teaching of Jesus,* 1931.
Oxford Studies in the Synoptic Problem, 1911.
E. F. Scott, *The Validity of the Gospel Record,* 1938.
V. Taylor, *Behind the Third Gospel,* 1926.
—— *The Formation of the Gospel Tradition,* 1933.
C. C. Torrey, *Our Translated Gospels,* 1936.
J. Weiss, *Das Alteste Evangelium,* 1903.

Paul:

M. Bruckner, *Die Entstehung der Paulinischen Christologie,* 1903.
M. Dibelius, *Die Weisterwelt im Glauben des Paulus,* 1909.
G. S. Duncan, *St. Paul's Ephesian Ministry,* 1929.
K. Lake, *The Earlier Epistles of St. Paul,* 1911.
—— *Paul, His Heritage and Legacy,* 1934.
W. Lütgert, *Freiheitspredigt und Schwarmgeister in Korinth,* 1908.
W. Morgan, *The Religion and Theology of Paul,* 1917.
A. S. Peake, *The Quintessence of Paulinism,* 1918.
—— *Paul the Apostle, his Personality and Achievement,* 1928.
—— *Paul and the Jewish Christians,* 1929.
(All these, and other O.T. and N.T. essays are republished in *The Servant of Yahweh and Other Essays,* 1931).

O. Pfleiderer, *Paulinismus,* 2nd ed. 1890, English transl. from 1st ed., 1877.

W. M. Ramsay, *St. Paul, the .Traveller and Roman Citizen,* 1896.

A. Schweitzer, *Geschichte der Paulinischen Forschung von der Reformation bis auf die Gegenwart,* 1911 (transl. *Paul and His Interpreters,* 1913).

—— *Der Mystik des Paulus,* 1930 (transl. *The Mysticism of Paul the Apostle,* 1931).

C. Anderson Scott, *Christianity according to St. Paul,* 1927.

General:

W. Bousset, *Jesus,* 3rd ed., 1907 (transl. from 1st ed. by J. P. Trevelyan, ed. W. D. Morrison, 1906).

—— *Kyrios Christos,* 1913, 2nd ed. (revised) 1921.

F. Büchsel, *Der Geist Gottes im N.T.,* 1926.

R. Bultmann, *Jesus,* 1926 (transl. L. P. Smith and E. Huntress *Jesus and the Word,* 1935).

F. C. Burkitt, *Christian Beginnings,* 1924.

—— *Church and Gnosis,* 1932.

—— *Jesus Christ, an Historical Outline,* 1932.

H. J. Cadbury, *The Making of Luke-Acts,* 1927.

Cambridge Ancient History, xi. 253-293, *The Rise of Christianity,* by B. H. Streeter.

A. Deissmann, *Licht vom Osten,* 4th ed. 1923 (transl L. M. Strachan, *Light from the Ancient East,* 2nd ed., 1927).

—— *Bibelstudien,* 1895, *Neue Bibelstudien,* 1897 (both vols. transl. A. Grieve, *Bible Studies,* 1901, 2nd ed. 1903).

J. Denney, *Jesus and the Gospel,* 1908.

C. Guignebert, *Jesus,* 1933 (transl. S. H. Hooke, *Jesus,* 1935).

M. Goguel, *La vie de Jésus,* 1932 (transl. O. Wyon, *The Life of Jesus,* 1933).

H. Gunkel, *Die Wirkungen des Heiligen Geistes,* 1899.

A. von Harnack, *Die Mission und Ausbreitung des Christentums in den ersten drei Jahrunderten,* 4th ed., 1924 (transl. J. Moffatt, *The Mission and Expansion of Christianity in the First Three Centuries,* 2nd ed., 1908).

P. N. Harrison, *The Problem of the Pastoral Epistles,* 1921.

M. Helm, *After Pentecost,* 1936.

O. Holtzmann, *Leben Jesu,* 1901 (transl. J. T. Bealby and M. A. Canney, *The Life of Jesus,* 1904).

A. Jülicher, *Gleichnisreden Jesu,* 1899.

K. Lake, *Landmarkes of Early Christianity,* 1920.

—— *The Resurrection of Jesus Christ,* 1907.

H. Leisegang, *Der Heilige Geist,* 1919.

W. Lütgert, *Die Irrlehrer der Pastoralbriefe,* 1909.

G. H. C. Macgregor and A. C. Purdy, *Jew and Greek,* 1936.

R. Otto, *Reich Gottes und Menschensohn,* 1934 (transl. *The Kingdom of God and the Son of Man,* 1938).
H. Preisker, *Neutestamentliche Zeitgeschichte,* 1937.
W. M. Ramsay, *The Church in the Roman Empire,* 1893.
D. W. Riddle, *Early Christian Life,* 1936.
K. L. Schmidt, *Der Rahmen der Geschichte Jesu,* 1919.
E. F. Scott, *The Epistle to the Hebrews, its Doctrine,* 1922.
A. Schweitzer, *Geschichte der Leben-Jesu-Forschung,* 4th ed., 1926 (transl. W. Montgomery, *The Quest of the Historic Jesus,* 2nd ed., 1931).
B. T. D. Smith, *The Parables of the Synoptic Gospels,* 1937.
P. Gardner Smith, *The Narratives of the Resurrection,* 1926.
H. L. Strack, *Jesus, die Häretiker und die Christen,* 1910.
G. Tyrrell, *Christianity at the Cross Roads,* 1910.
J. Weiss, *Christus, Die Anfänge des Dogmas,* 1909 (transl. *Christ, the Beginnings of Dogma,* 1911).
—— *Paulus und Jesus,* 1907 (transl. *Paul and Jesus,* 1909).
—— *Die Predigt Jesu vom Reiche Gottes,* 1892, 2nd ed., greatly revised, 1900.
—— *Das Urchristentum,* 1917 (transl. 2 vols., *The History of Primitive Christianity,* 1937).
P. Wernle, *Jesus und Paulus,* 1915.
H. Windisch, *Der Messianische Krieg und das Urchristentum,* 1909.
—— *Taufe und Sünde,* 1908.
W. Wrede, *Das Messiasgeheimnis,* 1901.

THE JEWISH BACKGROUND

J. Bonsivven, *Le Judaisme Palestinien au Temps de Jésus Christ,* 1935.
R. H. Charles [Ed.], *Apocrypha and Pseudepigrapha of the O.T.* (2 vols., 1913).
Cohn and Wendland, *Philonis Opera,* 1896-1915, with an *Index Verborum* by H. Leisegang, 1930.
Colson and Whittaker, *Philo,* in the Loeb Classical Library, in 9 vols., vol. vii. in 1937.
E. R. Goodenough, *By Light, Light,* 1935.
J. Juster, *Les Juifs dans L'Empire Romain,* 1914.
C. G. Montefiore, *Rabbinic Literature and Gospel Teachings,* 1930.
—— *Judaism and Paul,* 1914.
G. F. Moore, *Judaism in the First Three Centuries of the Christian Era, the Age of the Tannaim,* 3 vols., 1927-1930.
B. Niese, *Flavii Josephi Opera,* 1897, editio minor, 6 vols., 1888-1897.
J. Pascher, *Der Königsweg zu Wiedergeburt und Vergöttung bei Philo,* 1931.

E. Schürer, *Geschichte des Jüdischen Volkes im Zeitalter Jesu Christi,* 3 vols., 4th ed., 1901-1909 (transl. J. Macpherson, S. Taylor and P. Christie, *A History of the Jewish People in the Time of Jesus Christ,* 1885, from 2nd German ed.).

H. L. Strack and P. Billerbeck, *Kommentar zum Neuen Testament aus Talmud und Midrasch,* 1922-1928, four vols. bound as five.

H. St. J. Thackeray and R. Marcus, *Josephus,* in the Loeb Classical Library in 9 vols, vol. vi. in 1937.

THE GENTILE BACKGROUND

S. Angus, *The Environment of Early Christianity,* 1915.

—— *The Mystery Religions and Christianity,* 1925 and 1928.

—— *The Religious Quests of the Græco-Roman World,* 1929.

C. Bailey, *The Greek Atomists and Epicureans,* 1926.

E. Bevan, *Stoics and Sceptics,* 1913.

F. Cumont, *After Life in Roman Paganism,* 1922.

—— *Astrology and Religion among the Greeks and Romans,* 1910.

—— *Les Mystères de Mithra,* 3rd ed. (1913) (transl. from 2nd ed. by T. J. McCormack, *The Mysteries of Mithra,* 1903, 2nd ed., 1910); this reproduces the " conclusions " at the end of Vol. I of his great work on Mithra.

—— *Les réligions orientales dans le paganisme romain,* 4th ed., 1929 (transl. Grant Showerman, *The Oriental Religions in Roman Paganism,* 1911).

—— *Textes et Monuments figurés relatifs aux mystères de Mithra,* 1896, 1899.

S. Dill, *Roman Society from Nero to Marcus Aurelius,* 1905.

C. H. Dodd, *The Bible and the Greeks,* 1935.

W. Warde Fowler, *The Religious Experience of the Roman People,* 1911.

J. G. Frazer, *Attis, Adonis and Osiris,* in *The Golden Bough,* ed. 3, part iv, vols. 1 and 2, 1934.

T. R. Glover, *The Conflict of Religions in the Early Roman Empire,* 10th ed., 1923.

Jane Harrison, *Themis,* 1912, and *Prolegomena,* 1903.

H. Hepding, *Attis,* 1902.

A. D. Nock, *Early Gentile Christianity and its Hellenistic Background* (in *Essays on the Trinity and the Incarnation,* 1928).

S. Reinach, *Orpheus,* 1924, and in English (by F. Simmonds), 1930.

E. Rohde, *Psyche,* 8th ed. revised by F. Boll and O. Weinrich, transl. W. B. Hillis, 1925.

P. Wendland, *Die hellenistisch-römische Kultur in ihrer Beziehungen zu Jüdentum und Christentum,* in L.H.B., 1912.

INDEX OF MODERN AUTHORS

(*See also* Appendix D Bibliography)

20

GENERAL INDEX

Printed in Great Britain by Lowe & Brydone Printers Ltd., London, N.W.10

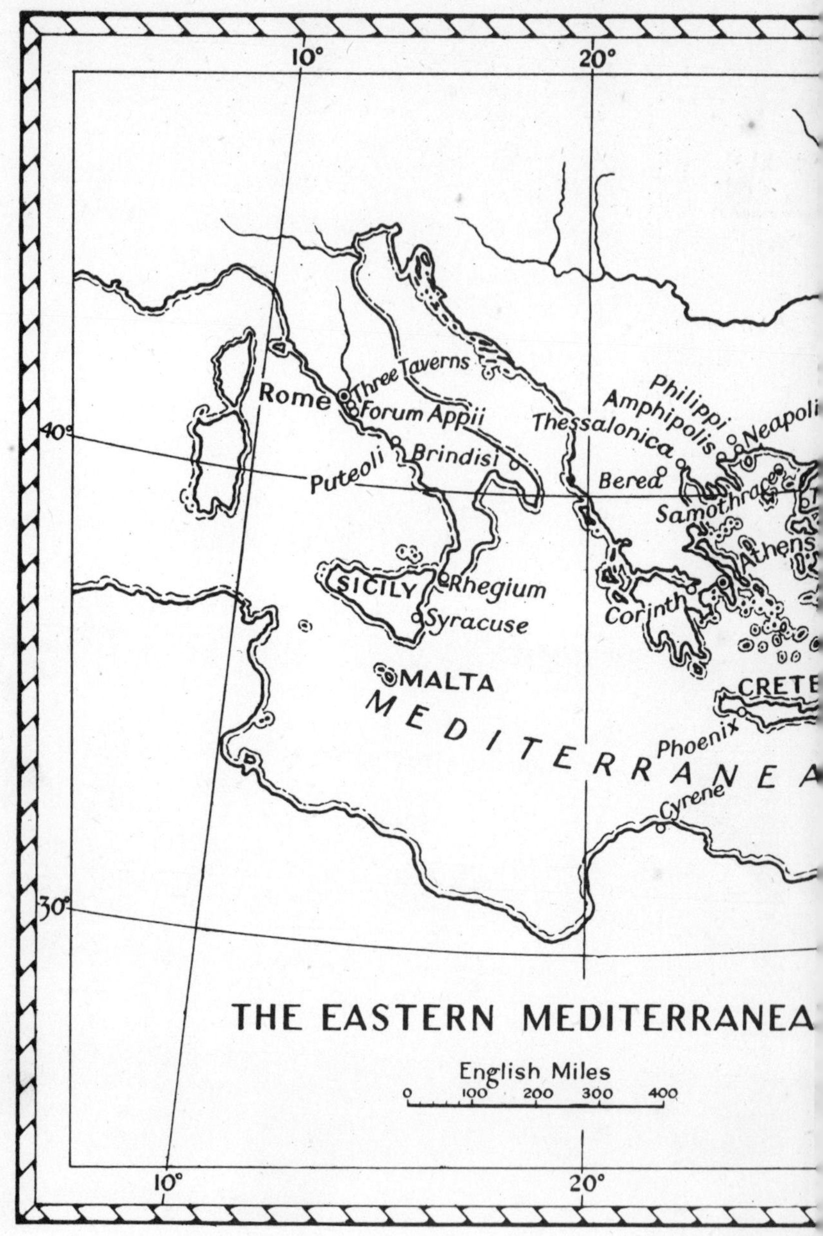
10°
20°
Three Taverns
Rome
Forum Appii
Philippi
Amphipolis
Neapoli
Thessalonica
40°
Brindisi
Puteoli
Berea
Samothrace
Athens
SICILY
Rhegium
Syracuse
Corinth
MALTA
CRETE
MEDITERRANEA
Phoenix
Cyrene
30°
THE EASTERN MEDITERRANEA
English Miles
0
100
200
300
400
10°
20°